SAGE was founded in 1965 by Sara Miller McCune to support the dissemination of usable knowledge by publishing innovative and high-quality research and teaching content. Today, we publish over 900 journals, including those of more than 400 learned societies, more than 800 new books per year, and a growing range of library products including archives, data, case studies, reports, and video. SAGE remains majority-owned by our founder, and after Sara's lifetime will become owned by a charitable trust that secures our continued independence.

Los Angeles | London | New Delhi | Singapore | Washington DC | Melbourne

ADVANCE PRAISE

Millennials are a unique generation from the workforce management standpoint. Professor Sharma's book provides an in-depth understanding into management aspects of the millennial workforce. A must read for all in the corporate world.

Lt Gen. Sanjeev Madhok, *PVSM, AVSM, VSM (Retd.)*
Former General Officer Commanding-
in-Chief, Army Training Command
Head Defence Business, Dynamatic Technologies Ltd

The book *How to Recruit, Incentivize and Retain Millennials* by Professor Dheeraj Sharma provides excellent approaches to manage and leverage millennial workforce for superior performance outcomes. This highly informative book provides exemplary guidelines on attracting, developing and retaining the most valuable assets, thereby paving the path for organizational growth. Unarguably, it will serve as a knowledge pool for the society as a whole.

Suresh Kumar, *President, Strategy and*
Human Resources, Polycab India Ltd

Professor Dheeraj Sharma's original research on the best experiences of the work environment with respect to recruiting and managing millennials is indeed laudable. Undoubtedly, the book will help bridge future generation gaps and provide a transformatory edge to both the 'millennials' and the organizations they work for.

Lt Gen. Manvender Singh, *PVSM, AVSM, VSM (Retd.)*

This book would prove to be a boon for understanding millennials and what makes them so different in their approach to lifestyles—personal and particularly in the work ethos. Understanding them has never been easy and this book aims to address some of those issues.

Lt Gen. Sanjeev Anand, *VSM, MECH INF (Retd.),*
Former Adjutant General, Indian Army

A book every HR professional should read and try to apply while dealing with the next generation. Well explained, well written and correctly linked to current and future challenges.

Ashok Priyadarshi, *Vice President, HR*
& CSR, Alkem Laboratories Ltd

A very informative read on a very pertinent topic. While millennials as a consumer group have been studied and written about ad nauseam, this is the first time millennials as employees have been studied by a renowned academician and researcher! A must-read for the managers of today!

Sonali Dhawan, *Chief Marketing Officer, Procter*
& Gamble, Indian Subcontinent

HOW TO RECRUIT, INCENTIVIZE AND RETAIN MILLENNIALS

DHEERAJ SHARMA

HOW TO RECRUIT, INCENTIVIZE AND RETAIN MILLENNIALS

Los Angeles | London | New Delhi
Singapore | Washington DC | Melbourne

First published in 2020 by

SAGE Publications India Pvt Ltd
B1/I-1 Mohan Cooperative Industrial Area
Mathura Road, New Delhi 110 044, India
www.sagepub.in

SAGE Publications Inc
2455 Teller Road
Thousand Oaks, California 91320, USA

SAGE Publications Ltd
1 Oliver's Yard, 55 City Road
London EC1Y 1SP, United Kingdom

SAGE Publications Asia-Pacific Pte Ltd
18 Cross Street #10-10/11/12
China Square Central
Singapore 048423

Published by Vivek Mehra for SAGE Publications India Pvt Ltd. Typeset in 11/14.5 pt Sabon by Fidus Design Pvt Ltd, Chandigarh.

Library of Congress Cataloging-in-Publication Data Available

ISBN: 978-93-532-8660-6 (PB)

SAGE Team: Manisha Mathews, Ankit Verma and Kanika Mathur

*To my family, which continues
to be my strength*

Thank you for choosing a SAGE product!
If you have any comment, observation or feedback,
I would like to personally hear from you.

Please write to me at **contactceo@sagepub.in**

Vivek Mehra, Managing Director and CEO, SAGE India.

Bulk Sales

SAGE India offers special discounts
for purchase of books in bulk.
We also make available special imprints
and excerpts from our books on demand.

For orders and enquiries, write to us at

Marketing Department
SAGE Publications India Pvt Ltd
B1/I-1, Mohan Cooperative Industrial Area
Mathura Road, Post Bag 7
New Delhi 110044, India

E-mail us at **marketing@sagepub.in**

Subscribe to our mailing list
Write to **marketing@sagepub.in**

This book is also available as an e-book.

CONTENTS

The author Dr Dheeraj Sharma, an eminent scholar of Management Science, defines the term 'millennials' as the set of individuals of age up to 18 years at the beginning of a century and born thereafter. In other words, in this century starting in the year 2000, millennials are the set of individuals born in or after the year 1982. By this definition, 19 per cent of the Indian population (approximately 385 million) falls under the category of millennials and constitutes a significant proportion of India's core demographic dividend. Therefore, India is presently one of the eight countries that are collectively termed as the 'Millennial majors' of the world.

The author, in this book of original ideas and application for India's contemporary organizations, urges that we find ways to leverage this demographic dividend efficiently and prevent it from converting into a demographic disaster. To manage the millennial workforce effectively, managers need to be trained to recognize and then implement this idea of special dividend of young population.

Millennials form a techno-generation that avoids face time. The tech savvy nature of millennials also influences the way they communicate. In a recent study that explored the communication preferences of millennials at work, it was found that 41 per cent of the respondents preferred electronic communication methods such as texts, instant messages and company intranet over outdated traditional methods such as face-to-face meetings and phone calls. Another study reported that millennials were more susceptible to the risk of developing chronic loneliness (15). The youth today spend a major chunk of their time communicating over social media and remain largely devoid of the human touch and feel factor that comes with a face-to-face conversation.

In my view, aspirants of corporate boards need nothing more than the resolve that Dr Sharma's book will be required reading to qualify as managers. The book is not about a theory of management, but the chapters provide a hands-on menu of options for developing the millennials for efficient management. I would call Dr Sharma's book a new dimension of innovation to help output of a corporate to up from one curve to one above for the same capital and labour inputs, thus not suffering from the law of diminishing returns.

Dr Subramanian Swamy (PhD Harvard)
Member of Parliament
New Delhi
1 June 2019

Can we just skip millennials and start hiring people belonging to different generations? This thought must have crossed the mind of legions of human resource executives who face the arduous task of hiring and managing millennials in today's workforce. This is a question that repeatedly gets asked to business leaders who have spent years providing leadership lessons to millennials.

I am well aware that today's millennials are painted as tech savvy, creative but prone to boredom, active but eclectic in their interests, physically solitary but part of large social media groups, wanting change but unenduring and so on. Millennials have a unique mindset of working together in a collaborative environment where new ideas are often shared to bring out the best product in the business. However, these are all possibly positive qualities that can make a good manager and citizen. Hence, millennials are likely to strive to become the crème de la crème of their organization as they possibly set very high standards for themselves and for the organization.

Millennials bring with them challenges to organizations as well. It is often said that they are obsessed with themselves and are not willing to be part of roles that they think are beneath their status. This becomes a double-edged sword for human resource professionals who are trying to recruit multi-dimensional talents that would perfectly fit the organizational hierarchy of companies. Challenges of overconfidence, excessive demands and distraction are other complicated areas cited by researchers where attention needs to be given by recruiting executives.

However, whether one likes it or not, millennials today have become the most important demographic entity in the hierarchy of any organization. They are mission-driven and have a bird's eye view of the opportunities lying ahead in the future. In a world increasingly dominated by technology, globalization and consumerism, millennials are at the forefront of the digital wave that is sweeping across multinationals eager to have a footprint in the increasingly customer-centric digital market today.

Millennials would play a critical role in India in the years to come as it strives to become one of the three biggest economies in the world. Additionally, nearly 50 per cent of the millennials are already primary breadwinners amongst Indian families. Millennials are the largest demographic segment in India today and, therefore, are going to be primary drivers of the Indian economy and Indian society. Consequently, a more nuanced understanding of millennials is vital to the growth of Indian economy as well as Indian society. This book fills the gap in understanding the psyche of millennials and suggests strategies to be adopted in retaining and managing millennials at the workplace.

Professor Sharma has spent years offering advice to multinational corporations, public sector organizations, government departments and ministries. Also, he has researched and published scientific papers in top journals in the domain of workforce motivation and management. Stemming from this rich experience, professor Sharma has come up with an excellent guide that would unravel many of the challenges that recruiters face in hiring and leveraging the qualities of millennials for maximizing outcomes for both individuals and their organizations. This book is, therefore, a must read for both professionals and recruiters alike to leverage key recruitment and retention strategies for success.

At the end, I heartily congratulate professor Sharma for this revealing, enriching and highly recommended book. I also thank him for giving me this privilege to write the foreword for this book. May God endow him with more strength to continue writing much beautiful pieces of work in the domain of world knowledge.

Dr Satya Pal Singh
New Delhi
10 June 2019

The quandary that millennials go through in their job search has often been an overlooked topic for both industry experts and academics. Many researchers believe that millennials are more eager to see and implement rapid change in their workplace. Although not only do they bring with them higher levels of values such as innovativeness, responsibility and credibility, but they also appear to have lower resilience and underdeveloped coping mechanisms. Some researchers claim that millennials define financial success as being debt-free rather than being rich. This brings to us the following important questions:

- Are millennials a truly unique generation in terms of their behaviour?

- What are the challenges that millennials face today at workplace?

- What can inspire millennials at workplace?

- How should organizations adapt to leverage on strengths of millennials while working around their inherent weaknesses?

- What strategies can organizations utilize to have an optimal person–organization fit?

This book attempts to address these pressing issues. It showcases why millennials today are different from previous generations. What are the specific differences between millennials and other generations? In Chapter 1, we define the term 'millennials' and offer a comparison between baby boomers, Gen Xers and millennials. Cases on the Indian Premier League (IPL) and Netflix have also been presented to showcase the increasing value that corporates hold for the unique viewpoint of the millennial generation. Chapter 2 discusses the difference in attitude and behaviour at workplace across different generations. Cases of IBM and Louis Vuitton have been presented to portray the initiatives that have already been taken to promote intergenerational harmony in organizations. Several initiatives are highlighted, which has allowed companies to lower the 'attrition rate' in workforce. In Chapter 3, we describe specific challenges that organizations face in dealing with millennials. Millennials make choices driven by a specific set of values and attitudes, which requires appropriate management. A case on Maruti Suzuki has been presented to highlight how out-of-control millennials caused violence in a workplace, resulting in increased difficulties in operations of a large organization. In Chapter 4, we delve into the role that parents and technology play in influencing behavioural outcomes of millennials. A case on the Blue Whale Challenge to highlight its effects of technology and aloofness in millennial community has been presented. Chapter 5 discusses current best practices in the industry to manage millennials. Cases on Deloitte and P&G have been put forth to showcase the holistic approach that companies have been taking to foster active employee engagement and mentoring of the millennial generation.

Many researchers contend that time-testing recruitment methods and techniques are increasingly unsuitable for millennials. In Chapter 6, we focus on specific strategies for recruiting millennials. We also make a point on why millennials need to be hired in a different way compared with previous generations. A successful case on Marriott International has been highlighted and why the initiatives it has taken have led to it being considered as 'one of the best places to work in' for millennials. Chapter 7 showcases the strategies necessary for incentivizing millennials. Many human resource (HR) experts contend that for millennials non-monetary incentives have become more important than monetary incentives. Several present contrary views. We also try to highlight best possible ways to incentivize millennials at workplace. A case on Google has been presented to emphasize the importance of happiness and productivity in the workplace as an alternate to traditional incentives at the workplace.

Retaining millennials is an extremely challenging task in organizations as many HR experts suggest that attrition rates are very high in millennials compared with those in previous generations. Chapter 8 focuses on this issue and recommends different strategies required to be followed by managers, recruiters and mentors for retaining millennials. A case on Facebook's unique retention strategies elucidates the points made in this chapter.

In Chapter 9, we discuss unique strategies that are needed to recruit the best millennial talent. Hence, cases on KFC, Walmart and Draper Inc highlight the importance of specific training methods and wellness programmes for maximizing employee well-being to harness millennial talent.

Employee branding is at the heart of an effective portrayal of a 'job position' by companies. Technology plays an important role in employee branding, facilitating a linkage between organizations and the millennial generation. Chapter 10 discusses the steps necessary for a positive job search campaign. Cases on Naukri.com and recruitment in IIMs have been put forth to highlight the essential characteristics of an online and offline job application. The last chapter introduces the concept of 'succession planning' in companies where millennials are expected to take over the reign of an organization from the previous generation. The reign of the millennial generation usually brings unique issues in terms of family dynamics as well as organizational dynamics. This requires meticulous planning and strategizing for a successful succession planning in the business where millennials are involved. Cases from Indian business families of Zydus Cadila and Reliance have been presented to showcase apposite succession planning when millennials are involved.

MILLENNIALS AND OTHER GENERATIONS

ORIGIN OF THE TERM 'MILLENNIALS'

Drawing its roots from American history, the term 'millennials' was probably first known to be used in the academic literature by Neil Howe and William Strauss in their book *Millennials Rising: The Next Great Generation* published in 2000 (1, 2). They referred to millennials as the set of individuals born in or after the year 1982. This book is recognized as one of the seminal works in the field. It offers a peek into the history of the development of the term 'millennials'. Its origin can be traced back to a poll conducted by abc.com that solicited prospective labels for this generation. Peter Jennings, a former leading journalist at *ABC World News Tonight*, reported in 1997 that the poll had received a several thousand suggestions from the people. The three proposals that topped the list were 'Millennials', 'Don't Label Us' and 'Generation Y', respectively. However, due to the majority preference for the term 'millennials' or 'millennium generation', it was finally chosen as the term for this cohort and is an accepted label used even today (1).

MILLENNIALS AT THE WORKPLACE

India boasts of being home to nearly 19 per cent (385 million) of the global millennial population and is one of the eight countries presently termed as the 'millennial majors' (3). It is imperative that contemporary organizations find ways to leverage this demographic dividend efficiently and prevent it from converting into a demographic disaster. To manage the millennial workforce effectively, managers first need to understand

and acknowledge the key distinguishing features of this cohort. Subsequently, customized systems and processes to deal with them need to be developed and implemented.

The popular press stereotypes millennials as lazy, disloyal, entitled, overly sensitive and so on (4). However, it is inappropriate to view each millennial in a similar light solely because of his (her) membership to a particular demographic group.

A recent survey conducted by BankBazaar reported that the top three aspirations of Indian millennials were wealth, health and fame, respectively. Surprisingly, women were found to have even higher aspirations than men (5). Another survey which seconds these findings revealed that money was the key motivator for millennials and that 83 per cent of Gen Y employees would consider switching their jobs for a salary hike (6). Despite such discouraging statistics, it is certain that organizations cannot ignore the interests of millennials as they are expected to constitute 50 per cent of the global workforce by 2021 (7). With the rise of the gig economy characterized by short-term employment contracts along with the intensifying war for talent, it becomes all the more crucial for organizations to attract as well as retain millennials. The following guidelines shed light on some of the concrete steps that organizations may take to boost the productivity and engagement of millennials at the workplace.

Several organizations have already started implementing innovative practices to attract and retain millennials. For instance, Infosys has scrapped the formal dress code and encourages its employees to wear smart business casuals. It has also come up with a new crowd-sourcing initiative known as 'Murmuring', which invites innovative business ideas that could contribute to the company's strategy. Likewise, Microsoft attempts to drive the culture of innovation at the internship phase itself by allowing interns to learn from experts directly. In a similar vein, IBM put forth an integrative tool known as 'IBM Verse', which integrates email, calendar, meetings, video chats and a lot of other capabilities on a single platform. IBM also has a well-developed reverse mentoring programme to engage millennials (8).

It is high time that other organizations also realize the significance of such initiatives and come up with advanced systems and processes that will help them get the best out of millennials.

KEY CHARACTERISTICS OF MILLENNIALS

The rise of the millennial population carries twofold implications for business organizations. Millennials not only make up a significant proportion of the workforce, but also form an essential segment of the customer base. Not surprisingly, organizations are rapidly trying to adapt themselves to cater to the needs of the millennial consumer, who is not easily satiated. Some of the millennial values that are shaping trends for the contemporary marketers have been discussed next. Organizations that have successfully reaped the benefits of these trends have also been presented in the form of an example to elucidate our claims.

Juggernaut Books is India's first smartphone publisher that provides a range of books on a digital platform, that is, a smartphone. The advantage it has over e-book readers such as Amazon Kindle is that the consumer need not purchase a specific device to read books. It offers the convenience of reading digital books on our very own smartphones. The books are also free or nominally priced, thus enhancing their appeal and reach amongst readers. Juggernaut Books even allows authors to publish their works. Its app has over a million downloads, and Bharti Airtel has also recently acquired a significant stake in the company (9).

In all, organizations need to be perpetually vigilant of the changing tastes and preferences of the millennials. They ought to continually innovate, provide personalized services and take up the responsibility of managing the best interests of their customers (10). Millennials are very likely to switch their service providers if they do not feel satisfied with the quality of goods and services. Hence, the key to attracting and retaining the millennial customer is to provide it with winning customer experience, even before the actual purchase takes place (11).

Some of the typical characteristics of millennials have been discussed as follows.

1. **Millennials make compromises**: Given the state of the job market for graduates, many millennials tend to make compromises while finding their first jobs. A recent survey conducted by PwC revealed that nearly 72 per cent of the respondents had made certain compromises to get into the job market (12). These compromises were especially rampant during the times of an economic downturn in 2008 and were expected to result in a turnover when the market would revive. The compromises could take many forms, ranging from accepting a lower salary to working outside preferred locations or job roles or industries. Turnover rates are also higher amongst millennials than those amongst other generations.

2. **Millennials value personal development and work-life balance over financial rewards**: This cohort is not driven primarily by financial rewards and monetary

incentives. A recent global survey reported that young professionals chose work-life balance over wealth and leadership opportunities (13). Millennials think about the expected levels of work-life balance even while considering which organization to work for.

3. **Millennials form a techno-generation that avoids face time:** The tech-savvy nature of millennials also influences the way they communicate. In a recent study that explored the communication preferences of millennials at work, it was observed that 41 per cent of the respondents preferred electronic communication methods such as texts, instant messages and company intranet over outdated traditional methods like face-to-face meetings and phone calls (14). Another study reported that millennials were more susceptible to the risk of developing chronic loneliness (15). The youth today spend a major chunk of their time communicating over social media and remain largely devoid of the human touch and feel factor that comes with a face-to-face conversation.

4. **The loyalty of the millennials:** In the job market, millennials are predominantly seen as job-hoppers who do not generally commit to one particular work organization for long. The reason behind such behaviour is possibly the incentive, that is, the pay rise associated with each switch. Millennials are ambitious, entitled and self-absorbed. Hence, if they do not see good salary hikes within a couple of years, they prefer to switch (16). The definition of 'loyalty' is different for this generation as compared to the earlier ones. They do not calculate loyalty in terms of years, but months.

A recent survey conducted in the North American context reported the existence of generational differences in brand loyalty and urged marketers to foster loyalty by providing personalized experiences (17).

5. **Millennials like to move up the ladder faster:** Career progression is a principal motivator for millennial professionals, which is reflected from the results of a recent survey that reports that 91 per cent of millennials consider career progression to be important while choosing a new job (18). Millennials look for instant gratifications and, therefore, do not believe in toiling for years to earn a promotion or pay hike. They are impatient, ambitious and entitled, which fuels their pursuit of reaching the top faster than other generations. Moreover, their individualistic and self-absorbed orientation prompts them to prioritize their interests over the interests of the organizations that they work for.

6. **Socially responsible brands influence millennials:** Millennials have a sense of purpose, and they are, therefore, more drawn towards philanthropic brands that practice socially and ethically responsible behaviour. The results of a survey substantiate this claim by indicating that 87 per cent of Americans would purchase a product if the organization advocated for an issue that they cared about (19). Corporate social responsibility (CSR) initiatives go a long way in not only attracting the right talent but also contributing to the bottom line by boosting sales. Organizations today not only spend money on social causes, but also allow their employees to take ownership of the process by giving them opportunities to volunteer. These measures make the millennial employees believe that not only are their organizations socially responsible, but they individually are also contributing towards generating a social impact.

7. **Wanderlust:** Millennials are characterized by a sense of wanderlust, that is, a strong desire to travel. The results of an official travel report revealed that millennials

travel much more compared with other cohorts (20). Millennials believe in splurging on authentic experiences rather than saving up and investing in big purchases such as buying a new home (21). Moreover, their openness towards new cultures and the passion for exploring the unknown takes them places. A new term known as 'bleisure', combing business as well as leisure has been recently coined in the millennial context. Millennials have changed the face of traditional business trips and now view them as personal leisure time while simultaneously travelling for business-related purposes (22).

8. **Accustomed to rapid feedbacks:** Millennials might get frustrated by the delayed responses from older employees. Older generations, on the other hand, may even be offended by a lack of face-to-face or voice-to-voice communication (20).

9. **Millennial stereotypes:** An essential element that contributes heavily to intergenerational conflicts is the accumulation of negative stereotypes in the minds of individuals of different generations. Baby boomers perceive millennials as lazy, impatient and unprofessional while millennials view baby boomers as old school or unapproachable (23). These beliefs ingrained in the minds of employees cloud their perceptions of cross-generational co-workers by directing all the attention from the individual towards the demographic group he (she) belongs to. Stereotyping gives rise to misunderstandings and miscommunication amongst co-workers, thus preventing employees of different generations from working together in a complementary fashion.

10. **Differences amongst millennials:** Not every millennial is the same. There emerge several individual-level differences within the cohort as well. Every individual is a

part of the broad demographic group but is also a unique bundle comprising of different experiences, skills, aspirations, talents and perspectives. Hence, it is advisable to consider the broad characteristics of this generation while simultaneously embracing individual differences when dealing with individuals. A recent study by Cucina et al. (24) has established that there are more within-generation attitudinal and behavioural differences as compared to cross-generation differences. Therefore, it is recommended that the best way to lead millennial employees is to ignore sweeping generalizations, focus on the individual under consideration, and find out what works for him (her) the most irrespective of demographic group memberships (25).

11. **Millennials are excellent employees:** Millennials carry some traits that are very unique to their generation. Therefore, if handled correctly, millennials can serve as excellent employees for business organizations. First, millennials are a bunch of curious minds. They are fascinated to learn new skills and are proactive in making efforts to improve themselves (25). This inclination to grow also helps the organization to grow in the long run. Second, born and brought up in nuclear families, the majority of the millennials unconsciously develop an individualized approach. Instead of treating this as an inhibitor, organizations can cash on it by providing individualized support, guidance and feedback. Third, millennials love collaborations. They are equipped to survive in teams and are comfortable working with others, learning from them and also competing with them. They like open-spaced offices instead of sitting in a cubicle eight hours a day, six days a week (26). Giving such work environments to millennials will satisfy their needs and will help foster loyalty.

12. **The meme generation:** Memes are the language of communication amongst millennials. The *Merriam-Webster* dictionary provides two meanings of the word 'meme'. A meme is 'an idea, behavior, style, or usage that spreads from person to person within a culture' or 'an amusing or interesting item (such as a captioned picture or video) or genre of items that is spread widely online especially through social media'. Memes are widely in circulation over social media, and they travel fast. Memes are an integral source of humour in the millennial life. Older generations view the humour of millennials as absurd, vulgar, weird or even meaningless (27). To sum it all, memes provide an extensive avenue for individual expressions, mood lightening and serve as an alternate medium for communication.

TYPES OF MILLENNIALS

Table 1.1 presents the types of millennials according to age.

TABLE 1.1 AGE SEGMENTS PROFILED

Teen millennials, ages 13–17	While it is true that teens are closer to their parents than ever before, their friends have an integral role in their social development. For the most part, parents are not seen as a force to rebel against but instead confidants and friends.
College-aged millennials, ages 18–22	These millennials are accustomed to high expectations and driven to succeed. Due to the increasing number of college applicants, the acceptance process has become quite competitive. Still, college-aged millennials have been told they are capable of great things and have no reason to believe they cannot deliver.

Young adult millennials, ages 23–25	As millennials reach young adulthood, they are beginning to take on adult responsibilities. However, as this is a generation that has mastered the art of prolonging adolescence, there has been an emergence of the boomerang child. This term refers to an individual who moves back home with his or her parents after graduating from college or entering the workforce. Those young adult millennials who are working do not let their lives revolve around their jobs and make social pursuits their main priority.

Source: Alves (n.d).

COMPARISON WITH BABY BOOMERS, GEN XERS AND GEN Y OR MILLENNIAL?

Table 1.2 presents a closer look at the main distinctions between boomers, Gen Xers and millennials (28).

BABY BOOMERS

Defining Characteristics

The baby boomer generational cohorts are the people born around the mid-1960s, that is, 1946–64. These groups of people, currently in their 60s, still comprise a large part of the workforce. A 2012 Nielson Report (29) predicted this group of employees to grow by 34 per cent by the year 2030.

The most remarkable feature of this generation is their hard-working nature and their competitive streak. Although a tad technologically challenged, they are investing effort in trying to learn the new technologies.

TABLE 1.2 GENERATIONAL DIFFERENCES

	Baby Boomers (1946–65)	Gen Xers (1966–78)	Millennials (1979–2001)
Characteristics	The 'me' generation • Narcissistic • Intellectual renaissance • Judgemental Baby boomers came of age post-Second World War, at the height of an intellectual reawakening in America. As youths, boomers rebelled against the establishment and the over-idealized, team-oriented generations that came before them.	Disillusioned cynics • Cautious and sceptical • Searching for self • Alienated and confrontational As a group, Gen Xers are a product of a strongly individualistic society. Thought of as a generation of slackers with little drive and no direction, Gen Xers are anti-rules and anti-groups. They rely on self over others.	Optimistic and confident achievers • Disciplined and accepting of authority • Well educated and competitive • Upbeat and open-minded • Entitled Reared in a youth-centric culture, millennials are self-assured and civic-minded. With sophisticated social awareness, millennials believe the community extends beyond their own backyard and feel empowered and compelled to make the world a better place.

	Baby Boomers (1946–65)	Gen Xers (1966–78)	Millennials (1979–2001)
Defining experiences	• Summer of Love • Civil Rights • Vietnam War • Sexual Revolution Social change and political pushback marks the baby boomer era. Boomers fought against race and gender inequality, participated in anti-war protests and supported sexual freedom, all within the refuge of an affluent America. This highly politicized generation was intent on challenging the status quo.	• Soaring divorce rates • AIDS • Recession Gen Xers were faced with a social climate in the midst of advancements in medicine and technology, the war on drugs, an unknown and deadly disease, times of recession and the splintering of the American family. Collectively, Gen Xers were not considered capable of rallying together to improve the state of the world.	• Digital age • Terrorism and natural disasters • A global economy Millennials have grown up in an environment where technology provides a platform for customization and immediate gratification in all aspects of life. News and information travel freely across continents, with recent acts of terrorism and natural disasters touching more than the people directly involved. As a result, millennials have been instilled with a far-reaching, global social conscience.

(continued)

(continued)

	Baby Boomers (1946–65)	Gen Xers (1966–78)	Millennials (1979–2001)
The state of the family	• Pampered children of stay-at-home moms • Defined gender roles • Affluent, stable families As children, boomers were indulged by their parents and grew up in households with clear and separate gender roles destined to be torn down and redefined. As parents, boomers' primary focus is on 'self' (i.e., self-improvement), which inherently positions the needs of the family unit in second place.	• Children of divorce • Latchkey kids • Loose adult supervision • Family as a source of conflict Gen Xers experienced their childhood in an adult-centric society where parents practised 'hands-off' parenting and were not always around. Gen Xer parents tended to concentrate on their own happiness rather than focus on their Gen X child's successes and disappointments.	• Highly involved parents • Strong family bonds • Nurtured at home • Family as a source of support Millennials came of age in a child-centric society. Both the increase in fertility treatments and the rise of youth advocacy in politics have helped establish that millennial children are valued and protected. The generation gap has all but disappeared, as parents and children understand one another and have more in common than ever before.
Personal measures of success	• Long-term employment • Job titles and promotions • Self-actualization	• Flexible work times • Jobs on their terms • Healthy and stable relationships	• Personal fulfilment at work • Active lives outside of work • Healthy and strong community

	Baby Boomers (1946–65)	Gen Xers (1966–78)	Millennials (1979–2001)
Personality traits	Ethical, determined and knowledgeable	Free-spirited entrepreneurial and adaptable	Self-directed (31), individualistic and pleasing
Life-events faced	Independence and partition of India; reorganization of Indian states on linguistic basis	Launch of the first Indian satellite, Indo-Pak war; invention of nuclear weapons	Multiple debt crises, introduction of the Internet
Work style	Get it done—whatever it takes—nights and weekends	Find the fastest route to results; protocol secondary	Work according to deadlines not necessary according to schedules
Authority	Respect for power and accomplishment	Rules are flexible; collaboration is important	Value autonomy
Leadership	Democratic leadership style	Advocates of collaborative leadership style	Less inclined to pursue formal leadership
Communication	Somewhat formal and through a structured network	Personal development and individual career goals	Personalized career development, quest for learning and drive for excellence (32)
Recognition and reward	Public acknowledgement in the form of advanced titles, special parking spaces, large private offices and career advancement	Not just materialistic rewards, liberty of exercising autonomy coupled with ample time off as a reward	Individual and public praise (exposure); opportunity for broadening skills

(continued)

(continued)

	Baby Boomers (1946–65)	Gen Xers (1966–78)	Millennials (1979–2001)
Work and family	To the importance and meaning of work	To individual career goals. Tend to switch jobs frequently	To the people involved with the project
Loyalty	To the importance and meaning of work	To individual career goals. Tend to switch jobs frequently	To the people involved with the project
Technology	Necessary for progress	Practical tools for getting things done	Multitasking generation knows nothing else but technology

Source: Hamidullah (2015).

State of Family

Baby boomers or the 60s child grew up in the safest of havens. They enjoyed a comfortable life, with their fathers earning the bread of the family and their mothers taking ample care of them. They were brought up with a lot of care and concern since they were born post-Second World War, thereby the name 'baby boomers' (33). After long periods of war and the fight for freedom, during which family life had come to a halt, the returning soldiers were eager to lead a settled life and build a household. Hence, their children were highly pampered and led healthy lifestyles.

That era was undergoing a major social change in the form of women entering the workforce. The gender roles were becoming more refined and called upon parents to jointly take efforts in raising the child. However, due to the changing gender dynamics, they faced severe conflicts relating to gender roles.

Life-Events Faced

Baby boomers grew up in the post-Second World War period, which was marked by stability. They were born in an independent India, hence were witness to the rapid growth and development of free India. There was a massive restructuring and reorganization of the Indian landscape, being advocated by the newly formed Indian government. Reforms were in place, and efforts were being made to dismantle the horrors faced during the British rule to push India towards progress, such as the Five-Year Plans (34). Hence, they were observers of India's path to development. The Indian Constitution was laid down, and for the first time, a government which was led by the people was elected in India.

The Indo-Pak partition was a major event and saw a relative period of confusion where people were separated from their friends and families. Furthermore, India was being divided into new states such as Bombay (now Mumbai), to facilitate governance. Article 370, granting special rights to Kashmir, was signed and saw Kashmir draft its own constitution in 1957, and within a decade in 1964, the cry for an independent Kashmir arose (35).

Work Style

The baby boomers are hard-workers and are purely dedicated to their work tasks. They have a knack for structure and formality in their tasks and prefer a peaceful and safe environment for work. They like to follow rules and are hard task-masters. They are comfortable working with others and are team players.

These individuals are highly involved with their work and derive satisfaction from their work. Baby boomers are more influenced by promotions at work and rewards. They find money to be fulfilling and hence work hard for it. They also demand a sense of job security and are steady in their work.

They have had the experience of working in the industrial economy, service economy and the current knowledge economy (33). Hence, they have tried to adapt according to the changing needs of the industry.

Work and Family

Baby boomers seem to have a lower desire for work-life balance as they are too deeply involved in the work they do. They have a work-focused orientation and allow their work to spill over to their after-work hours. They do not seem to delineate the two.

Loyalty

When it comes to loyalty, baby boomers are extremely loyal to the organization. They joined organizations when organizational loyalty was a valuable trait, and hence we see them stay for more than ten years at the same organization. They remain at their jobs, only seeking promotion and raise, and seldom do we find them switching jobs.

Technology

Baby boomers were already adults when technological advancements began, but we cannot scrape them off as being technologically unsound. They have rapidly taken to the adoption of new technology, and are focused on learning. They consider technology as a 'fountain of youth' (36) for themselves, which enables to maintain their sync with the present world. Although being a generation that has grown with the television sets, they have not failed to use the internet or other online services that technology brings them.

GENERATION XERS

Defining Characteristics

Generation Xers are born multitaskers, but at the same time are desirous of their work-life balance. They belong to the birth period of 1966–79 and currently in their 50s (37). Generation X group of working cohorts are more self-dependent and possess a quest for independence. They challenge the status quo and are unlikely to let others define them. To them, the self is more important, and they are more individualistic in nature. Self-achievement is their drive to work, but not at the cost of their general life satisfaction. They are fast and spontaneous and like informality within structures.

State of Family

The period in which Gen Xers grew up was marked by turmoil and unrest, which had a huge impact in shaping them up. They are children of parents who were more work focused, and thereby had little role to play in the bringing up of their children. Most families were witnessing a shift from large to nuclear families, and both parents were starting to work. Families were more concerned about earning and supporting the family and divorce rates were on the rise. As a result, the Gen X child grew up on his/her own and thereby their individualistic orientation. The familial and social insecurity they faced makes them think about themselves first, and they tend to possess only a small circle of trusted friends.

Life-Events Faced

Generation X cohorts have been participants in major, life-changing events, for example, India's war with Pakistan over Kashmir, culminating into the creation of the country of Bangladesh, in 1971. The country was suffering from multiple religion and community-based fights and riots. There were various protests against the government led by J. P. Narayan, supported by students and the well educated. Apart from that, there were major outbreaks in different parts of the country, such as the strikes by railway workers, peasant revolts in West Bengal and so on. The country was facing an economic slowdown with poor industrial development and unemployment being on the rise. The situation turned so grave that, in 1975, the then Prime Minister Indira Gandhi declared National Emergency in the country citing internal disturbances as the reason, which lasted for a period of 21 months (38).

Contrary to the political unrest, India also achieved major milestones in its scientific developments. It launched its first successful satellite, and ISRO was founded in 1969 (39). The country successfully completed its secret nuclear testing operation in Pokhran in 1974 (40). Moreover, the seeds of the Green Revolution were sown around this time, with the aim of boosting crop productivity to support farmers in 1966 (41).

Work Style

This generation is driven by competition and their drive for success. Despite coming from broken homes, their work values are intact. They have great problem-solving skills and work smartly. They desire autonomy at work and are self-motivated. The Gen Xers consider work itself to be rewarding, hence their high reliance on learning and development. They are extremely resourceful and self-reliant.

They have a high drive to inculcate new skills and are eager to learn new things. They do not need to be pushed for training but are rather on the lookout for the opportunities to grow themselves. However, they tend to show lesser involvement towards work since they like to maintain a healthy lifestyle. However, they desire satisfaction at work and do not want to be transformed into 'workaholics'.

Work and Family

Generation Xers are highly aware of the negative consequences work may have upon their family and health. Hence, they tend to maintain a strict division between their work and personal life. They believe in life outside of work as well and crave an overall life satisfaction. Their childhood was shaped up by parental conflicts and ignorance, and hence they crave to familial love and care. So, they try to fill the gap by giving more time to their family life.

Loyalty

Generation Xers, compared with the baby boomers, are less likely to display strong organizational loyalty. They consider themselves as 'free agents', and rather than loyalty to the organization, they are more loyal and attached to their professions and skills. Due to this orientation of Gen Xers, it becomes relatively difficult to retain them in a particular organization for long.

Technology

Generation Xers are not new to technology and are the first ones to use an electronic medium for communication. Although not as technologically sound as the millennials, they are not far behind when it comes to their technological orientation and digital responsiveness. Their use of social media is limited to keeping themselves updated (42) and are not as attached to their devices as the millennials. Although familiar with YouTube and other platforms, they still prefer their television.

GENERATION Y/MILLENNIALS

Defining Characteristics

Millennials or Generation Y, as they are technically called, are people born after 1980 (37). They have currently reached adulthood and are in their late 30s. Born multitaskers, millennials are strong-headed, but are thought to lack focus. They set their own goals and are steered by passion. They believe in the expression of self, and hence indulge in personal branding and self-promotion. They prefer to work alone but have strong group orientations as well. They nurture relationships at their workplace and enjoy working with others. They have a sense of community and are concerned about the political views of others, the internet and the newspaper. They are adventurous.

State of Family

This generational cohort has grown up in good times. Their parents were highly involved in their upbringing and paid extreme heed to their needs. They were brought up with a lot of love and care. As children, they received a lot of encouragement from family. During this period, the generational barriers were being overcome, and due to this their parents became more supportive. The friendly family environment nurtured them to do a lot of things on their own and shaped their mindset to be more accepting of things.

However, one cannot deny the adverse impacts of parental overindulgence in this generation. Their carefree way of life, retaliation towards things unacceptable to them and their strong sense of freedom and independence, finds its roots in the way they have been raised.

Life-Events Faced

The millennials grew up in a society engulfed in terrorism, warfare, globalization and recession. They witnessed a major presidential change in the United States, from George W. Bush to Barack Obama signifying a mix of ideologies (43). The 9/11 terror attacks in the United States engulfed the entire nation into sadness and trauma by witnessing the fallacy of a terrorist organization bombing up the World Trade Center building in the United States. So great was the loss of life and property and so deep was the fear amongst citizens following this terror attack that the United States announced a Global War on Terror (44) in order to eliminate these terror organizations. The entire world bore the brunt of this global war with the US forces invading the homes of many innocent people, but the terror attacks continued in different parts of the world. Even India was in its clutches as is privy by the 1993 Mumbai blasts (45), Akshardham Temple attack in 2002 (46), the 26/11 Taj Hotel blasts in 2008 (47) and a series of others.

With globalization, the nations of the world engaged in fruitful exchanges of financial, economic, political, technological and cultural resources. The United States and other developed nations expanded their businesses to developing countries, fostering investment in foreign trade. Increased interaction between nations increased work opportunities for them and led to the creation of more jobs, catering to diverse work groups. The Gulf War or the war for oil between the Arab countries, powered by the United States, led to the bombing of Iraq and a sharp increase in oil prices (48).

Work Style

The most striking character trait of millennials is their multi-tasking ability. Their brains are trained to do more than one thing at once. Very often, millennials might be found working on the laptop, using the cell device to answer text messages, with headphones plugged in listening to music, all at the same time. The millennial worker excels in the ability to switch tasks within seconds. They demand a fun-filled work environment (49) where they can work creatively in tandem with others. They prefer their work spaces to be a happy place where they can learn and grow.

Millennials work with passion and dedication and try to give in their best. They like to take upon challenging work tasks and are highly motivated by their need for success. They have an innate desire for growth and are hungry for success.

A slight fervour for self-promotion is also found within millennials where they want to carve out a niche for themselves in whichever field they are working in. At the workplace, they are team players since they are sociable and display sensitivity towards others. They are target-oriented, work hard to achieve those targets and then want instant gratification, which is like response on the work done. Due to their adaptable character traits, they are better in responding to changes in their work and stay composed in times of conflicting situations. This evolving technology has been a major factor in facilitating a shift in their thoughts and behaviours. The millennials possess greater job satisfaction.

Work and Family

Millennials prefer work-life balance to other generations. As highly dedicated as they might be towards work, they desire to have a gap between their work space and family life. They do not tend to bring their work home. They take time out from their schedules in order to spend time with family, take vacations, travel and hang out with their friends and so on.

Loyalty

Millennials, compared with the other generations, exhibit a lesser degree of organizational loyalty. Their desire for growth and learning makes them more prone to switching jobs rather than staying at the same job, if they perceive stagnation at work. Their perception of organizational support is rather low and likewise is their organizational commitment. They do not seem to give importance to valuing trust in organizations.

Technology

Millennials are technology's children. They have learnt to use computers in their schools and make use of them at their workplace. They have seen the internet becoming popular and telephones evolving into cellular phones, together bringing the world to their fingertips. They are comfortable with television and text messages, and are better off than their parents. They have grown up as the technology around them changed, which causes them to be extremely comfortable with technology. They have grown up seeing a shift from telephones to cellular devices to iPhones and smart devices. Compared with their previous generations, millennials are more adaptable to rapid technological changes.

The advancement of the internet during the era of the millennials greatly fostered the millennials towards a new level of organizational and personal life. Social media and various networking platforms now make the world a smaller place to live in where they can be connected to anyone at any point of the day. Social media platforms also provide them a way to make their voice heard, hence fuelling their need to express themselves. The introduction of chatbots, computerized systems, e-commerce and so on has reduced time, in addition to the reduced costs.

Millennials have grown up using Web 2.0 services and are extremely familiar with technological services of any kind. They thrive on the internet and networking. They have Wi-Fi, Bluetooth, high-speed internal calling, video calling and so on, which increase their connectedness with others at work as well as family. Their entire lifestyle runs around the word 'online', right from their work to entertainment and shopping.

The Case of Indian Premier League (IPL): Cricket for the New Generation

The IPL was first rolled out in 2008 as a disruptor in the game of cricket. Cricket is the most popular game in the Indian subcontinent. It is watched, played and ardently followed by people across all age groups. With the launch of the IPL, a completely unheard, the shorter 20-over format of cricket was introduced, which invited adverse reactions from people. Conventionally, Indians enjoyed the game of cricket in two formats—relatively longer test match and the shorter one-day match. Remarkably, the IPL changed the way in which cricket was marketed, and it was a complete shift from the cricket Indians had seen so far.

The IPL transformed cricket, making it a common man's gala event, from a mere sport. India, being a cricket-frenzy nation, responded in a remarkable way to the system of franchise teams, owned by corporate houses, where international and domestic players were made available for auction and sold to the highest bidder. The IPL bidding sessions saw the participation of various Bollywood stars, who added to the high dose of stardom and lustre. It saw an amalgamation of cricket, entertainment and high-end business. It is often said that India has two new religions (Bollywood and cricket), and both draw substantial public support. The IPL excellently combined the two, which helped it to become the cricketing giant it is today. As of 2017, the IPL brand is worth $5,500 million and is comparable to other cash-rich leagues in the world such as the National Basketball Association and the English Premier League (EPL) (50).

The IPL was extensively marketed as being full of 'cricketainment'. The cricket venues were strategically designed, and other events such as inauguration ceremony, after-game parties, cheerleader dance during the match and so on drew in a lot of attention. Celebrity involvement in the advertising and publicity was solely aimed at drawing in the crowds. Moreover, the cheap ticket costs coupled with the extensive advertisement of every game were impactful enough in making IPL the game of the masses.

One cannot help but find generational differences in the public reaction to the IPL. The baby boomers could not seem to identify with the publicity stunts being pulled off in cricket. For them, cricket was an elite game, and all the frenzy attached to it was taking away its actual value. The participation of cheerleaders in the game, who danced after every six and wicket, became a highly controversial issue. There were huge protests demanding that cheerleaders be removed from the game since it conflicted with the Indian value system. The incident also got political colours with the involvement of two national political parties demanding a ban against the dance by cheerleaders (51). The Gen Xers also seem to be drawn towards it since it gave them a chance to watch the game live at affordable prices. Some even indulged in taking families out for a match or casual outings.

Millennials showed the highest amount of acceptance for the unconventional format offered by the IPL. They saw it align with their free and 'fast' lifestyle. The concept of finishing a game in a few hours appealed to their way of life. The IPL became their place of hangout with friends or cousins. The idea of cheerleaders dancing on the tunes of latest Bollywood songs for every sixes, fours or wicket in the game appealed to this generation.

Started in 2008, IPL's television viewership crossed over 100 million in just 2016, making it one of the most viewed games in the world, growing exponentially at around 300 per cent during that time (50). The explosive success was attributed to the broad base of the millennial population in India, which are the highest viewers of the game.

Many other companies who launched special offers and promoted in collaboration with the IPL also benefitted massively. For instance, the app-based food-delivery company Swiggy, which primarily targets young tech-savvy millennial customers, started an ad campaign during the IPL season in 2018. This campaign yielded a 25 per cent growth in the orders to the company during the IPL (52). Overall, the IPL still has been a remarkable example of the business transformation of a conventional game to make it more acceptable to the modern youth.

Discussion Questions

1. Discuss the factors behind adoption of 20-20 format amongst millennials?

2. What changes can be recommended in the current format to make the IPL more acceptable to other generations?

....

The Case of Netflix: Winning over Millennial Customers

A recent report by *Business Insider* shed light on the research conducted by a market research firm, Morning Consult, on the values and ethics of millennial shoppers and their expectations for the brands that they shop. Consequently, the company surveyed millennials in the age group between 18 and 29 years old and requested them to fill a survey indicating their preference for over 1,000 brands to analyse how favourably or unfavourably they viewed them. Over 12,000 customers evaluated every single brand on the list. The results indicated that millennials had a natural affinity towards tech companies and that YouTube, Google, Netflix and Amazon were the most preferred (53). Specifically, in terms of TV content, Netflix was the flag-holder in the United States, with around 40 per cent of millennials preferring Netflix over the conventional cable TV. YouTube stood second in terms of TV content preference amongst US millennials (54). Netflix is pioneering the media industry, and these survey results indicate a new wave of change in this sector, which is marked by more and more millennials switching from the conventional TV content to online medium like Netflix. At this juncture, it is essential to ask, How Netflix managed to create a vast customer base comprising of millennials? What are the possible shortcomings? Lastly, what is the way forward for Netflix?

Netflix Inc is a company based in Los Gatos, California, USA. Founded in 1997 by Reed Hastings and Marc Randolph, Netflix is even older than the tech giant Google. Initially started as a DVD sales and rental service, Netflix migrated to online streaming media in 2007. Following their success in the United States, the company soon made its international debut in Canada in 2010. According to the *Wall Street Journal*, the company operated in about 190 countries of the world except for China, Syria, North Korea and Crimea as of 2016 (55). The company also boasts of producing customized media content under the banner 'Netflix Originals', specially targeted towards the millennial population. Overall, the company has amassed 130 million subscribers across the globe as of July 2018 (56).

In terms of the number of millennials, India ranks first in the world. In order to fulfil the demands of over 50 million millennial subscribers in India, Netflix has its unique content strategy (57). Netflix has planned to spend over $8 billion on content for the year 2018 and aims to bring out over a thousand original titles. In India, the company started off with the launch of movies such as *Love Per Square Foot*, followed by *Lust Stories*. The company made its debut Netflix Original Series, *Sacred Games* for the Indian audience. In an interview by chief content officer of Netflix, Ted Sarandos, the company believes in the philosophy of 'customer is the king', and its entry in India was the most difficult owing to the presence of many other competitors such as Amazon Prime, YouTube and Hotstar. However, the company focused mainly on the target segment, that is, millennials and created exclusive content for the same (57).

With regard to the growing competition amongst the online media streaming companies such as Netflix, Amazon Prime and Hulu, spending on original content is on the rise to earn the last dollar with their youngest subscribers—the millennials. However, these companies are facing problems with the millennials sharing their account password with others and hurting the companies' business and revenue models. A *CNBC* report suggests that over 35 per cent of millennial subscribers share their passwords for streaming services as compared to 19 per cent for Generation X customers and 13 per cent for baby boomers. At these password sharing rates, Netflix and other competitors are losing out on hundreds of millions of dollars in revenue. A more significant threat is the upcoming generation, that is, people below 21 years of age, amongst whom the password sharing rates are higher at 42 per cent. Such low willingness to pay is owing to the fact that these kids gain access to these services for free through their parent's account and continue to seek free service into their adulthood (58).

According to Media Partners Asia, a leading market research firm, once crippled by slow internet and low penetration, the Indian online streaming market is currently valued at over 700 million USD and is likely to grow to 2.4 billion USD in 2023. This sudden boom in online streaming is caused by a sharp drop in the mobile internet data prices pioneered by Reliance Jio, a leading telecom company owned by Mukesh Ambani. Consequently, once thrifty users of internet data are reportedly consuming 1.5 million terabytes of data per month (59).

With internet prices being low, subscribers have lower switching costs to migrate to other platforms for free content. Additionally, Indian customers have fewer incentives to migrate from the conventional TV content. This argument is based on the fact that in the United States, a monthly cable subscription costs more than $100 (60), thereby making online streaming more affordable. In India, Netflix is offered at the starting rate of ₹500 per month (approximately $7) for a single screen (61), which is very low compared to the United States, but is still higher than the cable TV services available in India. It has inadvertently created pressure for online streaming companies to stay competitive and profit making at the same time.

Thus, the journey of Netflix by far has been one of the most remarkable ones in terms of attracting and targeting millennial customers. However, coupled with the challenges of offering lower prices and password sharing, it has become increasingly difficult for online streaming companies to book profits.

Discussion Questions

1. How did Netflix manage to create a vast customer base comprising of millennials? What are the possible short-comings? What is the way forward for Netflix?

2. With the increasing rates of password sharing amongst millennials, how can Netflix manage to survive and stay profitable in India?

MILLENNIALS AND OTHER GENERATIONS

REFERENCES

1. Howe, N., & Strauss, W. (2000). Millennials rising: the next great generation. New York: Vintage Books.
2. Sharf, S. (2015, Aug 24). What is a 'millennial' anyway? Meet the man who coined the phrase. Forbes. Retrieved from https://www.forbes.com/sites/samanthasharf/2015/08/24/what-is-a-millennial-anyway-meet-the-man-who-coined-the-phrase/#6ce2508d4a05. Accessed on 11 Sep 2018.
3. Sillman, A., Mccaffrey, C.R., & Peterson, E.R. (n.d.) Where are the global millennials. ATKearney. Retrieved from https://www.atkearney.com/web/global-business-policy-council/article?/a/where-are-the-global-millennials-. Accessed on 11 Sep 2018.
4. Hayes, K. (2018, Jan 11). 9 ways young professionals can prove 'millennial stereotypes' wrong. Forbes. Retrieved from https://www.forbes.com/sites/katehayes/2018/01/11/9-ways-young-professionals-can-prove-millennial-stereotypes-wrong/#6276905c172b. Accessed on 11 Sep 2018.
5. Shetty, A. (2018, Aug 29). What do Indian millennials aspire? Forbes. Retrieved from http://www.forbesindia.com/blog/finance/what-do-indian-millennials-aspire/. Accessed on 11 Sep 2018.
6. PTI. (2018, May 1). 83% Indian millennials ready to switch jobs for pay hike: Report. Business Standard. Retrieved from https://www.business-standard.

com/article/jobs/83-indian-millennials-ready-to-switch-jobs-for-pay-hike-report-118050100600_1.html. Accessed on 11 Sep 2018.

7. PwC report. Millennials at work. Retrieved from https://www.pwc.de/de/prozessoptimierung/assets/millennials-at-work-2011.pdf. Accessed on 11 Sep 2018.

8. Ramanathan, A. (2015, Dec 1). The rise of millennials. Livemint. Retrieved from https://www.livemint.com/Leisure/ZxgufEOH9saYXk5RsmuhIP/The-rise-of-the-millennials.html. Accessed on 11 Sep 2018.

9. Balachandran, M. (2018, Mar 5). 2018 W-power trailblazers: Chiki Sarkar is a publisher of the millennials. Forbes. Retrieved from http://www.forbesindia.com/article/2018-wpower-trailblazers/2018-wpower-trailblazers-chiki-sarkar-is-a-publisher-of-the-millennials/49587/1. Accessed on 11 Sep 2018.

10. KPMG in India. (2017, Oct 24). CEOs need to rejig priorities to be prepared for the millennial customer. Forbes. Retrieved from http://www.forbesindia.com/article/special/ceos-need-to-rejig-priorities-to-be-prepared-for-the-millennial-customer/48479/1. Accessed on 11 Sep 2018.

11. Oracle (2017, Nov 3). How to win millennials in the digital age? Forbes. Retrieved from http://www.forbesindia.com/blog/business-strategy/how-to-win-millennials-in-the-digital-age/. Accessed on 11 Sep 2018.

12. PwC report. Millennials at work. Retrieved from https://www.pwc.com/co/es/publicaciones/assets/millennials-at-work.pdf. Accessed on 11 Sep 2018.

13. Mccabe, S. (2018, Jan 3). 'Work-life balance' top priority for millennials, global survey finds. Accounting Today. Retrieved from https://www.accountingtoday.com/news/work-life-balance-top-priority-for-millennials-global-survey-finds. Accessed on 11 Sep 2018.

14. Landrum, S. (2016, Nov 15). Millennials, here's why face time at work is still important. Forbes. Retrieved from https://www.forbes.com/sites/sarahlandrum/2016/11/15/millennials-heres-why-facetime-at-work-is-still-important/#66b202ba4992. Accessed on 11 Sep 2018.

15. Cosslett, R.L. (2018, Jun 20). Millennials, more face time could save our lives. The Guardian. Retrieved from https://www.theguardian.com/commentisfree/2018/jun/20/millennials-more-face-time-save-lives. Accessed on 11 Sep 2018.

16. Forbes Coaches Council (2017, Apr 4). Millennials and the death of loyalty. Forbes. Retrieved from https://www.forbes.com/sites/forbescoachescouncil/2017/04/04/millennials-and-the-death-of-loyalty/#371c80674562. Accessed on 11 Sep 2018.

17. Fullerton, L. (2017, Aug 7). Brand loyalty differs amongst millennials and GenZ but personalized experience resonates for both. The Drum. Retrieved from https://www.thedrum.com/news/2017/08/07/brand-loyalty-differs-amongst-millennials-and-genz-personalized-experience-resonates. Accessed on 11 Sep 2018.

18. Robert Walters. [Internet]. Retrieved from https://www.robertwalters.co.uk/career-advice/91-per-cent-of-Millennial-professionals-say-career-progression-is-a-top-priority-when-considering-a-new-job.html. Accessed on 11 Sep 2018.

19. Peretz, M. (2017, Sep 27). Want to engage millennials? Try corporate social responsibility. Forbes. Retrieved from https://www.forbes.com/sites/marissaperetz/2017/09/27/want-to-engage-millennials-try-corporate-social-responsibility/#e4fd99c6e4e4. Accessed on 11 Sep 2018.

20. Kundu, S. (2019, Apr 5). Opinion | Wanderlust for millennials is about more than pleasure. Livemint. Retrieved from https://www.livemint.com/

opinion/columns/opinion-wanderlust-for-millennials-is-about-more-than-pleasure-1554403217740.html. Accessed on 11 Sep 2018.

21. Mya, K. (2017, Feb 3). Why millennials have become the wanderlust generation. U.S. News. Retrieved from https://travel.usnews.com/features/why-millennials-have-become-the-wanderlust-generation. Accessed on 11 Sep 2018.

22. Landrum, S. (2017, Aug 17). Why millennials have a complicated relationship with travel. Forbes. Retrieved from https://www.forbes.com/sites/sarahlandrum/2017/08/17/millennials-and-their-complex-relationship-with-travel/#7c56ad7cc3b0. Accessed on 11 Sep 2018.

23. Gimbel, T. (2017, Apr 1). How to help millennials and baby boomers get along. Fortune. Retrieved from http://fortune.com/2017/04/01/leadership-career-advice-millennials-conflict-feud-mentorship/. Accessed on 11 Sep 2018.

24. Cucina, J.M., Byle, K.A., Martin, N.R., Peyton, S.T., & Gast, I.F. (2018). Generational differences in workplace attitudes and job satisfaction: lack of sizable differences across cohorts. J Manage Psychol. 23(8):891–906.

25. Patel, D. (2018, Jan 17). 7 Surprising traits that make millennials excellent employees. Entrepreneur India. Retrieved from https://www.entrepreneur.com/article/306860. Accessed on 11 Sep 2018.

26. Haden, J. (n.d.). A study of 600,000 people shows the secret to managing millennials is to quit thinking of them as millennials. Inc. Retrieved from https://www.inc.com/jeff-haden/a-study-of-600000-people-shows-secret-to-managing-millennials-is-to-quit-thinking-of-them-as-millennials.html. Accessed on 11 Sep 2018.

27. Bruenig, E. (2017, Aug 11). Why is millennial humor so weird? The Washington Post. Retrieved from https://www.washingtonpost.com/outlook/why-is-millennial-humor-so-weird/2017/08/11/64af9cae-7dd5-11e7-83c7-5bd5460f0d7e_story.html?noredirect=on&utm_term=.d65e65a4c1a1. Accessed on 11 Sep 2018.

28. The 2006 Cone Millennial Cause Study. The millennial generation: pro-social and empowered to change the world. Retrieved from https://blogthinkbig.com/wp-content/uploads/Cone-Millennial-Cause-Study-La-hora-de-cambiar-el-mundo.pdf. Accessed on 12 Sep 2018.

29. The Nielson Company (2012, Jun 8). Introducing boomers: marketing's most valuable generation. Nielson. Retrieved from https://www.nielsen.com/us/en/insights/reports/2012/introducing-boomers--marketing-s-most-valuable-generation.html. Accessed on 12 Sep 2018.

30. Hamidullah, M. F. (2015). Managing the next generation of public workers: A public solutions handbook. Routledge.

31. Keaveney, S. M. (1997). When MTV goes CEO: What happens when the 'unmanageables' become managers?. Marketing Management, 6(3), 21–24.

32. Chappelow, C. (2006). Dividends and interests: Learning from experience bridges the generations. Leadership in Action, 26(3), 19–20.

33. Yu, H., & Miller, P. (2005). Leadership style: the X generation and baby boomers compared in different cultural contexts. Leadership Org Dev J. 26(1):35–50.

34. Tiwari, A. (2019). India 3.0: the rise of a thousand million people. New York: Harper Collins; 2019.

35. Daily Excelsior (2019, Oct 4). Article 370 was lapsed in 1957, its existence is unconstitutional. DailyExcelsior.com. Retrieved from https://www.dailyexcelsior.

com/article-370-was-lapsed-in-1957-its-existence-is-unconstitutional/. Accessed on 12 Sep 2018.

36. McDaniel, C. (2019, Mar 9). Baby boomers eternal search for the fountain of youth. Golden Years Magazine. Retrieved from https://goldenyearsmagazine. com/baby-boomers-eternal-search-for-the-fountain-of-youth-p481-209.htm. Accessed on 12 Sep 2018.

37. Wallop, H. (2014, Jul 31). Gen Z, Gen Y, baby boomers: a guide to the generations. The Telegraph. Retrieved from https://www.telegraph.co.uk/news/features/11002767/Gen-Z-Gen-Y-baby-boomers-a-guide-to-the-generations. html. Accessed on 12 Sep 2018.

38. IndiaToday.in (2017, Jun 25). The 1975 Emergency completes 42 years today: 12 facts you should definitely know. India Today. Retrieved from https://www. indiatoday.in/education-today/gk-current-affairs/story/facts-about-the-1975-national-emergency-you-did-not-know-259595-2015-06-25. Accessed on 12 Sep 2018.

39. Bose, R. (2017, Feb 15). Here's a look at ISRO's evolution over the years and its major achievements. ScoopWhoop. Retrieved from https://www. scoopwhoop.com/Heres-A-Look-At-ISROs-Evolution-Over-The-Years-Its-Major-Achievements/#.jqm36h2yz. Accessed on 12 Sep 2018.

40. India Today Web Desk. (2018, May 18). Pokhran I: India's first nuclear bomb test was carried out underground and code named 'Smiling Buddha'. India Today. Retrieved from https://www.indiatoday.in/education-today/gk-current-affairs/story/pokharan-i-first-nuclear-atomic-bomb-test-of-india-324141-2016-05-18. Accessed on 12 Sep 2018.

41. Padmanabhan, V. (2018, Oct 23). Green Revolution and the decline of Congress in India. Livemint. Retrieved from https://www.livemint.com/Politics/mrZxS7dFqTKTzKF8L7IGNK/Green-Revolution-and-the-decline-of-Congress-in-India.html. Accessed on 12 Sep 2018.

42. Young, K. (2018, Mar 28). Three differences in how Zen Z and millennials use social media. We Are Social. Retrieved from https://wearesocial.com/blog/2018/03/three-differences-gen-z-millennials-use-social-media. Accessed on 12 Sep 2018.

43. Tisdall, S. (2019, Apr 28). Love, hate…indifference: is US–UK relationship still special? Guardian. Retrieved from https://www.theguardian.com/politics/2019/apr/28/britain-america-history-special-relationship-highs-and-lows-churchill-to-trump. Accessed on 13 Sep 2018.

44. Byman, D.L. (2007, Jul 1). Iraq and the global war on terrorism. Brookings. Retrieved from https://www.brookings.edu/articles/iraq-and-the-global-war-on-terrorism/. Accessed on 13 Sep 2018.

45. Karkaria, B. (2015, Jul 30). How the 1993 blasts changed Mumbai forever. BBC. Retrieved from https://www.bbc.com/news/world-asia-india-33713846. Accessed on 13 Sep 2018.

46. PTI. (2018, Nov 26). Accused in 2002 Akshardham temple attack in Gujarat arrested. The Hindu. Retrieved from https://www.thehindu.com/news/national/other-states/accused-in-2002-akshardham-temple-attack-in-gujarat-arrested/article25598887.ece. Accessed on 13 Sep 2018.

47. India Today Web Desk. (2017 Nov 26). How 26/11 Mumbai attack happened in 2008: from first eyewitness to Kasab. India Today. Retrieved from https://www.

indiatoday.in/india/story/how-2611-mumbai-terror-attack-happened-in-2008-from-first-eyewitness-to-kasab-1094473-2017-11-26. Accessed on 13 Sep 2018.

48. Henderson, D (2014, Jun 30). Who caused the August 1990 spike in oil prices? EconLog. Retrieved from https://www.econlib.org/archives/2014/06/who_caused_the.html. Accessed on 13 Sep 2018.

49. Steinhilber, B. (2017, May 18). 7 ways millennials are changing the workplace for the better. Better. Retrieved from https://www.nbcnews.com/better/business/7-ways-millennials-are-changing-workplace-better-ncna761021. Accessed on 13 Sep 2018.

50. Amin, R.(2017, Sep 5). How IPL became the third most expensive sports property in the world. Exchange4media. Retrieved from https://www.exchange4media.com/marketing-news/how-ipl-became-the-3rd-most-expensive-sports-property-in-the-world-70395.html. Accessed on 13 Sep 2018.

51. Rediff.com. (2015). Protests at Wankhede over foreign cheerleaders in the IPL. Retrieved from https://www.rediff.com/cricket/report/ipl-8-protests-at-wankhede-over-foreign-cheerleaders-in-the-ipl-harish-kotian/20150520.htm. Accessed on 13 Sep 2018.

52. Mansuri, M. (2018). Swiggy's IPL ad campaign yields 25% growth in orders during IPL. Retrieved from https://www.exchange4media.com/ipl-news/swiggys-ipl-ad-campaign-yields-25growth-in-orders-during-ipl-90467.html. Accessed on 13 Sep 2018.

53. Hanbury, M. (2018, Jul 23). These are the 25 brands that millennials love the most. Business Insider. Retrieved from https://www.businessinsider.in/these-are-the-25-brands-that-millennials-love-the-most/articleshow/65109743.cms. Accessed on 11 Sep 2018.

54. Schwarzbaum, E. (2018, Jul 7). Survey: more than one-third of millennials prefer to watch Netflix on TV over cable. Benzinga. Retrieved from https://www.benzinga.com/news/18/07/11982340/survey-more-than-one-third-of-millennials-prefer-to-watch-netflix-on-tv-over-cab. Accessed on 11 Sep 2018.

55. Ezequiel, M, Sharma, A. (2016). Netflix expands to 190 countries. The Wall Street Journal. Accessed on 11 Sep 2018. Retrieved from https://www.wsj.com/articles/netflix-expands-to-190-countries-1452106429

56. Netflix Q2 18 Letter to shareholders. (2018). Netflix Investor Relations. Retrieved from https://s22.q4cdn.com/959853165/files/doc_financials/quarterly_reports/2018/q2/FINAL-Q2-18-Shareholder-Letter.pdf. Accessed on 11 Sep 2018.

57. Joshi, N. (2018, Jun 30). Behind the rise of Netflix in India. The Hindu. Retrieved from https://www.thehindu.com/entertainment/behind-the-rise-of-netflix-in-india/article24292523.ece. Accessed on 11 Sep 2018.

58. Salinas, S. (2018, Aug 19). Millennials are going to extreme lengths to share streaming passwords, and companies are missing out on millions. CNBC. Retrieved from https://www.cnbc.com/2018/08/19/millennials-are-going-to-extreme-lengths-to-share-streaming-passwords-.html. Accessed on 11 Sep 2018.

59. Singh, M. (2018, Jul 5). Netflix and Amazon are struggling to win over the world's second-largest internet market. CNBC. Retrieved from https://www.cnbc.com/2018/07/05/netflix-and-amazon-are-struggling-to-win-over-indian-viewers.html. Accessed on 11 Sep 2018.

60. Graham, J. (2019, Jan 26). Even with price hikes from Netflix and Hulu, streaming still cheaper than cable. USA Today. Retrieved from https://www. usatoday.com/story/tech/talkingtech/2019/01/26/streaming-still-cheaper-than-cable-even-price-hikes-netflix/2684210002/. Accessed on 13 Sep 2018.

61. Ghosh, S. (2019, Mar 22). ₹250 for a month possible? Sure, says Netflix, which is testing low-cost subscription plan for mobile users in India. YourStory. Retrieved from https://yourstory.com/2019/03/netflix-tests-low-cost-subscription-india-jyonoms6lu. Accessed on 13 Sep 2018.

WHY ARE MILLENNIALS THE WAY THEY ARE?

FACTORS THAT MAKE MILLENNIALS DIFFERENT

The past two decades have witnessed a surge in scholarly as well as practitioner interest in the millennial generation. A significant amount of academic literature has accumulated within the domain of what is commonly referred to as inter-generational differences. Likewise, practitioners have also been intrigued by Generation Y, which is evident from the large volume of practitioner-based content that has been written over the past several years. The previous chapter reviewed the extant literature on generational differences and discussed at length the unique characteristics, attitudes and behaviours of the millennials. The takeaway that can be drawn from a review of the past literature is that millennials are significantly different from their former generations, that is, Generation X and baby boomers, in many respects. These differences present new challenges for work organizations that deal with millennials on a regular basis in the form of two key stakeholders, namely, Gen Y employees and customers. Moreover, the rise in the millennial population makes it all the more crucial for organizations to embrace and manage these differences effectively.

Given an understanding of the dissimilarity between millennials and other generations, an obvious question that may strike many is that of the reason behind these differences. While it has been widely accepted that millennials are different and need to be treated differently, the role of factors that have possibly resulted in this dissimilitude is not very clear. In-depth knowledge of the source of millennial differences may go a long way in understanding this generation and may also provide useful insights that would help in dealing with them effectively. The aim of this chapter, therefore, is to outline a pool of factors that may have contributed towards the development of unique characteristics of the millennial cohort.

The remainder of the chapter is organized as follows. First, we explicate the role that the parents of millennials have played in bringing up their children and how their unique styles of parenting have made the millennials so different. Next, we elaborate upon the role that technology has played in influencing the childhood as well as the adolescent phases of millennial life, thus moulding them into very different adults compared to their Gen X and baby boomer counterparts. Finally, we describe the role of historical events that took place during the lives of millennials and how these unique events or incidents have played their part in shaping millennials differently. We conclude with a case that elucidates our arguments by means of a real-world example.

THE ROLE OF PARENTS

Millennials are often criticized for their need to be coddled, their debt-ridden finances and their reliance on technology (1). In addition to anecdotal evidence, research by credible sources like the National Institutes of Health also reports the higher incidence of traits like narcissism amongst the millennials (2). Their parents are generally held responsible for such characteristics. This is because many of the distinct attributes of millennials are a product of the way that they were raised. Millennials are said to be the offspring of what is referred to as 'helicopter parents'. The academic literature defines helicopter parenting as 'a form of over-parenting in which parents apply overly involved and developmentally inappropriate tactics to their children who are otherwise able to assume adult responsibilities and autonomy' (3). In other words, heli-copter parents 'hover' around their children in the sense that they are overly involved in their children's lives and are exces-sively protective of them. This hyper-involvement is deeply rooted in the personal childhood experiences of helicopter parents who were born and brought up in a hands-off parent-ing style that made them feel neglected, unloved and ignored during their childhood. Driven by such experiences, helicop-ter parents try to overcompensate for all that they could not have by pampering their babies way too much. Instead of adopting a purely authoritarian style, helicopter parents try to be friends with their children. Additionally, cultural shifts in the form of the self-esteem movement increased awareness of child abductions, and experiences of economic collapses stimulated the rise of the helicopter parents (4, 5).

Extant literature has empirically investigated the impact of helicopter parenting on a host of outcomes for the targets of this parenting style. For instance, LeMoyne and Buchanan (6) found that helicopter parenting negatively impacted the psychological well-being of young adults and positively impacted their recreational consumption of pain pills as well as prescription medication use for anxiety/depression. Likewise, over-parenting was observed to be significantly correlated with maladaptive responses to workplace scenarios and lower student self-efficacy (7).

On a similar note, Odenweller et al. (8) reported a positive relationship between helicopter parenting style and undesir-able outcomes, such as millennials' neuroticism and interper-sonal dependency. They also observed a negative relationship between helicopter parenting and millennials' coping efficacy. Another study by Darlow et al. (9) noted the association between helicopter parenting and symptoms of depression and lower self-efficacy, which in turn were associated with lower levels of social and academic adjustment in college. While reviewing the literature that focuses on the dark side of helicopter parenting, it is important to demarcate the boundary of this parenting style from similar concepts. There is a fine line of difference between parental involvement and helicopter parenting. While the former leads to a range of positive outcomes such as higher engagement levels, reported educational gains, satisfaction and better college adjustment, the latter is an exclusive predictor of negative consequences discussed previously (10–12).

We now elaborate upon the specific factors pertaining to parenting that have played their part in making millennials the way they are. We also discuss the impact of these factors in shaping the millennial ways of life.

1. **The rise of nuclear families and its impact on individualism:** Millennials have grown up in a period that was marked by the disintegration of the traditional joint family system and the rise of nuclear families. A recent *Forbes* article sheds light on the distinct features of nuclear families in urban India. First, 88 per cent of nuclear households have three to four members along with the absence of senior citizens. Second, only 11 per cent of families have more than two children. The transition towards a nuclear family system was driven primarily by the surge in migration from villages to towns and cities in a quest for better jobs, financial stability and the need to incline children towards personal and academic development (13).

   This rise of the nuclear family made the childhood experiences of the millennials entirely different from those of their parents. Dual-earner couples in nuclear families spend a substantial portion of their day at work and consequently have little time left to devote to their children. They, however, try to compensate for this lack of time by micromanaging their children and providing them with a luxurious lifestyle. Long hours spent alone at home have sowed the seeds of individualism amongst millennials by making them habituated towards being alone, responsible and independent. This phenomenon is exacerbated by the fact that millennials are also devoid of the social networks that typically prevail within joint families. The lack of warmth and social support from grandparents, cousins and relatives gives birth to individualistic millennial adults who face difficulty in forging high-quality, long-term relationships, especially in their personal lives. A recent survey by *Comet* shockingly revealed that 41 per cent of the surveyed millennials were willing to give up on a relationship if it meant getting a life-changing promotion. Such trends can be traced back to the childhood patterns of millennials (14).

2. **Lone or emperor child syndrome and its impact on personality:** Lone child syndrome is a concept that emerged in China post the introduction of 'Lone child policy' in 1979. Individuals born after 1979 did not have any siblings as they were the only child to their parents. These individuals are primarily the millennials who are said to have been born after 1983. With the shrinking family sizes in urban India, where the majority of the households have fewer than two children, lone child syndrome has become a reality in India as well. This syndrome labels millennials as a generation that is selfish, spoilt, branded and misadjusted because of being the centre of attention for their parents and a lack

of siblings to rival or share with. Research also supports these anecdotes by establishing that only-children are actually less cooperative, more self-centred and less likely to get along with peers. Other studies also report that children who grew up without siblings were likely to have a different brain structure in comparison to their peers who have brothers and sisters. While only-children outperformed in terms of creativity, they were found to be consistently lower on the personality trait of agreeableness than children with siblings. Since a vast majority of millennials are single children, many of their habits, attitudes and behaviours can be attributed to the emperor child syndrome (15, 16).

3. **The culture of participation trophies and its impact on entitlement:** Millennials have truly earned the tag of being a 'Trophy Generation', and their parents can be rightly blamed for this. The concept of a trophy generation advocates the distribution of participation trophies not for winning but for merely showing up at competitions or events. Over the entire span of the millennial childhood, helicopter parents always tried to make their children feel that they were special. The generous distribution of participation trophies indicated to millennials that they deserved special treatment even if they failed to achieve anything. Millennials were accustomed to being handled with kid gloves all through their formative years. The real world, therefore, came as a shock to them as they stepped into the work domain. Their sense of entitlement has created a bagful of problems for their employing organizations. Millennials apparently crave for feedback at work but what they actually want is praise as they are incapable of dealing with negative feedback. They demand work-life balance and take it

to an extreme level where they leave work at dot 5 pm every day and refuse to answer work calls or emails over the weekend. Further, their obsession with making an impact and a lack of clarity over how to achieve the same makes them switch jobs so frequently, sometimes for no reason at all (17, 18, 19).

4. **Over-sheltering and its effect on underdeveloped skills:** The popular view about millennials is that they do not seem to have grown up fully. A recent survey seconds this view by reporting the perspective of millennials according to which millennials themselves do not feel grown up until they hit 27 years of age (20). Generation Y individuals receive a substantial amount of support from their parents even through adulthood. This phenomenon is even stronger in the Indian context where parents take pains to help their children settle down financially as well as personally, in contrast to the West where children leave home and are expected to be on their own once they reach adulthood. Not surprisingly, a recent survey by CBRE (Coldwell Banker Richard Ellis) revealed that nearly 80 per cent of Indian millennials within the age range of 22 to 29 years were still living with their parents (21). Moreover, millennials who live outside their hometowns for jobs spend a large portion of their salaries on rent and other discretionary expenses, and thus accept substantial financial support from their helicopter parents despite having a job (22).

This constant protection from hardships by parents makes millennials incompetent in solving their problems. Also, helicopter parents script the lives of their millennial children, thus transforming them into adults who cannot take independent decisions on their own and perpetually seek the approval of others for their actions.

ANECDOTAL EVIDENCE

An Analogy from the Mahabharata

Having discussed the unique styles of upbringing practised by helicopter parents, we realize that over-parenting is not a very recent phenomenon. In fact, we can also find some traces of over-parenting in ancient Hindu scriptures that were written thousands of years ago. The epic of Mahabharata is a classic example of the same. The powerful king Dhritarashtra had too many ambitions for his eldest son, Duryodhana, similar to the parents of modern times. Aware of the fact that his son walked on the path of *adharma*, Dhritarashtra turned a blind eye towards his son's imperfections. Blinded by extreme love for his son, Dhritarashtra did everything he could to support Duryodhana in his quest for the throne of Hastinapur. Such behaviour can be compared to those of helicopter parents who are also obsessed with their children's success and try to rescue their children from all their troubles and disappointments without acknowledging their weaknesses. Continually torn between the principles of dharma and love for his son, Dhritarashtra was always taken over by the love for his son.

Likewise, despite the challenges of their own lives, helicopter parents try to support their millennial children in every possible way across all spheres of life, be it financial, professional or personal. In doing so, they sometimes compromise on their own needs and values and do unjustified things in the name of parental love. Helicopter parents are the biggest cheerleaders of their children and regularly make their children feel that they are special. Such behaviour on the part of parents makes their children feel entitled to everything, as was the case with Duryodhana of the Mahabharata, and the millennials of today. The fate of Duryodhana is known to all. It is imperative that helicopter parents get rid of this parenting style to protect millennials from similar self-destruction (23).

An Analogy from Ancient Proverbs

'Nothing ever grows under a banyan tree.'

We conclude this section with an ancient Indian proverb that aptly describes the impact of helicopter parenting on millennials. The helicopter parents may be compared to a banyan tree that surely gives shade and comfort but makes it impossible for other plants to grow within its foliage. This is because it protects them from harsh sunlight and weather conditions which are necessary for the healthy growth of any plant. Likewise, helicopter parents, who overly protect their millennial children from hardships, rather end up crippling them in the long run.

THE ROLE OF TECHNOLOGY

Born and brought up during the digital age, millennials have literally grown up in the lap of technology. The most significant development that marked the childhood of millennials was the rise of the internet era. The internet entered India on 15 August 1995, with the launch of public internet access by Videsh Sanchar Nigam Limited (VSNL) (24). These technological advances have left an indelible impression on the young minds of the millennials. The impact of these technological forces on the Generation Y individuals persists even today and is reflected in their habits, attitudes and behaviours. We now focus on how the rise of technology has played its part in shaping millennial ways of life. We also elaborate upon the intergenerational differences that have emerged because of technological advancement.

1. **Millennials' brains are wired differently due to techno-logy use:** Millennials got introduced to smartphones and tablets during their formative years. According to scientists, the human brain continues to mature until the age of 25. Hence, it is likely that the use of technology by millennials, especially at an early age, might impact the process of brain maturity.

   In line with this argument, medical research has also observed that the constant interaction with technology influences brain development in several ways. Assaulted by backlit screens, the brains of millennials may not physically develop in a way similar to that of their parents. Neurologists suggest that there are certain parts of the developing brains, namely, the cerebellum, prefrontal cortex and parietal lobe, that get affected by the use of technology. The cerebellum coordinates and regulates muscular activity, the prefrontal cortex controls personality, cognition and social behaviour, while the parietal lobe is responsible for interpreting language and words. These functions of the human body are likely to be differently developed or even distorted in the case of millennials. Given the fact that a large number of millennials out there are disinterested, distressed and disengaged, neurological changes caused by technological use may be held responsible for the same (25).

2. **Techno-addiction and its impact on millennials' preferences:** Millennials have been exposed to smartphones and tablets ever since their childhood. They have spent a significant fraction of their childhood in front of the screens, playing video games over electronic gadgets. These youngsters grew up to become adults glued to their phones and trapped within the artificial world of social media, memes, web series and YouTube. The overexposure to

technology has completely transformed the ways of life of people born in the digital age to the extent that they have become addicted to it. The results of a recent survey revealed shockingly that millennials check their phone on an average of 150 times a day. Scientists have tried to investigate the motivation behind such behaviour. They found that social media posts, text messages and emails led to the release of a hormone known as 'dopamine' in the human brain, which creates a false sense of accomplishment. Another survey conducted by the Bank of America found four out of every 10 millennials to be having a closer relationship with their smartphones instead of the most important people in their lives. In a YouGov survey, more than half of the millennials themselves admitted to the fact that they were wasting too much time over their smartphones. Despite an acknowledgement of their shortcomings, millennials do not seem to care much about where they are headed. This is evident from the absurd findings of surveys which report that millennials chose to give up on things like physical hygiene, personal belongings, entertainment and caffeine rather than giving up over their smartphone for a week.

Such a dramatic shift in preferences carries unimaginable implications for the future that can unfold only with the progress of time (26–30).

THE ROLE OF HISTORICAL EVENTS

The characteristics of millennials cannot be generalized across the globe simply because these are a function of experiences. Since experiences of individuals belonging to a generational cohort vary with geographical boundaries, the resulting characteristics are also bound to differ. Hence, the events that influenced millennials in the United States may be very different from the events that influenced millennials in India. Having said that, we now flip through the pages of history to spot the most significant events that played a crucial role in shaping Generation Y in the United States and India.

Historical Events in the United States

1. **Political events:** In a recent survey, nearly 9 out of every 10 millennials (86%) reported the terrorist attacks of 9/11 as an important historical event of their lifetime (31). Likewise, the rise to power by the first black president, Barack Obama, was an event that was labelled as significant by as much as 47 per cent of the American millennials (31). The wars of Iraq and Afghanistan make to the list of top-10 historic events for 24 per cent of the millennials (31).

2. **Economic events:** The Great Recession hit the United States in December 2007 and ended in June 2009. The economic downturn was marked by a drop in the real gross domestic product and a surge in the unemployment rate.

3. **Social events:** The debut of MTV and its iconic show 'The Real World' was something that truly fascinated the American millennials and made them believe that anybody could come on TV. The launch of Facebook in 2004 touched the lives of many, and it soon became a part of everybody's lives (32).

4. **Legal events:** The Same-Sex Marriage Act was passed in the United States long back in 2004. Millennials belong to the unique generation that has been so accommodative and tolerant of all forms of diversity (32).

Historical Events in India (33)

1. **Economic changes:** An important economic factor was the opening up of Indian markets in the 1990s post-liberalization, which resulted in the establishment of multinational corporations in tier I cities. The growth of BPOs and MNCs in India led to economic growth, which pushed millennials to earn a good education in the pursuit of better employment opportunities

2. **Political changes:** A long list of events reflective of the political turmoil in India can be compiled. Millennials witnessed the occurrence of major political events such as the assassination of Indira Gandhi, report of the Mandal Commission resulting in the implementation of caste-based reservations and an increase in terrorist attacks. These events continue to haunt millennials, which is evident from the heated debates over social media platforms such as Facebook, Instagram and Twitter.

3. **Social changes:** The blurring of national boundaries led to the proliferation of Western culture amongst the Indian millennials. The rise of nuclear families, migration towards urban areas, increased women participation in the workforce and a heightened identification with work are indicative of the social changes that occurred during the lifespan of Indian millennials.

These economic, political and social forces have played their part in shaping millennial thoughts, ideologies and values and making Generation Y individuals into who they are today.

....

The Dark Side of Social Media: The Blue Whale Challenge

In the age of technological advancement marked by the rise of social media and the internet, online criminal activity and cyberbullying have taken the world by storm. The 'Blue Whale Challenge' is yet another entrant in the league of cyberbullying and internet crime. Incidents related to the infamous Blue Whale Challenge have been hitting the headlines for quite some time. The Blue Whale Challenge is believed to be an online dare-based game wherein the participants are required to complete a series of 50 psychologically twisted or self-harming tasks over a period of 50 days, the last task being suicide (34–36). While uncertainty still prevails regarding the existence of this notorious online game, hundreds of people across the globe, particularly youngsters, have reportedly died of it (37). Five teenagers in India have also been the alleged victims of this game, leading to the death of three of them. Taking a strict view of this deadly game, the government of India directed internet majors such as Google, WhatsApp, Facebook, Instagram and Yahoo to erase its links to prevent further deaths due to this game (38).

The lethal Blue Whale Challenge was developed in Russia in the year 2013 by a 22-year-old psychopath named Philipp Budeikin (39). Unlike other apps or games that can be downloaded over the internet, chosen victims in this game receive personal invitations in the form of links to participate in the challenge. These links are posted secretly in closed groups over social media platforms such as WhatsApp, Facebook and Instagram (40). Once the invite is accepted, the game begins between the administrator and the victim. The game starts off with the administrator brainwashing the participants by assigning them fairly easy daily tasks ranging from waking up at abnormal timings to watching horror videos. Over time, the tasks become increasingly difficult, such as cutting veins and carving the whale symbol on body parts. The final task of the game is to commit suicide (41).

Each participant must submit proof of completion of the task, in the form of photos and videos. If participants refuse to perform a certain task, they are threatened that their family will be harmed or their intimate information will be published over the internet (42). In other words, the participants are led to believe that there is no escape or exit from the game. The victims are chosen in a well-planned manner by the game administrators after having conducted thorough research about the potential participants. Teenagers who share a lot of their personal information online and appear to be more vulnerable or susceptible to persuasion and manipulation serve as soft targets for this challenge (41). The mastermind behind this challenge, Budeikin, is currently in prison after being sentenced to three years. In an interview in Russia, he revealed shockingly that he was wilfully inciting the youth to kill themselves. He added that he was doing it with the intent of cleansing the society of people who were adding no value to it. He coldly referred to those people as the 'biological waste' to the society and said that they were happy to die (39, 43).

Late millennials, who are presently teenagers (aged 15 to 19 years), are the most vulnerable to games such as the Blue Whale Challenge. Experts suggest that the high likelihood of being drawn towards such lethal games and challenges can be attributed to several distinguishing characteristics of millennials. First, contrary to the real world, the virtual world presents a lucrative platform for teenagers to exercise freedom. The lack of restrictions and the opportunity to do unimaginable stuff over the internet is sufficient to give them an adrenaline boost. Second, a large segment of teenagers is presently affected by poor mental health, which is evident from the rising cases of unhappiness, a sense of lacking goals and direction as witnessed by psychiatrists. Teenagers today have very low self-esteem and they constantly look for validation from their external environment. They are willing to go to any extent to project a certain image about them. The completion of such challenging tasks gives them a sense of purpose and blinds them towards the harm that it is doing to them. Third, considering the nature of jobs and the structure of families today, parents hardly have any time left to devote to their children, resulting in teenagers becoming more lost, lonely and depressed. This situation is exacerbated by the effortless availability of technological devices at the teenagers' disposal. Antisocial elements such as cyberbullies try to exploit this opportunity by brainwashing teenagers and making them believe that their life is not worth living (43).

The complex interplay of these critical factors causes young millennials to get trapped in such agonizing and deadly games (44).

Nearly a year after the notorious Blue Whale Challenge claimed hundreds of lives in Russia and abroad, the latest substitute of the same is all set to repeat history. This new online game, known as the 'Momo Challenge', is presently spreading rapidly over social media. Momo is the name of a social media account that uses the image of a grinning grotesque doll with large eyes and a wide mouth. The Momo Challenge begins with the participants receiving disturbing images over WhatsApp or Facebook. The scary images are accompanied by a piece of text saying 'I know everything about you'. Once initial contact is established with the participant, the victims are sent a series of challenges and activities that need to be completed in order to meet 'Momo'.

The challenges are absurd and provoke teenagers to engage in violent acts including suicide. Upon refusal to follow the orders of the game, participants are bullied and intimidated with scary images and dire consequences.

Given the rise of cyberbullying and online crime in the form of games like the Blue Whale Challenge and the Momo Challenge, it is the need of the hour to protect late millennials from such threats. Factors like addiction to social media, mental health issues and diminished attention from parents make late millennials all the more susceptible to such dangers. Parents and faculty need to take a series of steps including regular and open communication with youngsters to protect this generation from the negative influence of social media and the internet.

Discussion Questions

1. What other traits in millennials apart from those mentioned in the case can be responsible for the success of the Blue Whale Challenge amongst them?

2. Discuss the role of cyberbullying and deviant behaviours amongst the millennial generation?

REFERENCES

1. Bodker, I. (2017, Aug 15). How baby boomer parents molded the millennial generation. Retrieved from https://www.barkleyus.com/insights/baby-boomer-parents-molded-millennial-generation/. Accessed on 4 Oct 2018.
2. Stein, J. (2013, May 20). Millennials: the me me me generation. Time. Retrieved from http://time.com/247/millennials-the-me-me-me-generation/
3. Segrin, C., Woszidlo, A., Givertz, M., Bauer, A., & Taylor Murphy, M. (2012). The association between overparenting, parent–child communication, and entitlement and adaptive traits in adult children. Family Relations. 61(2): 237–52.
4. Wiley, F. (2016, Apr 13). Helicopter parents and millennials. Average Millennial. Retrieved from https://averagemillennial.com/2016/04/13/helicopter-parents-and-millennials/. Accessed on 4 Oct 2018.

5. Lythcott-Haims, J. (2015, Jul 9). The four cultural shifts that led to the rise of the helicopter parent. Business Insider. Retrieved from https://www.businessinsider.in/The-four-cultural-shifts-that-led-to-the-rise-of-the-helicopter-parent/article show/48006488.cms. Accessed on 4 Oct 2018.

6. LeMoyne, T., & Buchanan, T. (2011). Does 'hovering' matter? Helicopter parenting and its effect on well-being. Soc Spectr. 31(4):399–418.

7. Bradley-Geist, J.C., & Olson-Buchanan, J.B. (2014). Helicopter parents: an examination of the correlates of over-parenting of college students. Educ+ Train. 56(4):314–28.

8. Odenweller, K.G., Booth-Butterfield, M., & Weber, K. (2014). Investigating helicopter parenting, family environments, and relational outcomes for millennials. Commun Stud. 65(4):407–25.

9. Darlow, V., Norvilitis, J.M., & Schuetze, P. (2017). The relationship between helicopter parenting and adjustment to college. J Child Family Stud. 26(8): 2291–98.

10. Shoup, R., Gonyea, R.M., & Kuh, G.D. (2009, Jun). Helicopter parents: examining the impact of highly involved parents on student engagement and educational outcomes. In 49th Annual Forum of the Association for Institutional Research, Atlanta, Georgia. Retrieved from http://cpr. iub.edu/ uploads/AIR (Vol. 202009)

11. Lipka, S. (2007). Helicopter parents help students, survey finds. Chron High Educ. 54(11):A1, A32.

12. Klein, M.B., & Pierce, J.D., Jr. (2009). Parental care aids, but parental overprotection hinders, college adjustment. J College Student Retention: Res, Theory Practice. 11(2):167–81.

13. Consultants, T. (2017, Dec 12). Disintegration of the joint family system, emergence of nuclear family. Forbes. Retrieved from http://www.forbesindia. com/blog/beyond-the-numbers/disintegration-of-the-joint-family-system-emergence-of-nuclear-family/. Accessed on 5 Oct 2018.

14. Lutz, J. (2018, Feb 28). 41% of single millennials would end a relationship for a promotion. Forbes. Retrieved from https://www.forbes.com/sites/ jessicalutz/2018/02/28/41-of-single-millennials-would-end-a-relationship-for-a-promotion/#d03137bf302c. Accessed on 5 Oct 2018.

15. Dodgson, L. (2017, Sep 28). Only child syndrome is a real thing according to scientific evidence—but it might not be what you think. Business Insider. Retrieved from https://www.businessinsider.com/what-only-child-syndrome-really-is-2017-9?IR=T. Accessed on 5 Oct 2018.

16. Young, S. (2017, May 16). Only child 'syndrome': how growing up without siblings affects your child's development. Independent. Retrieved from https:// www.independent.co.uk/life-style/only-child-syndrome-no-siblings-traits-selfish-more-creative-study-chongqing-china-southwest-a7737916.html. Accessed on 5 Oct 2018.

17. Hosie, R. (2017, Feb 7). Millennials are struggling at work because their parents 'gave them medals for coming last'. Independent. Retrieved from https://www. independent.co.uk/life-style/millennials-struggling-work-careers-because-their-parents-gave-them-medals-for-coming-last-simon-a7537121.html. Accessed on 5 Oct 2018.

18. Bodker, I. (2017, Aug 15). How baby boomer parents molded the millennial generation. Retrieved from https://www.barkleyus.com/insights/baby-boomer-parents-molded-millennial-generation/. Accessed on 5 Oct 2018.

19. Tammy (2017, Apr 12). Millennials: the trophy generation. Learning in Bloom. Retrieved from https://learninginbloom.com/millennials-trophy-generation/. Accessed on 5 Oct 2018.

20. Turner, C. (2017, Apr 24). Millennials do not consider themselves 'grown up' until they are 27, survey finds. The Telegraph. Retrieved from https://www.telegraph.co.uk/education/2017/04/23/millennials-do-not-consider-grown-27-survey-finds/. Accessed on 5 Oct 2018.

21. PTI. (2018, Jan 15). Over 80% young urban Indians live with parents: survey. Business Line. Retrieved from https://www.thehindubusinessline.com/news/real-estate/over-80-young-urban-indians-live-with-parents-survey/article9378537.ece. Accessed on 5 Oct 2018.

22. Sanghvi, D. (2018, Jun 14). Parents' wallets still funding young millennial lifestyles. Livemint. Retrieved from https://www.livemint.com/Money/Dk9pThWk6WiHMdFXbIFULO/Parents-wallets-still-funding-young-millennial-lifestyles.html. Accessed on 5 Oct 2018.

23. Ramani, S. (2015, Aug 14). The story of how the Internet came to India: an insider's account. News18. Retrieved from https://www.news18.com/news/tech/the-story-of-how-the-internet-came-to-india-an-insiders-account-1039533.html. Accessed on 6 Oct 2018.

24. Zachos, E. (2015, Nov 14). Technology is changing the millennial brain. Public Source. Retrieved from https://www.publicsource.org/technology-is-changing-the-millennial-brain/. Accessed on 6 Oct 2018.

25. Brandon, J. (2017, Apr 17). The surprising reason millennials check their phones 150 times a day. Inc. Retrieved from https://www.inc.com/john-brandon/science-says-this-is-the-reason-millennials-check-their-phones-150-times-per-day.html. Accessed on 5 Oct 2018.

26. Barna, D. (2017, Oct 23). Millennials are more addicted to their phones than ever. MyDomaine. Retrieved from https://www.mydomaine.com/millennials-smartphine-addiction. Accessed on 6 Oct 2018.

27. Ballard, J. (2018, Jun 25). Over half of millennials say they waste too much time on smartphones. YouGov. Retrieved from https://today.yougov.com/topics/relationships/articles-reports/2018/06/25/smartphone-habits-millennials-boomers-gen-x. Accessed on 6 Oct 2018.

28. Bhardwaj, P. (2018, Jun 28). Almost half of millennials say they would rather give up shampooing for a week than stop using their phones. Business Insider. Retrieved from https://www.businessinsider.in/Almost-half-of-millennials-say-they-would-rather-give-up-shampooing-for-a-week-than-stop-using-their-phones/articleshow/64770639.cms. Accessed on 6 Oct 2018.

29. Stinson, A. (2018, Jun 29). Are millennials addicted to their phones? This new survey basically says yes and I feel seen. Elite Daily. Retrieved from https://www.elitedaily.com/p/are-millennials-addicted-to-their-phones-this-new-survey-basically-says-yes-i-feel-seen-9615363. Accessed on 6 Oct 2018.

30. Deane, C., Duggan, M. & Morin, R. (2016, Dec 15). Americans name the 10 most significant historic events of their lifetimes. Pew Research Center. Retrieved from http://www.people-press.org/2016/12/15/americans-name-the-10-most-significant-historic-events-of-their-lifetimes/. Accessed on 6 Oct 2018.

31. Rich, R. (n.d.). The Great Recession. Federal Reserve History. Retrieved from https://www.federalreservehistory.org/essays/great_recession_of_200709. Accessed on 6 Oct 2018.

32. Raina, R. (n.d.). What's different about the Indian millennial? People Matters. Retrieved from https://www.peoplematters.in/article/hr-ready/whats-different-about-the-indian-millennial-13231?utm_source=peoplematters&utm_medium=interstitial&utm_campaign=learnings-of-the-day. Accessed on 6 Oct 2018.

33. Express Web Desk (2017, Oct 21). What is Blue Whale Challenge? The Indian Express. Retrieved from https://indianexpress.com/article/what-is/what-is-the-blue-whale-challenge/. Accessed on 7 Oct 2018.

34. Mahadevaiah, M., & Nayak, R.B. (2018). Blue Whale Challenge: perceptions of first responders in medical profession. Indian J Psychol Med. 40(2):178.

35 Biswas, S. (2017, Aug 3). 13 reasons why Blue Whale Challenge is not the problem. India Today. Retrieved from https://www.indiatoday.in/fyi/story/blue-whale-challenge-suicide-game-death-13-reasons-why-1027849-2017-08-03. Accessed on 7 Oct 2018.

36. Express News Service (2017, Oct 21). What's the internet 'game' killing young people worldwide? The Indian Express. Retrieved from https://indianexpress.com/article/explained/whats-the-internet-game-killing-young-people-worldwide-pink-whale-4799981/. Accessed on 7 Oct 2018.

37. Express Web Desk (2017, Oct 21). Blue Whale Challenge: these are the 5 suspected cases in India. Retrieved from https://indianexpress.com/article/india/blue-whale-challenge-these-are-the-suspected-cases-india-4798745/. Accessed on 7 Oct 2018.

38. Jaini, A. (2017, Aug 2). Meet the 22-year-old creator of the 'Blue Whale' death game. The Times of India. Retrieved from https://timesofindia.indiatimes.com/india/meet-the-22-year-old-creator-of-the-blue-whale-death-game/articleshow/59860662.cms. Accessed on 7 Oct 2018.

39. NcprGov. FAQs: Blue Whale Challenge: what parents need to know. Retrieved from http://ncpcr.gov.in/showfile.php?lid=1499. Accessed on 7 Oct 2018.

40. Rossow, A. (2018, Feb 28). Cyberbullying taken to a whole new level: enter the 'Blue Whale Challenge'. Forbes. Retrieved from https://www.forbes.com/sites/andrewrossow/2018/02/28/cyberbullying-taken-to-a-whole-new-level-enter-the-blue-whale-challenge/#af1cb372673e. Accessed on 7 Oct 2018.

41. Baruah, J. (2017, Aug 20). Blue Whale Challenge and other 'games' of death. The Economic Times. Retrieved from https://economictimes.indiatimes.com/magazines/panache/blue-whale-challenge-and-other-games-of-death/articleshow/60135835.cms. Accessed on 7 Oct 2018.

42. Stewart, W. (2017, Jun 29). Man who invented Blue Whale suicide 'game' aimed at children says his victims who kill themselves are 'biological waste' and that he is 'cleansing society'. MailOnline. Retrieved from https://www.dailymail.co.uk/news/article-4491294/Blue-Whale-game-mastermind-says-s-cleansing-society.html. Accessed on 7 Oct 2018.

43. Kumar, P.M. (2016, Aug 23). Good to know: how to file a complaint against cyber bullying? The Logical Indian. Retrieved from https://thelogicalindian.com/good-to-know/government-awareness/report-cyber-bullying/. Accessed on 8 Oct 2018.

44. IANS. (2017, Aug 4). Blue Whale challenge: why teenagers are vulnerable to the game and what you can do about it. Hindustan Times. Retrieved from https://www.hindustantimes.com/health/blue-whale-challenge-why-teenagers-are-vulnerable-to-the-game-and-what-you-can-do-about-it/story-Yc91FxDuGBinBJj3LVBq4J.html. Accessed on 8 Oct 2018.

3

GENERATIONAL DIVERSITY IN THE ORGANIZATIONAL CONTEXT

Work values have been found to evolve over time, depending upon the meaning one attaches to work. During the 16th and 17th centuries, when religiosity was at its prime, appeasing God seemed to be the most significant work. The struggle towards attaining salvation initiated the pathway to being morally correct and working with dedication. Over due course of time, the ability to distinguish between the morally correct and wrong became intertwined with work. Values grew to become one's understanding of doing the right thing. Work values (conceptualized as an extension of values applicable in the organization) engulf employees' attitude at the workplace, which they look upon from time to time to appraise the situations and activities at work and meet the organizational goals (1). Sense of duty, hard work, sincerity, integrity, perseverance and so on all come to be associated values one needs to have at the workplace.

Every generation possesses differing work values owing to the different time periods in which they commenced work. Work values have played a pivotal role in the organizational content, as these values induce a person to act differently from the others. In most cases, how individuals behave at work is generally due to the work values developed by them in the organization. Every generation is accustomed to developing their own work value as per the socio-economic conditions experienced by them during their growing up years. As such, the developed work value becomes a characteristic of their generation. The baby boomers, Generation X and Generation Y all possess their striking work values, which are characteristic of their generational cohort (2).

These work values reflect in the different working styles at the workplace. It is often noticed that due to different working styles, which is relatively same for a particular generation apart from few personality changes, other generations cultivate certain misconceptions at the workplace regarding other cohorts (3). Owing to such differences as well as perceptual misunderstandings, the obvious clashes at the workplace increase, culminating in conflicts which need to be resolved. At any given time, there might be two to three generations working together on the same project. It becomes immensely important, then, to resolve those conflicts and make them work in concord.

Work values can be intrinsic or extrinsic. Intrinsic work values are those that are focused on deriving internal satisfaction from work, such as intellectual stimulation, learning and so on, whereas external work values provide an employee superficial satisfaction and arise as an outcome of work such as salary, status and so on. Apart from intrinsic and extrinsic, employees might also possess the social work value and status value (2). Every generation is bound to be marked by a different work value, whether intrinsic or extrinsic or others. Job acceptance, task performance, style of performing the task, group orientation, social tolerance, quitting the job and so on are all contingent upon the defining generational character trait towards work.

With respect to generational cohorts, every cohort has its defining work value. Studies have often revealed that baby boomers, growing up in optimistic and healthy times, focus on hard work and achievement. They value extrinsic rewards such as recognition and high salary more than anything else at work. They believe that they perform their task with utmost dedication, and this pays off. Gen X lays more emphasis on their skills and autonomy. Having experienced social change and familial insecurity in their childhood, they demand social security at the workplace as well as work-life balance from their place of work. Gen Xers also show a preference for social values apart from intrinsic values. The millennials, or the generation Yers, want their jobs to be more fulfilling for them, and include their work when counting on life satisfaction. They prefer work to be their calling, privy of their intrinsic work value. Even though Gen Y possesses high status orientation, their speediness and impatience towards fame, recognition and success can become more of a bane than a boon. These work values characterize their every move in the workplace, including their decision-making (3).

ATTITUDE TOWARDS WORK

We have already discussed the attitude towards work for the three generational cohorts. Baby boomers consider their work as their prime motive in life, Gen Xers regard work as a way to survive, while the Gen Y regard their careers as a means to satisfy daily needs and take no shame in having parallel jobs. Technology drives the Gen Y. Changing jobs is an everyday affair for the millennials, whereas it is considered degrading to one's career for baby boomers.

Examples: Let us consider the activity of online shopping as an example. Who would have thought that the simple activity of barter in order to procure something useful for oneself would undergo such a drastic change that it would become an entire industry on its own. Online shopping or e-commerce has emerged as one of the greatest changes of these times. One cannot simply overlook the generational causes attached to this mass culture. The baby boomers, honestly, could never imagine something like this, that is, sitting at home and getting whatever you want delivered to you with just a few clicks (4). The baby boomer generation has been so orthodox in its ways that they still find the concept of online purchasing amusing. The millennials, on the contrary, find it difficult to imagine life without it. Popularized by the corporate giants Amazon and Flipkart, e-commerce greatly flourishes in today's India.

The baby boomers, who grew up in a period which was a far cry from technology, have a nonchalant attitude towards online shopping. But the creators of such portals, having been the privileged Generation Xers, worked hard to develop and upgrade these portals. They invested time and effort to develop these websites and even greater effort to make them acceptable to the society. For example, Flipkart was initially working from a two-bedroom apartment as an online bookstore (5). Today, the company has become a multi-million-dollar business, selling everything from everyday eatables to luxury goods. The success of Flipkart is largely attributable to word-of-mouth publicity as well as the innate nature of the technology-loving millennials. They prefer having everything rather home-delivered to them. This is substantiated by the number of online websites and apps launched for the delivery of goods and services.

Oyo Rooms is another case where a millennial entrepreneur, Ritesh Agarwal, has changed the landscape of the travel industry in India through his sheer dedication and perseverance to his work. Ritesh had very humble origins and began his career by selling SIM cards on the streets of Odisha. Since then, he has come a long way, and today investors in his company hail him as a person who has great clarity of thought despite being so young. The ease with which he can handle everything, from strategic insights to the minute details of a property owner, is something that is often talked about in the company circles. His attitude towards work developed very early on through his Thiel Fellowship, where he learnt to 'think big and create an impact, without thinking if anybody has done it before' (6). This entrepreneurial nature of the millennials has fed the Indian economy with humongous tech-based apps, catering to every need of the consumer, giving the brick-and-mortar stores and other foreign companies a run for their money.

PERCEPTIONS OF GENERATIONS

When it comes to the workplace, we see people from different age groups working together in teams. The workplace has various profiles of employees working together to achieve long-term organizational goals. The modern organization witnesses diverse employee bases of varying race, religion, caste, ethnicity, educational background, sexual preferences, financial backgrounds and so on. Generational difference is but one more such diversity added to the list. Organizations always boast of employees working together happily in a nurturing environment and forging healthy relationships (7). But it is not always a sweet story. Apart from the other forms of diversity, generational diversity needs to be managed in the organization.

We have already mentioned the difference in work values of these generational cohorts. These characteristics, which speak for the generation, lead to a stark difference in job attitudes. With their affinity for structure, a baby boomer led-project team will greatly dispel the Xers who hate authority and want to work on their own. This is just a simple instance which could lead to rifts. Hence, it is important for the modern-day manager to acknowledge the existence of such differences and take them into accord in order to build a friendly organization.

In this section, we shall focus upon how the characteristics of each generation sets them apart from other generations.

The way they are perceived in the organization is highly a reflection of how they carry themselves, especially with regard to physical appearance, which speaks volumes about the individual. Here we shall see how each of these traits is responsible for the perception others have of them and how it affects their organizational life.

Millennials have already become the largest segment of the workforce. It is also estimated that they will make up 75 per cent of the global workforce by 2025 (8). Millennials have always had a tendency to chart out their own course and very often do not join the family business. A notable case is that of Aryaman Vikram Birla, son of business baron Kumar Mangalam Birla who chose cricket as his career over family business. He was picked up by the Rajasthan Royals for an impressive ₹30 lakhs in the 2018 IPL auction. His eldest sister, Ananya Birla, has also launched her own microfinance business and e-commerce luxury portal start-up, prompting everyone to believe that it is down to the youngest son who will inherit the Birla Empire. Another notable mention is that of Kavin Mittal, son of Bharti Airtel chairman, Sunil Mittal, who runs the Hike messenger app (9). This perception of doing things their own way has persisted amongst millennials for quite some time. Europe is a classic case where the next generation takes money and starts a new business altogether.

THE BABY BOOMERS VERSUS THE GEN Y

Today, the baby boomers mostly form the employer group or hold the top management positions in an organization. They are the major stakeholders in the company and we see them at managerial roles. In their late 50s and 60s, we hardly see them slogging out at lower positions in global houses (7). When it comes to India, the top family conglomerates, Tata and Birla see their businesses run by the second generation in the family, both in their 60s and 50s.

The Generation Y or the millennials consider the baby boomers to be old and strict. Millennials who are not fond of rules find them to be too rule abiding and adamant. Although they respect them, they do not want to be led by them due to the lack of flexibility in their leadership. Generation Y appears to detest the flak they keep receiving by their seniors and avoid getting into their bad books (7). The millennials feel that the baby boomers do not have a sense of urgency and are willing to devote days for a task which can be done by them in hours.

The Generation Y believe in the outcomes, rather than the means like the baby boomers. They want to finish their targets, rather than worry about how the target is to be achieved. Millennials do not understand why their appearance or reliance upon technology is criticized, since learning is not correlated with one's appearance. They like to come to the office, do their task and then go out and party, rather than slogging for hours like the baby boomers (10).

The baby boomers' deep commitment to one organization is not understood by the tip-of-the-finger millennials. They feel that in order to grow it is necessary for everyone to move out of their comfort zones, which contradicts how the boomer wants to stay in their own safe haven. They consider the old-fashioned baby boomers to be missing out on the thrill and adventures of life. Being too familiar with the concept of 'chilling out', even at the workplace, the millennials find the baby boomers way of life too conservative, fraught with tensions and burdens, which they themselves create (4).

The change in working style is prevalent in a management when the millennials start to enter the top management teams and hold executive positions in organizations. They come up with ideas and schemes centred on luring the millennial customer and focus on products and services that will attract the Gen Y (3). For example, Reliance Jio Limited brought on board 27-year-old Akash Ambani to capture the interests and needs of the younger generation population in the telecommunication industry (11). Hence, it is highly likely that organizational boards rely upon the out-of-the-box ideas of the Gen Ys to bring about change and an aura of freshness.

Although working together with employees half as young as themselves is viable for the best interest of the organization, baby boomers seem to face an internal conflict. Millennials reaching top positions, because of their years of hard work and toil, does not seem fair to the baby boomers. For example, Mr Abhishek, a sales employee who worked for five years in an organization before reaching the status of an expert, suddenly found a young entrant, just completing six months in the organization, being assigned the same status. Since it was an advertising firm, it was deemed important to get the perspective of the youth of today, leading to the recruitment of Amit. The young entrant, Amit, had worked for three different companies in a year and was a star performer in all the positions he held. Working on a project together was becoming difficult for Abhishek, who could not understand the aggressive strategies Amit would come up with. Amit's ideas always found favour with the top bosses, which made Abhishek feel undermined at his job. Although he sometimes tried to question Amit, Amit always came up with some reasonable explanation. The game changed when the strategy devised by Amit actually bore good returns and was able to bring in a lot of customers.

Millennials are seen by the baby boomers as slackers. The care-free millennials, who focus on performing the job smartly, are often criticized by the baby boomers for their fast life (4). From their working styles to their choice of clothes, everything is remotely opposite to those of the baby boomers. Hence, both these generations seem to be at loggerheads with one another.

The millennials' sense of freedom and life are perceived to be slanderous by the baby boomers. Sitting at a desk and working hours on a certain job is not the style of millennials. They would rather prefer to complete the task within a few hours, using technology. Baby boomers also see them as too reliant upon technology. One can often hear them remark that millennials are too frivolous. Millennials believe in smart work. Google is a part of their everyday lives and they do not think twice before looking up something on the internet, a luxury not available to the baby boomers. Hence, they are always considered as being too reliant upon the internet and the technology and having no mind of their own. However, that is not the case as the millennials are very sharp and intelligent (12).

The appearance of millennials is also criticized. Being causal at the workplace is not something millennials shy away from. They prefer wearing jeans and tee at work, accessorized by causal chappals. The conservative baby-boomer, who considers the workplace to be pious, considers the millennial's dressing style to be unruly and rustic, a sign that they are not serious about work. Such is the free spiritedness of the millennials, as reflected in their attire, that top global organizations, such as Facebook and Google do not have a mandatory dress code. On a weekday, one can find a male employee in casual tees and shorts, wearing slippers, with headphones plugged in, walk in the offices of Google (13). The same boy might be heavily criticized by his grandfather, working in the Tata Group, over his attire. Although cherishing the fact that his grandson works for one of the topmost companies of the world, he would think that he is not disciplined.

A millennial also believes in multitasking, which is considered by the baby boomers as a sign of less dedication. They come across as being less serious about work and having low focus. When these millennials become managers, they have a hard time dealing with baby boomers, who try to find faults with their managerial skills due to their perceptions (12). The tendency of the millennial to possess low organizational loyalty is unwarranted by the baby boomers. They feel that this is a very fast generation, possessing no form of attachment to anything and wanting to live only for themselves.

The entrepreneurial knack of the millennials is such that they make their offices their homes or, rather, their homes their office. Their laptops become their office, where they remain glued to it, working day in and day out (10). The decision to start their own company itself becomes a concern for baby boomers as they do not understand how quitting one's high-paying job to live in months of financial crisis can be acceptable to some. Always thriving on the lump sum pay for their hard work, they fail to understand how someone would not want to join a big organization and give up the perks of work to open up their own firm.

THE BABY BOOMERS VERSUS THE GEN X

The boomers or the orthodox ones are set in their ways. They are found to be hard to please and very custom oriented. The Gen X finds dealing with them a tough job, warranting extra effort. The freedom-loving Xers are in stark contrast to their structure-loving boomer managers or employers. The boomers have worked hard to reach the position they are at and feel they deserve respect and credit along with a right to be stern. However, it is this same lack of autonomy that the Xers detest. Although they work under them, Xers find it hard to cooperate with the boomers and consider them to be strict task managers. They also feel that they are less appreciative of their counterparts (14).

The work ethics of the baby boomers are highly esteemed in the organization. Their dedication, honesty and integrity are something they take pride in. Though Gen Xers consider these traits to be assets, they feel that doing smart work is the need of the hour. They perceive baby boomers to be competent, but slow at adapting to changing or challenging situations.

Gen Xers being the children of the Baby boomers see a need for a quicker pace in their tasks. They feel that they are too rigid and are unaccepting of change. The Gen Xers consider them a tad slow. They want to bring changes in the norms, but the boomers oppose those. Hence, sometimes, boomers are also viewed as hindrances in the work of the Xers (14). The Xers as managers want to create an environment for everyone to perform their tasks as per their wish. However, baby boomers need order and autonomy, and working sans proper leadership and guidance hinders their productivity. The baby boomers' love for hierarchy does not befit the Xers.

A significant difference in attitudes between them lies in their friendliness with technology. Gen Xers grew up in the era when the technology was developing and are hence more comfortable with it. Compared to the Xers, baby boomers are more comfortable doing tasks mechanically or manually. Modern organizations rely entirely on computers and technology for work. Even the manufacturing industries take the assistance of software to functionalize the work and production. Hence, they do not want to lag behind and have learnt to access technology to match with the times. Although some have become very adept in functioning with technology, the question lies if we can still consider them at par with other generations (13). The Gen Xers ability to work without question gives them an edge over the boomers. They do not wish to perform tasks mechanically, as can be seen in the mechanization of all the jobs.

The State Bank of India faced a massive challenge from its employees when it shifted to computerized systems. The employees, who were not technologically adept, had to be trained accordingly to use the banking software. They felt it was a laborious task for them to learn at their age.

The Gen Xers value their work-life balance immensely, unlike the baby boomers. The baby boomers had to work hard, work extra shifts in order to fund themselves and their family, resulting in work-family conflict. Moreover, the terms work-family conflict, work-life balance and so on were not in existence then (10). Although some baby boomers might approve of the Xers concern for their families, most regard this as being flaccid about work, and putting family above work.

Baby boomers consider the Xers to have less value for work. Since the Xers have greater regard for their skills and learning, they work accordingly in the organization to harbour that. Their love for the comforts of life, their philosophy of 'work to live' does not find concord with the baby boomers prophesizing 'live to work'.

Baby boomers like appreciation for their task and want to climb their career ladder slowly. They value promotion as a return of their hard work. When a Gen X, having completed one project successfully, competes for a work promotion, baby boomers feel they are not entitled to it. They feel like the Xer seeks a job promotion in a short span of six months, in contrast to their generation where they would get promoted at the end of a year or more.

To illustrate the above differences, we take the case of a hypothetical manufacturing plant. The plant has several quality control software employed to check the final quality of the product. Mr Ghemawat had been working in the quality control department of the organization and, for years, had been overseeing everything manually. When a new 35-year-old CEO is appointed, he decides to install quality control software, which will make the manual testing redundant. Mr Ghemawat is asked to go for a 15-day training programme to learn the working of the new tool, which he finds difficult to learn at his age. His younger counterparts who had been taking advice from him previously are able to learn the operations quickly, since they are more comfortable with technology. Additionally, Mr Ghemawat does not approve of the software and is bent on using his manual techniques again to gauge the operations more effectively. He is told that the software is efficient enough, but he does not oblige. He belongs to the baby boomer generation and feels more comfortable doing things in a set predefined way, and trusts his judgement more than that of the machine. On the contrary, his Gen X counterparts feel more comfortable with the software, since it simplifies their job. They feel happy at work and begin to look forward to the leadership of the new CEO. The company also feels that although incurring huge costs, installing the software to oversee the task boosts productivity, by cutting down the slack time.

Hence, we see how a difference in opinions between the Gen X and the baby boomers can lead either of the generations to suffer.

THE GEN X VERSUS THE GEN Y

The Generation X and Y have various similarities amongst them since they both are the technology friendly generation.

Their work attitudes also connote at some point and both believe in the philosophy of life satisfaction. Yet, the easy-going ways of the millennial seem to be at a discord with the Gen X. The millennials, too, consider Gen Xers to be quite individualistic and production oriented in their ways. Although the Gen X seek autonomy, they never question the working of their superiors unlike the millennials. Millennials are quick to question every move and decision taken by the supervisors and co-workers alike and do not withhold themselves from giving an opinion. Because of this character trait, they do not come across as laidback, but rather as overconfident and ungrateful (3). Millennials are undaunted and consider their managers and supervisors to be equals to them.

Gen Xers identify with the millennials to a certain extent and feel that they need a role model and a sense of direction. Their work skills and ability to perform a task prove their capabilities in front of their Gen X managers, but still they feel that a lot more can be taught to them. The Gen Xers feel that they lack in professionalism to a certain degree and can do much better if properly trained and counselled. Not possessing a high sense of attachment to the organization themselves, the Gen Xers do not disregard their preference for their work. Notwithstanding, they find the millennials to lack a sense of ownership to a certain degree (4). Although millennials are socially cooperative and tolerant towards others, they bear less organizational responsibility.

Coming across as arrogant, the millennials consider their previous generations to be difficult to deal with. Although the Gen Xers prepare themselves to be examples for the millennials, the millennials consider them to be trying too hard to prove themselves. They feel that Gen Xers are quick to learn but are somewhat more concerned about their safety and security. The deep need for work-life balance makes the millennials think of Gen Xers as being lesser career driven. However, in sharp contrast to the millennials, the Gen Xers have well sketched out career paths. Focusing on self-fulfilment from work, millennials go easy with the rules and are willing to bend them whenever possible, unlike the Gen Xers (12). Requiring lesser structure at the workplace, the millennials prefer to work in teams, but the Gen Xers perform well on independent tasks.

In this technology-driven era, millennials consider technology to be their right-hand. Right from job hunting to hunting for food, there is no activity that the millennials do not rely upon technology for. In contrast, Gen Xers, although not intimidated by technology, are not tech-freaks. They rely more upon their problem-solving skills, but are not afraid to avail technology if and when required. With their skill-based approach, the Gen Xers even view technology as a learned skill, rather than as an essential to the task.

The Gen X manager is always wary of the way Gen Y carry themselves at the workplace. They do not want the company culture to be affected by their wayward lifestyle. A Gen X manager is also aware of how easy it is for the Gen Y employee to switch jobs. They value them for the skills they bring to the organization, but they know that they cannot keep Gen Xers bound to the same organization (13). Moreover, it is simpler for a millennial, even in high positions, to quit their jobs in search of better opportunities or starting their own ventures. Being the children of parents who faced job loss during recession, millennials are highly motivated to be self-sufficient and give less importance to traditional jobs in a company.

Considering the need for the current generation to be independent and self-reliant, the government of India has launched its Start Up India initiative to fund scalable entrepreneurial projects to help them to become big businesses. Ever since the initiative was started in 2015, the government has funded 129 start-ups successfully. Such initiatives have widespread effects, so much so that the situation has become cyclic and self-fulfilling. With the promise of funding and investment, grants increase and more people are encouraged to become employers rather than employees (15).

Retention of such millennials becomes a difficult activity in light of their work values. Their extensive job-hopping, in the hope to quickly advance in their careers, encourages the Gen X managers to invest more time in trying to keep them at their respective jobs. Infosys faces the problem of higher attrition rates, especially amongst employees who complete two–four years at work. The management needs to earn the organizational loyalty of the millennial generation, by showing their care and concern not just for profits but the triple bottom line as well.

A 2018 Deloitte Millennial Survey reveals that millennials seek that their managers and leaders act aggressively and pro-actively take decisions for the betterment of the society as a whole. The younger workforce's disappointment with their business leaders who are only concerned about profit and are working less for the society is visible in the survey. Only a small fraction of 28 per cent want to stay in the organization for more than five years and yearn that their companies and employers provide them with a prospect of return good enough to make them stay. These reasons involve not just guaranteed share of profits, but their leaders offering them flexibility, appreciating their diversity and making them adept at the innovative nuances of Industry 4.0 (14).

....

The Case of IBM: Managing Generational Diversity in the Workforce

International Business Machines Corporation (IBM) is an American multinational computer manufacturing company operating in around 170 countries. The company sells computer hardware and software parts and also provides consultancy services. In 2017, the company had over 380,000 employees and is considered one of the largest companies in the world (16). Employees of the company or popularly known as 'IBMers' are highly diverse in terms of culture, religion, nationality, gender and age, amongst others. Managing such a vast, diverse and multigenerational workforce located across the globe is a big challenge for the company.

The increasing longevity rates, decreasing birth rates and improving working conditions have resulted in higher employee longevity. As a consequence, modern workplaces comprise of cohorts of millennials, baby boomers, Generation X and Generation Z. As employees of various generations work alongside each other, there exist several critical challenges in managing them. A recent survey of HR managers in organizations with more than 500 employees reported that 58 per cent of managers have experienced conflict between younger and older employees (17). Thus, understanding of multigenerational workforce is crucial for managers to handle the disputes and create an inclusive and productive workplace.

With the aim of managing the generational diversity in the organization, the company launched its 'Diversity and Inclusion Programme'. In 2007, it undertook a massive campaign in line with the Generational Workforce Strategy, to understand the 'Mature age' employee, that is, their organizational needs and ways to retain them (18). At a time when companies were facing tremendous attrition rates, IBM was able to sustain its employees by providing them with a company culture favourable for their growth. The company believed that the right way to go forward while managing diversity is by making every employee feel valuable in the organization. IBM tried to build a corporate culture where the needs of every age group were addressed. Respect for one another is a trend at IBM, where people get together to celebrate others.

IBM provided the benefits of flexitime to the young breed of workers, apart from the freedom to choose one's working schedule on their terms. Being a technology-driven company, it leaves no stone unturned to capture the budding talent of today. The primary value of the company lies in building an environment susceptible to growth; its corporate strategy is to allow individuals to 'think'. It meets the needs of all the generations and enables them to learn and develop by providing them a culture of innovation, compensation equivalent to their performance, work-life balance, flexibility and leadership opportunities.

There is no doubt that IBM left no stones unturned to adjust the management styles to improve the effectiveness amongst the generations. However, in certain countries, such multigenerational differences can accommodate up to five generations and in Asian countries these differences are very stark and visible. A younger boss is unacceptable and considered disrespectful in many cultures. Thus, within such a cultural context, can the diversity and inclusion programmes to mitigate intergenerational differences like those by IBM ever be fully successful?

Discussion Questions

1. Can such programmes be replicated across different cultures? If yes, what factors will determine the success of such programmes?

2. Does the IBM's programme to mitigate multigenerational differences work in India? Provide justifications for your answer.

....

Perception of Luxury: Louis Vuitton Handbags

Louis Vuitton is a French-based luxury fashion brand. Offering a wide range of products, from handbags, shoes, watches, leather goods, belts, accessories, perfumes and so on, it is a highly renowned brand. Regarded as a status symbol, Louis Vuitton goods are priced at a premium and are only considered fit for the clientele from the upper social strata (19).

It has been observed that differences exist across generations in their perceptions of luxury goods and brands. Luxury is regarded as something rare, more desirable and premium priced, associated with skyrocket prices. Traditionally, brands like Louis Vuitton or Mercedes-Benz had an aura of being exclusive and elitist. Only a few selected, the top-notch, the crème de la crème of the society could lay their eyes and hands on these. Even so, the brands were always very hushed up in their affairs, and their communication was very close. Back then, this worked for those luxury brands (19).

Taking the example of Louis Vuitton handbags, 50 years back, the average Indian consumer could not imagine buying one. They exuded the aura of being too expensive, which in reality they were, giving them an unattainable quality. Baby boomers considered these handbags to be items connected to the rich. Moreover, the economic conditions were such that these items were not sought after. It may not have come as a surprise that many claimed not to have heard of these branded bags. Perceived to be classy, the baby boomers considered them to be a fashion statement. The traditional baby boomers did not want to spend their hard-earned pay on the statement items. They believed these items were for the wealthy and regarded them as show-offs. Regarding them as far-fetched, they did not have the craving to possess them.

However, with the changing times, luxury brands no longer hold the same status. Millennials have a different mindset. For them, luxury is something that signals the fulfilment of their aspirations. They associate luxury handbags with a life-goal fulfilment and place it on their bucket list. Additionally, luxury handbags are not just an add-on item in their closet, but a life experience on their own. They simply do not want to become owners of things. The happiness they derive out of the possession of the good, no matter the cost, also holds great emotional value to them.

The social media-frenzy generation wants things that help to amplify their image and view these luxury items as one. Notably, with technology making everything seem so close, these handbags no longer remain exclusive. Social media marketing on channels such as YouTube, Instagram and so on, including company websites, have placed them just a click away. Moreover, the luxury industry segment is also growing as marketers want to reach out to the masses. Although still a tad too highly priced, the fashion brand has moved away from being detached. Marketing strategies to attract the average-earning millennials revolve around being accessible and amicable to them. The booming economy of the country and the organizations' global expansion have brought the Western world products closer to home.

Discussion Questions

1. What do different generations value? Can employers create different value propositions across generations?

2. How can a company like Louis Vuitton mitigate inter-generational differences?

REFERENCES

1. Smola, K.W., & Sutton, C.D. (2002). Generational differences: revisiting generational work values for the new millennium. J Org Behav. 23(4):363–82.
2. Schwartz, J. (2010, Jan 1). Talking about whose generation? Deloitte Insights. Retrieved from https://www2.deloitte.com/insights/us/en/deloitte-review/issue-6/talking-about-whose-generation-ages-and-attitudes-among-the-global-workforce.html. Accessed on 13 Sep 2018.
3. Knowles, H. (2017, Nov 3). The importance of generational targeting: from millennials to baby boomers, one message won't compute. Madison Ave Collective. Retrieved from https://medium.com/madison-ave-collective/the-importance-of-generational-targeting-from-millennials-to-baby-boomers-one-message-wont-69b18c563d3a. Accessed on 13 Sep 2018.
4. Rampton, J. (2017, Oct 17). Different motivations for different generations of workers: boomers, Gen X, millennials, and Gen Z. Inc. Retrieved from https://www.inc.com/john-rampton/different-motivations-for-different-generations-of-workers-boomers-gen-x-millennials-gen-z.html. Accessed on 13 Sep 2018.
5. From 2BHK to 8.3 lakh sq feet: The Flipkart story so far. The Economic Times. 2018 May 9. Retrieved from https://economictimes.indiatimes.com/news/company/corporate-trends/from-2bhk-to-8-3-lakh-sq-feet-the-flipkart-story-so-far/a-look-back/slideshow/64092726.cms. Accessed on 27 Sep 2018.
6. Chanchani, M. (2015, Aug 3). Ritesh Agarwal's journey from being a SIM-seller to the helm of OYO Rooms. The Economic Times. Retrieved from https://economictimes.indiatimes.com/small-biz/entrepreneurship/ritesh-agarwals-journey-from-being-a-sim-seller-to-the-helm-of-oyo-rooms/articleshow/48322588.cms. Accessed on 26 Mar 2019.

7. Johnson, M. (2016, May 11). When baby boomers meet millennials: finding common ground at work. Bridgepoint Consulting. Retrieved from https://bridgepointconsulting.com/8000-2/. Accessed on 13 Sep 2018.

8. Beheshti N. (2018, Nov 29). The clash of the baby boomers and millennials: how can we all get along? Forbes. Retrieved from https://www.forbes.com/sites/nazbeheshti/2018/11/29/the-clash-of-the-baby-boomers-and-millennials-how-can-we-all-get-along/#56276012f9e2. Accessed on 26 Mar 2019.

9. Narayanan, C. (2018, Feb 1). What does it take for family businesses to last generations? The Hindu. Retrieved from https://www.thehindubusinessline.com/specials/people-at-work/what-does-it-take-for-family-businesses-to-last-generations/article22612817.ece. Accessed on 26 Mar 2019.

10. Moore, G.R. (2013, Jul 11). Baby boomers, generation 'X' and generation 'Y' in the workplace: a melting pot of expertise. Resource1. Retrieved from https://www.resource1.com/baby-boomers-generation-x-and-generation-y-in-the-workplace-a-melting-pot-of-expertise/. Accessed on 14 Sep 2019.

11. Block, D. (2019, Feb 1). Data plans. The Caravan. Retrieved from https://caravanmagazine.in/reportage/government-helping-reliance-jio-monopolise-telecom. Accessed on 13 Feb 2019.

12. Miles, E. Does generation Y have it easier than the baby boomers? Mccrindle. Retrieved from https://mccrindle.com.au/insights/blogarchive/does-generation-y-have-it-easier-than-the-baby-boomers/. Accessed on 13 Sep 2018.

13. Stewart, J.B. (2013, Mar 15). Looking for a lesson in Google's perks. The New York Times. Retrieved from https://www.nytimes.com/2013/03/16/business/at-google-a-place-to-work-and-play.html. Accessed on 13 Sep 2018.

14. The Deloitte Millennial Survey 2018. Retrieved from https://www2.deloitte.com/global/en/pages/about-deloitte/articles/millennialsurvey.html. Accessed on 11 Feb 2019.

15. Singh, V. (2018, Sep 2). PMOs Startup India Initiative is paving the way for a new crop of entrepreneurs. Entrepreneur.India. Retrieved from https://www.entrepreneur.com/article/319403. Accessed on 27 Sep 2018.

16. IBM recruitment process. GeeksforGeeks. Retrieved from https://www.geeksforgeeks.org/ibm-recruitment-process/. Accessed on 27 Sep 2018.

17. Servicefutures (n.d.). The barriers of managing a multigenerational workforce and how to break them. Retrieved from https://www.servicefutures.com/barriers-managing-multigenerational-workforce-break. Accessed on 27 Sep 2018.

18. Falkingham, N. (2015, Apr 16). IBM training and the truth about the millennial generation. IBM. Retrieved from https://www.ibm.com/blogs/ibm-training/ibm-training-and-the-truth-about-the-millennial-generation/. Accessed on 27 Sep 2018.

19. Ganapathi, M. (2018, Oct 23). Even a fake Louis Vuitton is a status symbol in India. Quartx India. Retrieved from https://qz.com/india/1433172/even-a-fake-louis-vuitton-is-a-status-symbol-in-india/. Accessed on 27 Sep 2018.

CHALLENGES
OF A
MILLENNIAL
WORKFORCE

KEY CHALLENGES ORGANIZATIONS FACE WHILE DEALING WITH MILLENNIALS

Over the past two decades, a substantial amount of literature has accumulated in the realm of intergenerational differences. Particularly, the millennial generation has been argued to be starkly different from the rest in terms of attitudes and behaviour. A recent report by the Pew Research Center gauged the sea of change that has occurred across generations by comparing the activities and experiences of the silent generation (born in the years 1928–45) and the millennials during their early adulthood. Millennials in the United States have come a long way from the manner of living of their grandparents (i.e., the silent generation) in terms of education, women participation in the workforce, marriage preferences, fondness towards metropolitans and willingness to serve in the Army (1). On a similar note, other works also observe a striking dissimilitude between the ways of life of millennials and their parents (Generation Xers and late baby boomers) (2). Some of the apparent departures from tradition are that millennials avoid cooking, prefer to learn online, share private details like salary with others, crave instant recognition, cohabitate before marriage and rely on Google for all sorts of advice.

The varied ways of life of millennials are also reflected in work settings. Millennials enter the workforce with unique needs, characteristics, expectations and personalities. These differences pave the way for new challenges that contemporary organizations encounter on a regular basis. Few of these differences may even create problems for other stakeholders, such as supervisors, co-workers or even the organization on the whole.

Much has been said about the hassles caused by millennials in the popular press or blogs. However, the academic articles backed by sufficient theory or empirical analysis are relatively limited. In Table 4.1, significant academic contributions outlining the challenges that millennial employees pose to their employing organizations have been reviewed and presented. The focus of each of these academic articles with regard to the millennial challenges they discuss has also been provided in a separate column for the convenience of the reader.

A review of the table offers a glimpse into the difficulties that emerge while working with the Generation Y employees. Apart from the research conducted by academicians on the dark side of the millennials, millennial bashing is the reality experienced by thousands of Gen Y employees out there. Though each generation has to deal with its fair share of negative comments from its predecessors, millennials have been the most heavily criticized lot. This submission is evident from the fact that the internet is flooded with articles containing titles such as '8 Reasons millennials are the worst' and 'Five really good reasons to hate millennials'. A recent article in the *Forbes* magazine carried excerpts from a letter written to the author by a millennial employee who had recently joined her first job. The letter spoke about the harsh comments that her elder co-workers used to make against her generation of employees while blatantly ignoring her presence in the room (13). Many more like her were also probably in the same shoes.

Contrary to such millennial-bashing articles, there exists another stream of literature that argues in favour of millennials by putting forth the view that not every person born in Generation Y is identical and that stereotypes do not hold true for every millennial. Proponents of this view corroborate

TABLE 4.1 KEY ACADEMIC WORKS

Authors (Year)	Context	Main Challenge Discussed	Notable Findings
Twenge & Campbell (2008)[3]	–	Millennial psychological traits	The paper reviewed data spanning more than 80 years (1930–2007) from 1.4 million people that were contained in previous research reports. Findings revealed that Generation Y exhibited higher self-esteem, anxiety, depression, a more external locus of control and a lower need for social approval. Women were also found to possess more agentic traits. The authors cautioned managers to expect more employees with a high need of praise, unrealistically high expectations, a difficulty with criticism, casual dress, job-hopping, ethical scandals, an increase in creativity demands and a shift in workplace norms for women.
Barkin et al. (2010)[4]	–	Millennial obesity	The authors drew from the statistics stating the dramatic rise in obesity levels in the United States to estimate the impact of obesity on millennials. The paper contended that the millennial cohort is affected by obesity like no other. It also put forth the view that obesity may have lasting implications for millennial employees as well as their organizations in terms of productivity and aggregate lifetime earnings.

Authors (Year)	Context	Main Challenge Discussed	Notable Findings
Twenge (2010)[5]	–	Work ethic and work-related values of Gen Y	Based on a review of past literature, the study propounded that the Generation Y (also referred to as GenMe) placed more value in leisure, rated work as less central to their lives and expressed a weaker work ethic in comparison to its predecessors. Generation Y was found to be predominantly higher on individualistic traits.
Twenge & Foster (2010)[6]	USA	Millennial narcissistic personality	The nationwide meta-analytic study reported a significant increase in the narcissistic traits of American college students over the generations. The authors hold the cultural changes pertaining to education, parents, media, family life and rise in individualism as responsible for this increase.
Coffin et al. (2012)[7]	USA	Millennial reactions to feedback	Intergenerational differences on the concept of feedback were explored in the study. Millennials reported themselves to be most motivated by informal feedback (39.0%) followed by mentoring (33.3%), formal feedback (30.9%) and pay raise (8.0%). Conversely, baby boomers and millennials perceived that the best form of feedback to millennials was informal feedback (61.2%), followed by formal feedback (25.4%) and pay raise (13.4%). Likewise, differences were found in the ways millennials reacted to criticism and praise in organizations in comparison to how their predecessors expected them to react.

(continued)

(continued)

Authors (Year)	Context	Main Challenge Discussed	Notable Findings
Westerman et al. (2012)[8]	USA	Millennials' high expectations and entitlement	The study reported higher levels of narcissism amongst millennial university students in comparison to students in the past. The narcissism levels were noted to be even higher amongst business students than amongst psychology students. Business students who were high on narcissism additionally held significantly higher expectations in terms of jobs, salary and promotion.
Becton et al. (2014)[9]	USA	Millennial mobility behaviours	The article compared the behaviours of three generations (baby boomers, Generation X and the millennials) at the workplace. Baby boomers were found to exhibit fewer mobility behaviours relative to their successors. Additionally, more instances of compliance-related behaviours were noted for baby boomers.
McGinnis Johnson & Ng (2016)[10]	USA	Millennial sector-switching intentions	The paper investigated the relationship between actual pay, perceptions of pay and sector-switching intentions amongst millennial employees working in the non-profit sector. Millennial managers enjoying pay increases were less likely to switch sectors relative to their underpaid counterparts. Hence, it was concluded that high pay was the driving force that attracted millennial managers as well as those possessing educational degrees to the nonprofit sector. This was, however, not the case with millennial employees earning lower pay or lacking a strong education.

Authors (Year)	Context	Main Challenge Discussed	Notable Findings
Jassanwalla & Shashittal (2017)[11]	USA	Millennials' conflicts with other generations	Most millennials were found to initiate conflicts with older supervisors and co-workers in the workplace. These conflicts were rooted in hurt caused by perceptions of unfairness by supervisors. Millennials were observed to take an aggressive stand in conflicts within vertical dyads. They also developed a duplicitous impression of the organization and concluded that conflict was necessary to protect them from unfairness and manipulation.
Kim (2018)[12]	–	Millennials cyberloafing at the workplace	Given the fact that millennials have grown up in the internet era with unparalleled access to technology, this study analysed the use of technology for non-work-related reasons by millennials at the workplace. The paper discussed two approaches to manage this issue and offered practical guidance to organizations to deal with cyberloafing while simultaneously attracting and retaining millennials.

Source: Twenge & Campbell (2008).

their claims by presenting survey statistics such as those which state that 59 per cent of the respondents were committed to their current jobs for over three years (14). Research of this sort attempts to break the popular stereotypes regarding millennials. The present piece of work also refrains from a stereotypical view of millennials. However, it also supports the contention that certain habits and tendencies run across the majority of the people belonging to this generational cohort (15). These characteristics may be positive or negative, but since the focus of this chapter is on the challenges associated with millennial employees, the negatives have been elaborated upon further.

The popular press has noted the following bad habits of millennials. These habits and ways of life invite troubles for their hiring organizations as well as cross-generational organizational members.

1. **Millennials make demands instead of requests:** While voicing their opinions in organizations, Gen Y employees start out by making rigid demands instead of requests, which is highly undesirable especially in the earlier phases of their career. Employers perceive such behaviour as disrespectful and insubordinate (15).

2. **Millennials are obsessed with technology:** Born and brought up in the laps of technology, millennials are constantly plugged in, to the extent that they are believed to be addicted to technology. A recent survey reported millennials to be the most distracted by technology even during mealtimes. It is common to find millennials constantly checking their phones amidst a conversation or using their tablets during meetings, which may seem really annoying to elder co-workers and supervisors (15, 16).

3. **Millennials exhibit overconfidence:** Millennials have been referred to as the 'trophy generation', which signifies that the Generation Y has grown up receiving trophies for merely showing up at events irrespective of their actual achievement in them. Hence, their expectations and sense of entitlement persist and rather inflate in organizational settings. Millennials carry a sense of delusional confidence but are ironically incapable of handling even small setbacks. Their exhibition of unfounded confidence reflected by overestimation of their skills and abilities may be perceived as overconfidence and arrogance by more knowledgeable and experienced colleagues.

   Such perceptions may cause irritation to them and result in unnecessary conflict (15, 17, 18).

4. **Millennials are a pampered cohort:** Born to 'helicopter parents' who have coddled them throughout their childhood, millennials have grown up to become adults who are terribly incapable of surviving in the real world on their own. Parents of millennials have always been overprotective of their children and remain overly involved in their lives, thus delimiting their potential of functioning as independent adults. Millennials, therefore, feel unequipped to solve even little problems on their own or adjust at the workplace. A recent article in the *Forbes* magazine seconds these contentions by revealing that millions of millennials today feel unengaged at work and find themselves incapable of saving for a rainy day, keeping a job for more than 18 months or fostering meaningful friendships and relationships (19–21).

5. **Millennials are the multitasking generation:** Millennials are characterized by a tendency to multitask or attempt to do several things at the same time. Research

has already demonstrated the side effects of multitasking, namely impairment of cognitive function, distraction, divided attention, sabotaged performance and many more. In fact, it is also argued that multitasking rewires the human brain and snatches its ability to think creatively and deeply. Neurologists have also concluded that multitasking can lower the intelligent quotient by as many as 15 points while simultaneously trashing the emotional quotient. The results obtained by performing multitasking are similar to those which are produced by a brain deprived of a night's sleep. These multitasking tendencies of millennials carry implications for organizations as well as they have to deal with 40 per cent less efficient, emotionally unintelligent, less attentive, stupider and mildly brain-damaged employees (22–24).

STRATEGIES TO RESOLVE GENERATIONAL TENSIONS

The older generations may have a lot against Generation Y. The millennial employees are often rightly accused of continually showing up late for work, leaving early, always turning down overtime requests and wondering why they had not been promoted after just one year on the job. Not surprisingly, millions of employers out there are finding it increasingly frustrating to manage their younger employees (25). Millennials have truly changed the face of work and jobs in the business landscape and have shaken up the organizations that they work for.

It is high time that business organizations learn to embrace the change brought about by the millennial employees instead of cribbing about it. In a recent article published by the *Forbes* magazine, it has been recommended that dismissing younger employees as lazy or entitled is not the best way to understand or motivate them (26). Organizations have no choice but to accept the Generation Y the way they are as they constitute a majority of the workforce, and the numbers are expected to shoot up even more in the future. It would be wiser as well as more advantageous for employers to change their perspective towards the millennial employees and focus on developing strategies to get the best out of them wilfully and without conflict. Doing so is in the best interests of both the parties. The millennials will not feel compelled to conform to the ways of life established by their predecessors, and their successors will be able to leverage on the positive qualities of millennials and extract quality work out of them.

There are several steps that organizations may take to understand and subsequently resolve the generational differences and tensions. Some of the broad guidelines for addressing the challenges posed by the Gen Y workforce have been presented below.

1. **Try to understand the millennials:** It is crucial for employers to understand the millennials—their values, needs, aspirations, characteristics and so on—before trying to manage them. Such an endeavour can be facilitated by the process of segmentation of the workforce with the aid of metrics and benchmarks. Doing so would help the employers get a clearer picture of what the younger employees desire compared to the Gen Xers and baby boomers. Once the knowledge of their desires is at the employer's disposal, incentives fulfilling those desires may be used to motivate and stretch the employees to their fullest potential. Additionally, organizations need to regularly float surveys capturing the engagement levels of employees across age groups (27). Data from these surveys would be useful in carrying out predictive analyses focusing on what could engage and retain the millennials. Finally, the HR department

needs to assume a strategic role in the organization by forecasting the talent requirements and continually developing and updating the talent pipelines. The same efforts also need to be communicated to the employees to demonstrate the organization's concern in actively managing its employees' careers.

2. **Get the 'deal' right:** The terms and conditions of the exchange relationship between the employee and the organization need to be discussed openly at the time of hiring itself. Both the parties should try to reach a consensus over the rights and responsibilities of each of them. Organizations must be open while stating what they are offering and what they are expecting in return. Doing so substantially decreases the possibility of breach of psychological contract, which refers to the perception that the other party has failed to fulfil the obligations promised earlier (27). Since psychological contract breach has been found to be unfavourably related to a host of work-related attitudes (job satisfaction, organizational commitment and turnover intentions) and behaviours (organizational citizenship behaviour and in-role performance) (28), it is very critical for organizations to keep their promises.

3. **Help millennials grow:** Millennials are increasingly attracted to jobs that offer opportunities for them to progress in their careers. A recent Qualtrics-Accel Partners survey reported that millennial employees were willing to commit to a particular organization for even 10 years if the company offered annual pay hikes and upward career mobility (29). These findings are quite in contrast to the job-hopping reputation that millennials are infamous for. Hence, it can be implied that millennials do not have a fetish for exploration and rather desire stability. It is,

therefore, necessary that organizations bust their myths about millennials and focus on providing them the things which are the most important to them. Contrary to a popular stereotype which suggests that millennials are attracted to cool workplaces and free artisanal lunches, the truth is that long-term job security and opportunities for climbing the organizational ladder are the real things millennials cherish (30). Organizations can, therefore, design jobs for their younger employees in a manner that maximizes the possibilities of their growth. Millennial employees do not believe that growth in the form of career advancement is contingent upon seniority and the time of service. Their need for instant gratification also makes them want career advancement quicker than other generations. Hence, organizations could start by adding more levels, grades or other badges so that the step-by-step rise over the levels makes millennials believe that they are progressing in their careers.

4. **Feedback, feedback and more feedback:** Because of their tendency to seek instant gratification, millennials crave feedback and recognition probably more than any other generation. Since millennials want to know how they are doing more regularly, supervisors should provide them with honest feedback in real time. They should also make it a point to highlight the positive contributions made by the employee and suggest if any improvements were required. Employers should also make efforts to make the employees realize their key competencies and help them to excel at them.

5. **Set them free:** Millennials prefer autonomy and freedom. Organizations must ensure that their systems and processes do not compromise on these fundamental millennial values. More and more millennials are demanding

the provision of flexible work schedules in pursuit of a better work-life balance. A recent study conducted at Bentley University reported that nearly 77 per cent of the millennials believed that a flexible work schedule would enhance their productivity. Millennials are the generation that does not believe in the typical 9-to-5 jobs and is of the opinion that productivity should be measured not by the input number of hours but the work output.

Millennials are highly attracted to jobs that provide alternate working arrangements such as telecommuting, part-time scheduling, flexible scheduling and freelancing (31). In addition to these facilities, employers should give clear instructions and set concrete, mutually agreed upon targets for the younger employees. The target setting meetings must also clearly lay out the deadlines. The 'how' portion of meeting the deadlines should be left upon the sole discretion of the employees.

6. **Provide millennials with learning opportunities**: Although their learning styles differ, millennials place much value in continual learning. Most millennials are driven by a high need for achievement, as per the McClelland's theory of needs. A recent survey suggests that Generation Y employees are not even pursuing job satisfaction. Being individualistic in nature, they look for their own development and expect their employing organizations to help them build their careers (32). Rather than viewing such preferences in a negative light, organizations should try to set congruent goals, the achievement of which helps in the growth of both the employee and the organization. Additionally, millennials may be assigned rotational assignments frequently to provide them with a variety of experiences.

They may be further encouraged to exercise their creativity by challenging them to come up with innovative solutions to business problems. Millennials may also be included in intergenerational teams, thus allowing them the opportunity to learn personally from senior managers. Millennials have a strong desire to work overseas, and they may be provided such opportunities to help them develop a global career.

7. **Expect millennials to go:** Contemporary organizations have to make peace with the fact that millennials are bound to leave them one day. Their average span with each organization is probably much less than that of their parents and grandparents. A survey conducted by Visier supports these claims by revealing that members of the millennial cohort were twice more likely to quit their jobs in comparison to non-millennials (33). Another study, 'The 2018 Millennial Survey', conducted by Deloitte seconds these findings by reporting that nearly 43 per cent of the millennials plan to ditch their current jobs within two years. Only 28 per cent of the Gen Y respondents were planning to stick by in their current roles for the next five years (34). The surprising factor is that not always do millennials have strong reasons to quit. Job-hopping is the latest trend amongst Generation Y employees.

It is high time that employers come to terms with this harsh reality and learn to adjust to it. Turnover also brings with itself the opportunities for hiring new talent, infusing fresh perspectives and rejuvenating the organization. Organizations may also formulate the best of policies and processes to attract the crème de la crème to them and achieve a competitive advantage over rivals. Examples of the same could be attractive policies across all the functions of human resource management (HRM), namely, compensation, recruitment and selection, learning and development and so on.

The aforementioned recommendations are expected to go a long way in helping Generation Xers and baby boomers in dealing with the challenges of a millennial workforce. The proper introduction and implementation of the right bundle of HR practices and policies may prove to be highly beneficial in managing the millennial talent.

....

The Case of Maruti Suzuki in Haryana: Violence at the Workplace

Maruti Suzuki India Limited (MSIL), formerly known as Maruti Udyog Limited, is an industry giant operating in the Indian automobile sector (35). MSIL is a subsidiary of the Japanese auto giant Suzuki Motor Corporation, with the Japanese multinational holding 56.21 per cent of its stake (36). The company is currently headquartered in New Delhi and is engaged in the business of purchase, manufacture and sale of passenger motor vehicles, automobile components as well as spare parts (33, 37). MSIL is presently the market leader in the Indian auto sector and has successfully captured 51 per cent of the market share as of 2018, thus remaining far ahead of rivals such as Hyundai Motor India (16.2%), Mahindra & Mahindra (7.3%) and Tata Motors (7%) (38). The manufacturing facilities of MSIL are located in Gurugram and Manesar regions of Haryana, with regional and area offices across the country (37).

Despite being an exemplar of growth and success, MSIL was encountered with an infamous controversy in 2012 at its Manesar plant and took the entire nation by storm. In a shocking act of violence in July 2012, an HR executive (Awanish Kumar Dev, aged 49) was set ablaze and burnt to death by a mob of workers at the plant (39). Nearly a hundred employees and nine police officers sustained life-threatening injuries during the riot, and the office complex was also burnt down, leading to a shutdown of the plant for one month (40). The Manesar plant previously boasted of an annual production of 550,000 cars, accounting for one-third of MSIL's total production (41). This unfortunate incident was a major blow to Maruti, causing it a loss of over $500 million worth of production, coupled with a massive drop in its share prices. The automobile sector, once highly regarded by the investor community, lost its trust and charm. The violence was seen as damaging to the global car manufacturer's sentiments to invest in India's growing domestic automobile market in a bid to become the largest low-cost export base (41).

The roots of this heinous industrial crime date back to the times when several arguments were ongoing between the members of the trade union and the management of MSIL. These arguments were triggered by a disciplinary action against one of its employees (39). Moreover, due to the labour law situation in India, several experts also believe that companies like Maruti were excessively relying on contract labourers, who are easy to fire and get fewer wages and benefits than permanent workers. According to the *Economic Times*, around 50 per cent of the workers at the Manesar plant were temporary contractual workers earning a meagre salary of ₹6,000 per month—which is approximately 33 per cent of a permanent worker's pay (41). Execution of disciplinary action and the company's labour policy were considered the primary reasons behind this violent incident. Subsequently, trade unions made calls to reinstate the defaulter employee along with demands of equal pay for contractual labours, accusing MSIL of 'anti-worker and anti-union activities', erupting in massive violent protests (41).

Apart from these main factors, there are few other implicit factors at the individual level which led to workers getting violent. These factors may include worker and management attitudes, intolerance, lack of proper communication amongst the stakeholders, lack of understanding and most importantly 'generational differences'. Millennials formed a major chunk of the contractual blue-collar workers in the Manesar plant and the 147 blue-collar employees arrested after the violence were all millennials (42). A majority of these arrested workers were in the age group of 20 to 34 (42). Also, the management positions were traditionally filled on the basis of seniority, and thus comprised majorly of Generation X employees.

The above incident is an eye-opener for firms managing the millennial workforce and offers a glimpse of the violent form that resentment may take in the case of millennials. In the case of MSIL, company policies pertaining to labour management were poorly framed. Additionally, the management also failed to understand the underlying attitudes and behaviours of its employees towards their work. For instance, trade unions comprising of millennials tend to make rigid demands in place of requests to the management. Such insubordination is perceived unruly by their Generation X seniors who occupy positions in company management. For MSIL, the majority of its executives are from Generation X, and thus the importance of building a healthy relationship despite such generational differences becomes all the more crucial. Another point of import is the way that millennials deal with their anger and frustration.

Research has found that millennials tend to initiate conflicts with older supervisors and co-workers. It suggests that these conflicts are usually rooted in the hurt caused by perceived unfairness on the part of supervisors, and millennials feel that conflicts are necessary to protect them from such unfairness and injustice (43). Thus, in the case of MSIL, disparity of pay amongst the contractual and permanent blue-collar employees was perceived as highly unfair by the millennial workforce which provided moral grounds for such a violent conflict.

Recently, in March 2017, the Court of Additional District and Sessions judge in Haryana convicted a total of 31 workers in the case and sentenced 13 of them to life imprisonment under the charges of murder, rioting and destruction to property (44). The case of MSIL provides an example of how the ineffective management of the millennial workforce can create havoc for even the best of organizations. Had MSIL formulated and implemented better policies to manage their millennial employees, several lives including that of the deceased employee and his family would have been spared. For organizations, such situations prove to be highly detrimental to their growth and success. Thus, the challenges posed by the millennial workforce are critical to success, and company's HR policies should take enough steps to appropriately address them considering the fact the millennials will constitute a significant part of the global workforce in the coming years and firms need to be prepared for this radical change.

Discussion Questions

1. Are millennials more prone to violence at workplace? What are some critical interventions necessary at workplace to reduce violence in millennials?

2. What policies should have been at place in MSIL so that such a menace can be prevented?

REFERENCES

1. Fry, R., Igielnik, R. & Patten, E. (2018, Mar 16). How millennials today compare with their grandparents 50 years ago. Pew Research Center. Retrieved from http://www.pewresearch.org/fact-tank/2018/03/16/how-millennials-compare-with-their-grandparents/. Accessed on 28 Sep 2018.

2. Business Insider. 11 things millennials do that their parents wouldn't recognize. Business Insider. Retrieved from https://www.businessinsider.in/11-things-millennials-do-that-their-parents-wouldnt-recognize/Instead-of-waiting-for-an-annual-performance-review-millennials-crave-more-frequent-feedback/slide show/63236196.cms. Accessed on 28 Sep 2018.

3. Twenge, J.M., & Campbell, S.M. (2008). Generational differences in psychological traits and their impact on the workplace. J Manag Psychol. 23(8):862–77.

4. Barkin, S.L., Heerman, W.J., Warren, M.D., & Rennhoff, C. (2010). Millennials and the world of work: the impact of obesity on health and productivity. J Bus Psychol. 25(2):239–45.

5. Twenge, J.M. (2010). A review of the empirical evidence on generational differences in work attitudes. J Bus Psychol. 25(2):201–10.

6. Twenge, J.M., & Foster, J.D. (2010). Birth cohort increases in narcissistic personality traits among American college students, 1982–2009. Soc Psychol Pers Sci. 1(1):99–106.

7. Coffin, J., McGivern, S., Underwood-Price, L., Xiong, S. & Zander, H. (2012). Feedback in an intergenerational workplace. Available at: http://wp.stolaf.edu/sociology/files/2013/06/Feedback-in-an-Intergenerational-Workplace.pdf

8. Westerman, J.W., Bergman, J.Z., Bergman, S.M., & Daly, J.P. (2012). Are universities creating millennial narcissistic employees? An empirical examination of narcissism in business students and its implications. J Manag Educ. 36(1):5–32.

9. Becton, J.B., Walker, H.J., & Jones-Farmer, A. (2014). Generational differences in workplace behavior. J Appl Soc Psychol. 44(3):175–89.

10. McGinnis Johnson, J., & Ng, E.S. (2016). Money talks or millennials walk: the effect of compensation on nonprofit millennial workers sector-switching intentions. Rev Public Pers Admin. 36(3):283–305.

11. Jassawalla, A., & Sashittal, H. (2017). How and why millennials are initiating conflict in vertical dyads and what they are learning: a two-stage study. Int J Conflict Manag. 28(5):644–70.

12. Kim, S. (2018). Managing millennials' personal use of technology at work. Bus Horizons. 61(2):261–70.

13. Ryan, L. (2017, May 4). The real reason people hate millennials. Forbes. Retrieved from https://www.forbes.com/sites/lizryan/2017/05/04/the-real-reason-people-hate-millennials/#4749db34767b. Accessed on 28 Sep 2018. Accessed on 28 Sep 2018.

14. Johnson, K.H. (2018, Jun 19). Enough with the millennial bashing. Forbes. Retrieved from https://www.forbes.com/sites/kevinhjohnson/2018/06/19/enough-with-the-millennial-bashing/#6acb0511a3d0. Accessed on 28 Sep 2018.

15. Demers, J. (2017, Oct 5). 7 Bad workplace habits millennials need to stop making. Entrepreneur India. Retrieved from https://www.entrepreneur.com/article/301069. Accessed on 28 Sep 2018.

16. Mayyasi, A. (n.d.). Which generation is most distracted by their phones? Priceonomics. Retrieved from https://priceonomics.com/which-generation-is-most-distracted-by-their/. Accessed on 28 Sep 2018.

17. Alsop, R. (2008). The trophy kids grow up: how the millennial generation is shaking up the workplace. New York: John Wiley & Sons.

18. Byrne, K. (2017, Sep 17). Millennials: 'Their overconfidence at work can look delusional'. Independent.ie. Retrieved from https://www.independent.ie/life/millennials-their-overconfidence-at-work-can-look-delusional-36133512.html. Accessed on 28 Sep 2018.

19. Wong, B. (2018, Sep 28). What millennials say about their parents during therapy. HuffPost. Retrieved from https://www.huffingtonpost.in/entry/what-millennials-say-about-their-parents-during-therapy_us_5ad0f6d1e4b0edca2cb99211. Accessed on 28 Sep 2018.

20. Koslow, S., & Weaver, C. (n.d.). The terrible 22s. AARP. Retrieved from https://www.aarp.org/home-family/friends-family/info-2016/millennials-boomers-reaching-adulthood.html. Accessed on 28 Sep 2018.

21. Kruman, Y. (2018, Feb 26). Curing helicopter parenting: how to help your millennial or Gen Z kid to launch and thrive. Forbes. Retrieved from https://www.forbes.com/sites/forbescoachescouncil/2018/02/26/curing-helicopter-parenting-how-to-help-your-millennial-or-gen-z-kid-to-launch-and-thrive/#328b39d47baa. Accessed on 28 Sep 2018.

22. Beaton, C. (2017, Jan 27). The millennial workforce: how multitasking is changing our brains. Forbes. Retrieved from https://www.forbes.com/sites/carolinebeaton/2017/01/27/the-millennial-workforce-how-multitasking-is-changing-our-brains/#7173c9053605. Accessed on 30 Sep 2018.

23. Zetlin, M. (2016, Jul 30). Constant multitasking is damaging millennial brains, research shows. Inc. Retrieved from https://www.inc.com/minda-zetlin/constant-multitasking-is-damaging-millennial-brains-research-shows.html. Accessed on 30 Sep 2018.

24. Lee, A. (2017, Jan 19). Multitasking on their smartphone: millennials in the workplace. Huffpost. Retrieved from https://www.huffingtonpost.com/entry/multitasking-on-their-smartphone-millennials-in-the_us_5880b58ee4b0fb40bf6c46f0. Accessed on 30 Sep 2018.

25 Sujansky, J.G. (2009). Spoiled, impatient, and entitled: why you need strong millennials in your workplace. Retrieved from https://www.atmosphereci.com/blog/spoiled-impatient-entitled-millennials-workplace/. Accessed on 30 Sep 2018.

26. Johnson, K.H. (2018, Jun 19). Enough with the millennial bashing. Forbes. Retrieved from https://www.forbes.com/sites/kevinhjohnson/2018/06/19/enough-with-the-millennial-bashing/. Accessed on 30 Sep 2018.

27. Robinson, S.L. (1996). Trust and breach of the psychological contract. Admin Sci Quart. 41(4):574–99.

28. Zhao, H.A.O., Wayne, S.J., Glibkowski, B.C., & Bravo, J. (2007). The impact of psychological contract breach on work-related outcomes: a meta-analysis. Pers Psychol. 60(3):647–80.

29. The Millennial Study. Accel + Qualtrics. Retrieved from https://www.qualtrics.com/millennials/. Accessed on 2 Oct 2018.

30. Overfelt, M. (2017, May 11). Millennial employees are a lot more loyal than their job-hopping stereotype. CNBC. Retrieved from https://www.cnbc.com/

2017/05/10/90-of-millennials-will-stay-in-a-job-for-10-years-if-two-needs-met. html. Accessed on 2 Oct 2018.

31. Taylor, T.C. (2017, Dec 7). Workplace flexibility for millennials: appealing to a valuable new generation. Forbes. Retrieved from https://www.forbes.com/sites/adp/2017/12/07/workplace-flexibility-for-millennials-appealing-to-a-valuable-new-generation/#469c212e7fe6. Accessed on 2 Oct 2018.

32. accel5 (2017, Sep 15). Going micro: how companies can meet millennials' desire for continual learning. EBSCO. Retrieved from https://www.ebsco.com/blog-corporate/article/going-micro-how-companies-can-meet-millennials-desire-for-continual-learnin. Accessed on 2 Oct 2018.

33. Kline, D.B. (2018, Jun 7). This is why so many millennials quit their jobs. The Motley Fool. Retrieved from https://www.fool.com/careers/2018/06/07/this-is-why-so-many-millennials-quit-their-jobs.aspx. Accessed on 2 Oct 2018.

34. Freidman, Z. (2018, May 22). 43% of millennials plan to quit their job within 2 years. Forbes. Retrieved from https://www.forbes.com/sites/zackfriedman/2018/05/22/millennials-quit-job/#13d46b2c57f1. Accessed on 2 Oct 2018.

35. Maruti Suzuki. Indian Brand Equity Foundation. Retrieved from https://www.ibef.org/industry/india-automobiles/showcase/maruti-suzuki. Accessed on 2 Oct 2018.

36. PTI. (2013, Apr 1). Suzuki Motor's stake at Maruti Suzuki goes up to 56.21%. Times of India. Retrieved from https://timesofindia.indiatimes.com/business/india-business/Suzuki-Motors-stake-in-Maruti-Suzuki-goes-up-to-56-21/articleshow/19323285.cms. Accessed on 2 Oct 2018.

37. Maruti Suzuki Corporate Office. Retrieved from https://www.marutisuzuki.com/corporate/reach-us/all-offices.

38. Taumar, D., Nangia, P., & Mishra, S. (2019, Feb 12). Complete Indian auto sales analysis 2018: CV sales cross one million mark. The Economic Times. Retrieved from https://auto.economictimes.indiatimes.com/news/industry/complete-india-auto-sales-analysis-2018-cv-sales-crosses-a-million-mark/67549073. Accessed on 14 Feb 2019.

39. Dhankhar, L. (2017, Mar 10). Maruti factory violence verdict: a brief history of the case. Hindustan Times. Retrieved from https://www.hindustantimes.com/gurugram/maruti-factory-violence-verdict-a-brief-history-of-the-case/story-hXMxAHf6I3DuJHCflV47YN.html. Accessed on 3 Oct 2018.

40. Raj, A. (2017, Mar 18). Maruti Manesar violence case: 13 workers given life imprisonment. Livemint. Retrieved from https://www.livemint.com/Companies/jwJ5Go9HdMxzDvoF9b20iP/Maruti-Manesar-violence-case-13-workers-given-life-imprison.html. Accessed on 3 Oct 2018.

41. Bawa, P. (2017, Mar 10). 2012 Maruti factory violence case: manager killed, factory burnt, 31 convicted—10 facts. NDTV. Retrieved from https://www.ndtv.com/india-news/verdict-today-for-maruti-workers-in-deadly-haryana-riot-10-facts-1668232. Accessed on 3 Oct 2018.

42. Sampath, G. (2016, Sep 2). The saga of jailed Maruti Suzuki workers. The Hindu. Retrieved from https://www.thehindu.com/business/Industry/the-saga-of-jailed-maruti-suzuki-workers/article8005256.ece. Accessed on 3 Oct 2018.

43. Jassawalla, A., & Sashittal, H. (2017). How and why millennials are initiating conflict in vertical dyads and what they are learning: a two-stage study. Int J Conflict Manag. 28(5):644–70.

44. Behl, A. Maruti Suzuki case: 13 given life sentence for violence at Manesar plant in 2012. Hindustan Times. Retrieved from https://www.hindustantimes.com/gurugram/maruti-violence-case-13-murder-accused-given-life-sentence/story-RoGa1LKCw6pEyM9IePEumM.html. Accessed on 3 Oct 2018.

5

STRATEGIES OF MANAGING MILLENNIALS: INDUSTRY'S BEST PRACTICES

With the varying kinds of workforce at the helm of an organization's affairs, it is essential to ensure that these generational cohorts stay engaged at work. Industry-wide organizations have realized that to sustain a proper work culture they need to appreciate generational diversity and are looking out for ways to make diversity a priority. This culminates in a push to seek the best formulae to manage and ultimately retain the millennial worker (1).

When attempting to build generational coherence, one cannot but ignore the fact that more often than not, these differences arise from the stereotypes we hold of one another. Whenever a senior fellow employee is unable to understand our perspective, we blame it on the generational gap and brush it off as 'You won't understand'. Or whenever a younger counterpart walks in the office sporting a funky hairstyle, we quickly label him as the 'unprofessional and reckless lot'. How is it that we fail to understand the huge difference in the life values that sets them apart?

The perceptions and preconceived notions we form of each other is the cause of rifts and tensions, whether at the workplace or elsewhere. When working in a group, it is highly likely that we superimpose our perceptions onto the other members, substituting what they truly are with how we see them. Such narrow mindset and way of looking eventually leads to conflicts amongst the group members. The stereotypes and unconscious biases that we hold of one another at work need to be overcome as the first step to managing the cohorts. Having a four-generational workforce working as a team will prove efficient only when every distinguished member sheds their stereotypes and becomes more accepting and tolerant towards the others. The key is to instil in them the eye to appreciate, value and respect every individual.

Managing the different generations of employees starts with the acceptance of their differences and a withdrawal from the 'all-in-one-box' syndrome. As we have identified previously, different generations, owing to their different value systems, have their own motivation and aspirations. Their drive for work, their lifestyle and life goals differ. The role of the manager here then gets tied up with identifying the unique needs of not just every generation, but also every individual (1).

The best way to manage the workforce in today's scenario is to focus on the individual employee. Strategies and schemes incentivized to meet their work preferences and ambitions is the way out in the long run. Although a tedious task, it is not one that cannot be done. Here again, the onus lies on the managers at all levels, and the employers to make each one feel wanted, valued and special in their organization. After all, each employee wants the same thing out of their work, which is, a promising career and engaging work, with only the definitions of 'promising' and 'engaging' changing person to person.

As our discussion points out, managing generations, the millennials in particular, is a two-way path, first being the elimination of conflicts by removing the biased perceptions and, second, through customization of strategies to meet every individual need. Let us now see in detail how this can be brought about.

MANAGING INTERGENERATIONAL TENSIONS

Research points out that in order to manage intergenerational conflicts, it is essential to identify the orientations of every group. Managers need to learn to engage both, a 60-year-old employee, who has dedicated his entire life to the organization, and a fresh out-of-college graduate, in his early 20s, who joins the organization having already decided on the next company he wants to move to.

TABLE 5.1 STRATEGIES TO MANAGE INTERGENERATIONAL TENSIONS (2)

Specific Strategy (First-Order Categories)	Strategy Category (Second-Order Categories)
Focusing on communication style: Individuals consciously flex their tone of message, communication medium or language usage	Achievement-oriented
Performing proficiently: Individuals refer to results or achievements that are important to other generations and that they have either accomplished recently or are upcoming	
Being visible: Individuals make sure that their work efforts are noticed by others by being present during normal working hours (also involves maximizing contact with those in other generations)	Image-oriented
Managing information to control image: Individuals utilize (or do not provide) select pieces of information or ideas to give them or their generation a positive image of others	
Protecting needs: Individuals focus on ensuring that their needs are met in an interaction	Ego-oriented
Removing self: Individuals walk away from and ignore (or layoff/terminate in extreme cases) others to avoid unproductive interactions	

Source: Urick et al. (2016).

STRATEGIES FOR MANAGING GENERATIONS

Managing millennials is all the more a tedious task, especially with their 'fleeting' attitude. It is now time to explore newer possibilities and move out of our comfort zone to change with the changing workforce.

Focus on the Similarities

The Bentley University Survey on managing the multigenerational workforce points out a very important aspect (3). For building a strong inclusive culture, it is necessary for the leader to highlight the similarities. Knowing a point of coherence imparts a similar-to-me effect, which helps to eradicate the differences and stereotypes. More often than not, an individual's personality differences contribute more to one's diverse opinions. Hence, even with generationally dissimilar working styles, individuals might share similar ideas or may support other's opinions. Even when one considers the differences, it is to be reiterated that generational distinctiveness can actually be capitalized positively.

Establishing Common Communication Channel

To eliminate misunderstandings and perceptual errors in the workplace, it is vital to establish common channels of communication if and when employees are unable to be on the same page when communicating with one another.

MANAGING THE MILLENNIALS

Align with the Company's Vision

Millennials need for recognition can be capitalized here to catch their attention. Making them know that the task they have been assigned, or their role in the organization, is crucial in instilling a sense of purpose in them. Knowing that their contribution to the firm is high and that they occupy a meaningful position makes them feel valued. It is primarily the task of the manager and team leaders to show them the significance of their job and their part in the organization's performance. If the leaders are able to convey how their job role or responsibility is aligned with the vision of the company at the beginning itself, it will no doubt provide a sense of meaning in the task and an engagement with the task.

Instant Feedback, Encouragement and Personal Interaction

Millennials are a generation that needs feedback on their work. Not just that, they want immediate gratification. They seem needy and brash in this respect, where they want an instant recognition of their tasks. Since millennials have received constant response and feedback by everyone around them since childhood, they have grown accustomed to it, and hence feel the urge to seek feedback. Whether it is simple words of praise like 'good job' or 'you have improved' or constructive criticism, they like to know how they are performing on the professional front. They want to know how they can improve themselves at their work. It also acts like a driving force for them to know how far or near they are from the goal they have set for themselves. Remotely, it also fulfils their desire of achievement and recognition. It is a form of individual interaction that goes a long way in keeping them motivated at their tasks.

Millennials seek out feedback for work-related improvement (4). Interestingly, a study done by Gallup in 2016 shows that only 19 per cent of the employees receive feedback from their leads, out of which only 17 per cent consider that feedback to be useful. But the loophole lies in the fact that even though they need feedback, they do not approach their leaders and ask upfront, since only 15 per cent respondents in the same study agree to having asked for feedback from their bosses (5). This is the gap which the managers need to fill by spreading the importance of feedback amongst the bosses and team lead.

Growing up in an era of social connectivity, millennials are also highly propelled by regular personal interactions with their managers and bosses. Ideally, day-to-day interaction can reap benefits but the most effective interactions are the ones done on a weekly basis. Meeting their supervisors every week serves as a strong form of engagement at work. It not only shows them that their bosses pay attention to them and are personally involved in their work, it also serves the purpose of constant monitoring and performance review for the employee, rather than a ne-time review/appraisal.

Time to Nurture Personal Ideas and Passion Projects

Millennials need time to work on their personal projects or rather 'passion projects', which are not related to their job tasks. Young employees are more creative and have a knack of entrepreneurial spirit and hence want time to develop their ideas. A dedicated time and space provided to them to nurture their innovative spirit by the organization boosts their job engagement. Companies such as Google have been implementing this by offering their employees a chance to work on their mini ideas post their job tasks. Google wants its employees to dedicate 20 per cent of their work time to other projects aside from their main jobs, especially ideas that are going to prove advantageous to Google itself (6).

Such an arrangement which promotes intrapreneurship is a two-way ship and helps both the organization and the employee alike. The employee feels a sense of attachment with the company and towards his/her work and the organization benefits by greater innovation, happier employees and fewer exits. Google CEO, Larry Page, says that such schemes help to empower their creative employees and help the organization in retaining their in-house talent. Such initiatives make the employer–employee relationship stronger (7).

Engagement in Community Service and Philanthropic Activities

Time and again, studies have found that millennials patronize community service and giving back to the society. They engage in the most charitable work amongst all the other generations, so much so that they are being classified as the most generous generation (8). They believe in the responsibility they owe towards the society and the less privileged and needy.

The changing socio-economic circumstances coupled with the technology-led ease of giving have led to the scenario of millennials spending more time in volunteer services and philanthropic activities. They are also more aware of the needs of others and how they can contribute to making society better for everyone. They want to make the world a better place for the current and coming generations.

Providing a Sense of Fulfilment

This points out to answering the 'why' of their jobs. They need to find meaning in the work they do. Employers and managers must be able to answer how the job/their role helps to meet the purpose of the organization and the greater goal of life. Millennials work in an organization not just for the salary. They seek fulfilment in everything they do and they even demand it from their jobs. For millennials, their job must provide them with a sense of purpose. In order to retain a millennial at their job, it is important to understand that instead of the employer, they bear attachment and loyalty to the job. Hence, not just monetary benefit but an assurance of doing something big appeals more to the millennials (9).

To understand why millennials change their jobs, we have been working under the assumption that millennials are job-hoppers. But are they really so? The answer to this question is 'no'. If not all millennials are quick to shift jobs; one can identify what it could take to retain a millennial. A survey by Gallup identifies that millennials leave jobs due to lack of engagement at work.

For the millennials, customization is important. The answer to derive the most out of the millennials lies in providing them with what they need the most from their organization, designed to suit the needs of the millennials that aligns with their passion. It is duly important to understand what makes them stick. David Kurzmann, CEO of Women's Best, notices that more than financial benefits, millennials seek a good work ambience and appreciation for their work (4).

Reverse Mentoring

Being one of the newer trends on the block, reverse mentoring purports to pairing an older generation employee with a millennial who acts as the mentor. The millennial's task remains to familiarize them with the new technological software and tools, so that the boomers do not lag behind. The younger employees also benefit through this interaction since it provides them with the domain knowledge and learning, professional expertise and career assistance which the senior member brings to the table. The sharing of ideas brought about by mixing of the generations is an implicit long-term investment the company makes by capitalizing on diversity. Forming the largest generation in the workforce, the millennials make the correct candidates to assist the top-tier managers to formulate business strategies leveraged to make the most in this digital era (10).

Pioneered by Jack Welch, the former CEO of General Electric, reverse mentoring is an effective strategy to leverage internal resources to make the less tech-savvy employees possess technological know-how. In his initial attempt at reverse mentoring, Welch formed 500 pairs of junior–senior employees. He was hopeful that his endeavour would benefit both the members through sharing of expertise and technical know-how. And rightly enough, the strategy proved fruitful and ever since was aptly adapted by the organization, with other big companies following suit (11).

Reverse mentoring defies the hierarchy since it practically overturns the traditional norm of mentoring. Since the younger employees are the main imparters of knowledge and are considered 'experts', it heightens their morale. They feel more visible and valued in the organization and thereby perceive more career prospects, which increases their chances of continuation in the company. It also helps to hone their leadership skills (12).

Reverse mentoring is a good form of intergenerational collaboration to bridge the gap between the generations. Since both generations work together and there is an obvious sharing of experiences, it helps to remove the stereotypes and biases both parties carry. Along with the immediate advantage to the young mentor and the senior mentee, it is a good way to build the spirit of comradery and teamwork in the workspace. The organization also gains a rapid upskilling of their workforce, ready for the challenges to be encountered. Even though most organizations incorporate reverse mentoring programmes to different extents and have different approaches, the main purpose should always be identified before the implementation for it to contribute significantly.

The Case at Deloitte: Performance Review System for Millennial Workforce

In 2015, Deloitte Touche Tohmatsu Limited, or better known as Deloitte, captured people's attention when it announced its endeavour to introduce a new performance review system (13). This professional service giant was not the first multinational to do so. Deloitte closely followed in the heels of companies like Accenture, Adobe and Microsoft, which had revamped their performance management systems. An employee survey conducted by the company itself had pointed out the flaws in the ranking-and-rating review systems (14). It was revealed that these forced systems, where employees are pitted against their colleagues, do not serve the purpose of evaluations correctly or capture their performance effectively. These systems bore no impact on the employee engagement and did not seem to increase their motivation at work. Rather, the systems' evaluation of their goal achievement was seriously flawed, in addition to being time-consuming and redundant. These ultimately led Deloitte to think about ways to redesign its system for a much more holistic and effective review system.

Deloitte is a UK-based private company, comprising of a family of independent firms, operating globally (15). It provides an umbrella of professional services consisting of auditing, consulting, human capital services, legal advisory, financial advisory, regulatory services, risk management, tax services and technology services. Having a history of more than 180 years, this company has evolved to become one of the leading consultancy firms, instituting itself as one amongst the 'Big Four' league of consulting organizations.

Deloitte has a strong focus on its work culture and people management. Moreover, considering the nature of the firm, its economy is driven by knowledge workers, who bring their respective capabilities and skills to the workplace. The traditional ranking systems are highly goal based, and abide by the one-size-fits-all approach, which does not consider the individual skill set and learnings into account. The changing business dynamics, too, do not offer a supporting hand to the current performance review system. These processes only test the employees based upon the tasks they complete and evaluate them against other colleagues, which happens once a year. A vital component of learning and overall development is largely ignored.

Deloitte was until then implementing the conventional performance review system, which fit the demands of the baby boomers. At the beginning of every year, an employee had a target set for him/her. The feedback about the employee was provided on a rank-and-rate basis by the supervisor after each project. The supervisor evaluated if the target was met, how well it was met and what could be the scope of improvement for the employee. These interim evaluations were then combined at the end of the year into a consolidated rating. Finally, in the lengthy meetings that were held at the end of the year, counsellors compared the performance of each employee with their co-workers, after which the final annual rating would be given. The entire process of multiple ratings, comparison with peers and meetings for evaluation were a tedious process. In addition, the evaluation was highly subjective such that it was based upon the supervisor's perception of the employee. All these made it detrimental to the employee morale.

Following the survey, Deloitte realized the need to shift from this system to one which factored other parameters of evaluation (15). To meet the needs of the largely millennial workforce, it implemented a system which fostered employee engagement, was less subjective and provided scope for actual learning. Keeping these in mind, Deloitte's redesigned the system centred around continuous collaboration, including the aspects of coaching, feedback and development. This kind of approach brought the managers to the forefront and made them active participants in the performance evaluation process. The focus was to shift the time involved in discussing others to invest in time nurturing others. Conversations with the respective employees are fruitful in enhancing performance. The revamped system also decoupled performance evaluation from compensation.

The millennial generation needed mentors and coaches, rather than evaluators. Hence, it was only relevant that managers played an active role in the overall development and learning of the employee instead of simply evaluating them. With the new system, the managers were involved in monitoring the employees and giving them feedback about their work on a continuous basis. Instead of reviewing the past performance, the process was regulated to help employees become better in the future. Advice about improving performance and setting career goals were made part of the process. Effective internal feedback also excluded the need for millennials to seek guidance from external sources. Regular check-ins with the leaders and supervisors set clear expectations regarding the task, which engaged both the parties and instilled transparency.

The system is so devised that every employee, including the manager, becomes more aware of his or her own role in the organization. Managers find themselves more engrossed in the development of the employee, which in turn pushes the manager towards better performance. The emphasis upon one's own contribution is also utilized in removing subjectivity from the assessment. Managers have to decide their actions towards a particular employee, given a particular situation, instead of assessing the employee based upon their thoughts and feelings of them. This is done objectively through a set of questions, the response data of which are then analysed to put forth a performance-pattern analysis. The results of the analysis are used by the company to decide upon the grey areas and the course of action.

Discussion Questions

1. Do you think Deloitte's new performance system will be successful? Enlist reasons for your answer.

2. Given the high attrition rates amongst the millennials, do you think performance evaluation measures will help to reduce it? Substantiate your answer.

....

Reverse Mentoring at P&G

The Procter & Gamble Company is the largest consumer packaged goods company in the world (16–19). Founded in 1837 and incorporated in 1905, the company is headquartered in Cincinnati, United States It is the home of 65 brands of products which are categorized into 10 segments: (i) baby care, (ii) fabric care, (iii) family care, (iv) feminine care, (v) hair care, (vi) home care, (vii) grooming, (viii) oral care, (ix) personal health care and (x) skin and personal care. It occupies the number one market share when it comes to millennials. Also known as P&G, it has a global reach spread in 180 countries. Its worldwide net sales account for $65.1 billion, of which $23.7 billion comes from its US sales. It boasts of a consumer base of five billion; its products are sold primarily through department stores, grocery stores, pharmacies, e-commerce, specialty beauty stores and so on.

P&G has been successful in implementing reverse mentoring in its various diversity endeavours targeted at increasing workforce diversity (20). Reverse mentoring refers to an initiative wherein the older executives of the company are paired with younger employees for mentoring on topics such as technology, social media and so on. Reverse mentoring programmes have helped the senior-level employees to gain new perspectives, relatively necessary for strategies which are specially targeted at attracting and retaining the younger generations. By pairing junior members with the senior managers, P&G has been able to create a culture which operates from trust and respect and does not succumb to irrational biases. These initiatives bring to fore the challenges of the other party, so that strategy makers can make the workplace better for them. Hence, to provide the top management team better insights about the needs and aspirations of the millennials from diverse walks of life, reverse mentoring acts as an effective tool.

The younger generations seek to associate with organizations that are more than just a company (21, 22). The brand should be able to provide them with a sense of fulfilment. The youth-centric range of products also calls for new insights which can only be provided by actually understanding the consumers of today. Hence, to align itself with the needs of the employees and the consumers, getting to know them is important. Reverse mentoring provides with learning and development opportunities for the senior executives, thereby helping them to strike a chord with the young in order to develop effective strategies, devising youth-centric marketing and advertising, redesigning products, fuelling innovation, attracting youth consumers and ensuring brand loyalty and employee loyalty.

P&G's Mentor Up is a classic example of a reverse mentoring strategy adopted by an organization (23–25). P&G rolled out its Mentor Up initiative to increase the representation of females at the top management level. Mentor Up fulfilled a twofold agenda (i) bringing fresh perspective to the table and (ii) increasing the female representation in the top management. P&G had high female attrition rates at the lower and mid-managerial levels (almost double that of the male), which culminated in low women members in the top management. As a response to this issue, P&G decided to have mentorship programmes to guide and train young female employees so that they could hold leadership positions in the organization in the future. But when they spoke to the female employees, they found the traditional mentorship did not serve the cause.

Based on an initial survey, it was found that although men and women received similar performance ratings, yet women were less satisfied with the work environment (26). Further, a secondary survey revealed that the women felt that their top management had little information about the actual problems these women faced. Apart from that, they also felt that since the top management did not take accountability for increasing women representation, they had very few role models and hence their career paths were bleak. To retain females, it was necessary to know the reason why they were quitting, which could be found out by delving deeper into what they wanted from the organization. Hence, a reverse mentoring programme called Mentor Up was introduced.

The reverse mentoring programme was initiated under the wing of Advancement of Women Task Force. Mentor Up grouped senior executives with junior female employees. Through their interaction, the problems faced by women at the workplace were brought to light for effective redressal. The junior females acted as mentors and provided suggestions and advice on improving the condition of women in the organization. The main aim was to involve the men as well as women, to take feedback and develop an understanding of the issues women face at work.

The programme helped to remove the generational differences by eliminating the biases and misunderstandings about the younger women (27). It also helped to develop healthy work relationships between the male and female counterparts. The mentor–mentee bonding made the senior members aware about the different aspirations and goals of the younger generation of female employees. Since mentoring relationships are based on two-way communication, the junior employees were exposed to the challenges encountered by the top executives. It prepared the female employees at the start of their career for future leadership roles in due course of their tenure in the organization. These programmes proved as strong foundation for ongoing initiatives such as Corporate Women's Leadership Team and Men Advocating Real Change (28). Such programmes coupled with other benefits nurture women and cater to their needs in such a way that the females are tempted to continue working in the organization.

The reverse mentoring programme Mentor Up was successful and saw an upsurge in the young female employees (29). So much so, P&G has currently earned a spot on NAFE Top Companies for Executive Women List 2019 and Working Mother Best Companies for Multicultural Women 2019 (USA) with a 35 per cent of women corporate executives and 36 per cent of women board members (30). It also features at rank 141 on the Forbes List of World's Best Employers 2018 and at rank 22 on the Forbes List of Best Employers for Diversity 2019. Due its various endeavours, P&G has become one of the pioneers for improving diversity (31).

Discussion Questions

1. Can programmes such as reverse mentoring be applicable across various cultures? What caution needs to be kept in mind while implementing such programmes?

2. Describe strategies similar to reverse mentoring which can be used to reduce differences amongst the young and the older employees of the organization?

Table 5.2 shows HR strategies to help organizations capitalize on the strengths of each generation.

TABLE 5.2 ACQUISITION, DEVELOPMENT AND RETENTION STRATEGIES TO HANDLE BABY BOOMERS, GENERATION X, AND MILLENNIALS

Generation(s)	Acquisition Strategies	Development Strategies	Retention Strategies
Baby boomers	They are committed and focused. Negotiation is for public acknowledgements. Ambition-driven employees can be evaluated either on their KSA's past performers, length of service and experience or through a routine recruitment and selection process.	Talent-driven learning, team assignments and initiatives can be given to them. Executive coaching programmes such as assessment, feedback and coaching to guide executives in improving their work performance and business bottom line results.	Scheme of sabbatical leave, for specified purposes such as pursuing higher education, taking care of children/family members; relaxation in the eligibility criteria in the matter of length of service for promotion purposes; long-term retirement benefits may be offered.
Generation X	Merit and competency-based placements are required on the basis of technical knowledge, skills, psychometric tests and adaptability.	Sponsorships programmes, performance-driven learning; team coaching and team building programmes for improving group performance, team coaching and team building abilities; Offering creative and challenging tasks.	Providing option of flexible working hours; fast track promotions; Group financial rewards, ranging from leave encashment, retirement gratuity, pension plans and provident fund; Providing good quality of work-life and short-term retirement plans.

(continued)

(continued)

Generation(s)	Acquisition Strategies	Development Strategies	Retention Strategies
Millennials	Selection on the basis of paper/pencil tests, dexterity test and personality test; potential and aptitude and attitude for growth is another important factor on which they are evaluated.	Training programmes focusing on balanced development of business and managerial perspectives; Schemes for encouraging employees to pursue professional and computer education through correspondence, part-time, distance learning where course fees may be reimbursed and cash incentives may be awarded, on successful completion of the course; Multitasking assignments and broad skill set training.	Financials rewards for individuals demonstrating excellence in performance against predefined goals; Staff suggestion schemes to encourage ideation process amongst employees; for example, offering incentives for innovative suggestions that are in tune with organization priorities and concerns; Flexible work shifts, home-based work through tele communication, internet for work-life balance may be offered.

Effective communication	• Judicious blend of formal and informal communication should be adopted while communicating with mutigenerational workforce. • Technology can form an appropriate backbone for all forms of formal and informal communication in the organization. • Thus, appropriate technological and non-technological platforms can be developed to create disseminate and communicate ideas taking into consideration the development through technology information.
Eliminating chances of perception errors	• Organizing informal information sharing sessions from time to time giving a chance to employee for getting acquitted with each other. • Creating data for HR competency maps in the organization can be effective solution to formalize the process and systems in the organization.
Develop two-way coaching and mentoring	• There is need for setting up two-way flow of knowledge and support, wherein experience, knowledge and skill sets may be shared, both up and down the organization hierarchy. • This, in whole, can boost up the morals of the employee, enabling them to perform their task in a better manner. Online support and a system through intranet and extranet and video conferencing facilities can be appropriate platforms for such learning.
Make policies and programmes flexible	• Refining policies and programmes and tailoring them in a manner to better meet the needs and expectations of multigenerational workforce has become need of the hour. • Therefore, it should include polices related to financial and non-financial benefits, career management and succession planning and work-life balance.
Learning and training	• Creating a mixture of function and project assignment appeals to all generations. Since traditionalist are functional experts, boomers are best at team assignments and Gen X are free spirited and independent, creative by nature and can be assigned challenging tasks that question the existing status quo.

STRATEGIES OF MANAGING MILLENNIALS

(continued)

Create mix of function and project-oriented assignments	• Looking beyond the formal and classroom setting or online experiences and pairing up experienced staff with the younger ones' hand and vice versa will make employees benefit from the knowledge and experiences of all.
Knowledge retention initiatives	• Retaining the wisdom of older employees requires brainstorming sessions, conferences and workshops from time to time to further understand eminent issues.

Source: Chawla (2015).

A Talent Management Approach to Managing a Millennial Workforce

Align your business plan and talent strategy	• Talent strategy should be aligned with the overall business plan strategy. Recognize the importance of millennials in your business plan.
Face the future	• A strategic people planning approach is in place to help you understand the needs or shortages. • Check whether current talent management fits the business plan and considering millennials while formulating a plan. Have a strategic people planning approach to understand the talent shortages.
Pay attention to pivotal roles	• Get the talent that creates disproportionate ability to create (or destroy) business value. Have a succession plan in place to move millennials in crucial roles.
Focus on the financials	• Make measurement, benchmarking and analysis part of your plan. Look for return on investment (ROI) of talent, track the cost of replacing lost millennial talent and measure the impact of losing talents on your strategic priorities.

Source: Millennials at work reshaping the workplace (2011).

Millennial females have higher organizational commitment levels than their male counterparts (33). Thus, managers should consider hiring millennials with graduate degrees and, more specifically, females because of their higher organizational commitment levels. Women understand that they are a marginalized group in the workforce and are committed to keeping their job. Women tend to treat their organization as their extended family and are very committed.

A study from the reverse mentoring programme for boomers and millennials suggests that HRD professionals require to gain an understanding about what motivates and drives today's multigenerational workforce to work with passion so that organizations can adopt policies and programmes such as reverse mentoring that can help organizations achieve the same (34).

The following five strategies will help you overcome the challenge of managing millennials and raise their productivity (35).

1. Pay attention to the process of onboarding employees; provide a quick tour on policy and guidelines review for new employees. Empower them through company history, culture, mission and products and services that spans 6 to 12 months. Include socialization opportunities, projects, multimedia presentations and multiple learning and development experience on onboarding programmes.

2. Create cool workplace through creative communication, open work spaces, state-of-the-art technology, workplace flexibility and social networking opportunities. As a result, the work environment is made dynamic, interesting, challenging and fun.

3. Challenge them at the workplace. Provide incentives for projects in various ways to help them do well and receive recognition for their work. High expectations stem from high volume feedback and encouragement.

4. Coaching differently help them understand their unproductive behaviour to increase their success. Whenever

you are solving a problem, involve them directly to strengthen overall value to the organization. Track their progress and modify their behaviours to improve their performance.

5. Plan a career path. Not only do millennials expect to do well in their jobs, they desire to rise quickly in the organization, which might strike many older co-workers as arrogance. However, this can help managers as a key tool to engage their younger employees fully. Managers can help them to formulate a career plan by directing them to follow the plan and reach the top. Other career-related guidance can also be provided by the organization such as educational benefits. As a result, millennials can better understand how their efforts fit into the company mission and motivate them to perform better or become a top performer in a job.

REFERENCES

1. Higginbottom, K. (2016, Mar 17). The challenges of managing a multi-generational workforce. Forbes. Retrieved from https://www.forbes.com/sites/karenhigginbottom/2016/03/17/the-challenges-of-managing-a-multi-generational-workforce/#94c04717d6ac. Accessed on 10 Oct 2018.
2. Urick, M.J., Hollensbe, E.C., Masterson, S.S., & Lyons, S.T. (2016). Understanding and managing intergenerational conflict: An examination of influences and strategies. Work Aging Retire. 3(2):166–85.
3. Center for Women and Business at Bentley University (2017). Multi-generational impacts on the workplace: A curated research report.
4. Patel D. (2017). 5 costly mistakes leaders make when managing millennials. Retrieved from https://www.forbes.com/sites/deeppatel/2017/11/07/5-costly-mistakes-leaders-make-when-managing-millennials/#132dc84f19f. Accessed on 10 Oct 2018.
5. Adkins, A., & Rigoni, B. (2016, Jun 2). Managers: millennials want feedback, but won't ask for it. Gallup. Retrieved from https://www.gallup.com/workplace/236450/managers-millennials-feedback-won-ask.aspx. Accessed on 10 Oct 2018.
6. Robinson, A. (n.d.). Want to boost your bottom line? Encourage your employees to work on side projects. Inc. Retrieved from https://www.inc.com/adam-robinson/google-employees-dedicate-20-percent-of-their-time-to-side-projects-heres-how-it-works.html. Accessed on 15 Oct 2018.

7. Mcalone, N. (2016, Apr 24). Google is building an in-house startup incubator called 'Area 120'. Business Insider. Retrieved from https://www.businessinsider.in/Google-is-building-an-in-house-startup-incubator-called-Area-120/articleshow/51970347.cms. Accessed on 10 Oct 2018.

8. Wheeler, J. (2018, Aug 15). How millennials are changing philanthropy. Forbes. Retrieved from https://www.forbes.com/sites/theyec/2018/08/15/how-millennials-are-changing-philanthropy/#3e104db87c68. Accessed on 10 Oct 2018.

9. Moore, K. (2014, Oct 2). Millennials work for purpose, not paycheck. Forbes. Retrieved from https://www.forbes.com/sites/karlmoore/2014/10/02/millennials-work-for-purpose-not-paycheck/#22fc590b6a51. Accessed on 10 Oct 2018.

10. Steimle, J. (2015, May 5). Reverse mentoring—investing in tomorrow's business strategy. Forbes. Retrieved from https://www.forbes.com/sites/joshsteimle/2015/05/05/reverse-mentoring-investing-in-tomorrows-business-strategy/#59d1a5346769. Accessed on 10 Oct 2018.

11. Wingard, J. (2018, Aug 8). Reverse mentoring: 3 proven outcomes driving change. Forbes. Retrieved from https://www.forbes.com/sites/jasonwingard/2018/08/08/reverse-mentoring-3-proven-outcomes-driving-change/#3f2068118b51. Accessed on 13 Oct 2018.

12. Cosgrove, E. (2016, Sep 13). Reverse mentoring: 'you need help!' LinkedIn. Retrieved from https://www.linkedin.com/pulse/reverse-mentoring-you-need-help-emily-cosgrove/. Accessed on 13 Oct 2018.

13. Buckingham, M. & Goodall, A. (2015). Reinventing Performance Management. Harv. Bus. Rev. Retrieved from https://hbr.org/2015/04/reinventing-performance-management.

14. Garr, S. (2014, Mar 4). Performance management is broken. Deloitte. Insights. Retrieved from https://www2.deloitte.com/insights/us/en/focus/human-capital-trends/2014/hc-trends-2014-performance-management.html. Accessed on 13 Oct 2018.

15. Deloitte UK website. Retrieved from https://www2.deloitte.com/uk/en.html. Accessed on 13 Oct 2018.

16. P&G Careers. Retrieved from https://www.pgcareers.com/about-us. Accessed on 13 Oct 2018.

17. P&G Profile. Reuters. Retrieved from https://www.reuters.com/finance/stocks/company-profile/PG. Accessed on 13 Oct 2018.

18. P&G, Forbes. Retrieved from https://www.forbes.com/companies/procter-gamble/#635657404165. Accessed on 13 Oct 2018.

19. P&G US website. Retrieved from https://us.pg.com/. Accessed on 13 Oct 2018.

20. Tesseras, L. (2015, Jul 9). How to take advantage of reverse mentoring. Xeim. Retrieved from https://www.marketingweek.com/2015/07/09/how-to-take-advantage-of-reverse-mentoring/. Accessed on 13 Oct 2018.

21. Danziger, P.N. (2017, Oct 24). How can P&G be so clueless about what customers want? Forbes. Retrieved from https://www.forbes.com/sites/pamdanziger/2017/10/24/can-pg-be-so-clueless-about-what-customers-want/#67e545bc762e. Accessed on 14 Oct 2018.

22. Bourke, J., Garr, S., Berkel, A.V., & Wong, J. (2017, Feb 28). Diversity and inclusion: the reality gap. Deloitte Insights. Retrieved from https://www2.

deloitte.com/insights/us/en/focus/human-capital-trends/2017/diversity-and-inclusion-at-the-workplace.html#endnote-sup-30. Accessed on 14 Oct 2018.

23. Young, J. (2018, Feb 15). How reverse mentoring can help your business. Peakon. Retrieved from https://peakon.com/blog/learning-development/reverse-mentoring/. Accessed on 14 Oct 2018.

24. Biss, J.L., & DuFrene, D.D. (2006). An examination of reverse mentoring in the workplace. Business Education Digest (15):30–41.

25. Cosgrove, E. (2016, Sep 13). Reverse Mentoring: 'You Need Help!' LinkedIn. Retrieved from https://www.linkedin.com/pulse/reverse-mentoring-you-need-help-emily-cosgrove/. Accessed on 14 Oct 2018.

26. Stromei, L.K. (Ed.). (2001). Creating mentoring and coaching programs: twelve case studies from the real world of training. Alexandria, VA: American Society for Training and Development.

27. Ashton, J., & Petrin, R. (Fall 2010). Who's the mentor now? A word of caution about reverse business mentoring. Insights Magazine, Northeast Human Resources Association. Retrieved from https://www2.usgs.gov/humancapital/ecd/mentoringreadinglist/ReverseMentoringArticle.pdf. Accessed on 14 Oct 2018.

28. Citizenship Report, Procter & Gamble, 2018. Retrieved from https://us.pg.com/diversity-and-inclusion/. Accessed on 14 Oct 2018.

29. P&G. Retrieved from https://www.forbes.com/companies/procter-gamble/#635657404165. Accessed on 14 Oct 2018.

30. P&G (2019, Mar 5). Working mother. Retrieved from https://www.workingmother.com/best-companies-procter-gamble. Accessed on 14 Oct 2018.

31. Millennials at work reshaping the workplace. (2011). [online]. New York: PWC. Retrieved from https://www.pwc.com/m1/en/services/consulting/documents/millennials-at-work.pdf. Accessed on 11 Dec 2017.

32. Chawla, G. (2015). HR Strategies for Managing a Multigenerational Workforce: A Conceptual Study. In Advances in Management and Technology. New Delhi: McGraw Hill Education (India) Private Limited.

33. Kaifi, B.A., Nafei, W.A., Khanfar, N.M., & Kaifi, M.M. (2012). A multi-generational workforce: managing and understanding millennials. Int J Business Manag. 7(24):88.

34. Chaudhuri, S., & Ghosh, R. (2012). Reverse mentoring: a social exchange tool for keeping the boomers engaged and millennials committed. Hum Resour Dev. 11(1):55–76.

35. Bogosian, R., & Rousseau, C. (2017). How and why millennials are shaking up organizational cultures. Rutgers Bus Rev. 2(3):386–94.

6

STRATEGIES FOR RECRUITING MILLENNIALS

HRM, also referred to as people management, is a discipline that is 'concerned with all aspects of how people are employed and managed in organizations' (1, p. 4). A comprehensive definition of HRM describes it as 'the process of acquiring, training, appraising, and compensating employees, and of attending to their labor relations, health and safety and fairness concerns' (2, p. 4). It is evident from the above definition that the HR department in an organization is responsible for a wide range of functions, such as workforce planning, recruitment and selection, learning and development, performance and reward management, amongst several others. The present chapter focusses on one of the core functions of HRM, namely, recruitment and selection in organizations. Past research has drawn clear lines of distinction between the processes of recruitment and selection. While recruitment refers to the process of attracting applicants, the selection is the process of choosing amongst them (3). The entire sequence of events that occur during the recruitment and selection process can be segregated into three broad stages. The first stage, also referred to as the 'attraction' stage, begins with the posting of job advertisements by the organization to make potential applicants aware of the vacancy and encourage them to apply for it. The second stage, known as the 'recruitment' stage, involves the screening of applicants, resulting in sieving of those who fail to meet the eligibility criteria for that job. The third and final stage, labelled as the 'selection' stage, comprises a rigorous set of assessments to choose the most promising and suitable applicants for the job (4).

Over the past two decades, there has been a striking change in the way organizations perform their recruitment and selection activities. The explosive growth of the internet has completely revolutionized the hiring process in business organizations.

With the advent of the internet, the recruitment industry has rapidly evolved from Craigslist and Monster of the 2000s to LinkedIn and social media platforms that are in vogue today (5). The entire process of recruitment and selection starting from the posting of job advertisements by organizations to candidates applying for them, submitting their CVs and even appearing for interviews has been completely digitized. While there is a plethora of literature that discusses the impact of technological forces in transforming the hiring process, the role of demographic trends has been relatively under-examined. Particularly, the academic research studying the impact of increasing population within the millennial cohort on the recruitment and selection processes in organizations is fairly limited. We attempt to bridge this gap in the literature by shedding light on how the patterns of organizational recruitment and selection are changing against the backdrop of a rising Generation Y population.

The objective of this chapter is threefold. First, we explain how the rise of the millennial population is transforming the way recruitment and selection processes are carried out in business organizations. In doing so, we elaborate upon the changing expectations of millennial candidates with regard to the hiring process. Second, we present a range of strategies that organizations can adopt to effectively recruit and select millennials into their pool of human resources. Finally, we conclude with a case study that illustrates the efforts of a real-world organization that actually excelled in recruiting and selecting millennials into its workforce.

HOW ARE MILLENNIALS SHAPING THE RECRUITMENT LANDSCAPE IN ORGANIZATIONS?

Over the years, it has been widely accepted by scholars as well as practitioners that millennials are a unique set of individuals with different attitudes, values and preferences vis-à-vis their predecessors. These differences are often reflected in the world of work as well. Millennials step into the workforce with a very different set of expectations and a unique way of looking at things. Contemporary organizations, therefore, are tailoring their efforts specifically to suit the needs and expectations of millennials. Doing so is especially important because of the following reasons. First, millennials have substantial bargaining power over employers as they constitute a large proportion of the working population and the numbers are expected to rise further in the future (6). These demographic trends make it next to impossible for organizations to ignore the interests of millennials.

Second, the 'war for talent' continues to be fought with organizations leaving no stone unturned to attract, engage and retain the best talent (7). Classic academic works have asserted that the accumulation of valuable, rare, inimitable and non-substitutable resources allows an organization to gain a sustained competitive advantage over its rival firms (8). Lately, it has been recognized that talent, too, may be a source of competitive advantage for organizations (9). Given the fact that other competing organizations are putting in dedicated efforts to manage millennial talent effectively, no organization can afford to lose that edge by lagging behind in such initiatives. Hence, a complex interplay between demographic trends and competitive pressures is driving organizations to tailor themselves to cater to the needs and expectations of the Generation Y workforce.

One of the core functions of HRM that have undergone considerable changes over the past few years is recruitment and selection. We now elaborate upon some of the unique preferences of millennials that have been instrumental in changing the face of the recruitment landscape. In doing so, we also discuss the examples of few organizations that have taken care of these millennial preferences and have appropriately addressed the same by incorporating relevant changes in their hiring process.

1. **Millennials are involved in technologically advanced modes of job search:** Millennials have grown up in an age dominated by a series of technological developments such as the introduction of devices such as computers, smartphones and tablets coupled with the phenomenal growth of the internet. These technological forces have had a marked influence on the lives of millennials and have completely transformed the way they do things. The same holds true even for activities like looking for a job. Millennials are starkly different from baby boomers and Generation Xers in their job search patterns. In a recent survey conducted by Talent Trends, a majority of the millennials reported that they visited social media for job-related information, preferred electronic communication over physical methods, and believed that they should be able to apply for jobs over smartphones or tablets (10). Not surprisingly, a large number of job search apps like Naukri.com, Monster jobs, Glassdoor, LinkedIn and Simply Hired have come up during the past few years. Organizations are trying to cater to the changing job search preferences of millennials, which is evident from the number of jobs that are posted on these platforms each day.

2. **Millennials prefer shorter hiring process and the use of sophisticated hiring techniques:** Several studies in the marketing literature have demonstrated that millennials are impatient consumers and have an impaired ability to delay gratifications (11, 12). These tendencies are also reflected in other spheres of millennials' lives such as their preference for shorter hiring processes. In a case study conducted by KPMG, it was observed that more than one-third of the 400 job applicants found the hiring process excessively long to the point of frustration (13, 14). On the one hand, millennials demand a reduction in the length of the hiring process. On the other hand, the length of the entire recruitment process has increased from an average of 13 days in 2011 to 23 days in 2015 (15). Given the frustration and uneasiness millennials experience due to the length of the hiring process, organizations are trying to respond to these concerns through a host of strategies. First, organizations are using sophisticated technologies such as applicant tracking systems (ATS) to automate the hiring process. ATS offers a range of benefits such as easy job postings, quick filtering capabilities, time and cost savings, and a broader reach (16). Technologies such as ATS reduce the manual effort often consumed in activities such as screening resumes, which in turn helps in shortening the hiring process. Second, organizations are doing away with traditional interaction methods such as face-to-face interviews and are taking the help of technology to screen potential hires. Organizations such as Goldman Sachs are replacing the initial rounds of campus interviews and opting for virtual meetings such as Skype interviews (15, 17). The adoption of such techniques is a crucial step in the direction of shortening the hiring process and meeting millennial expectations.

3. **Millennials are increasingly focused on corporate culture:** Millennials place a lot of value in the culture of the organization they would be working for. Hence, it is vital for organizations to take crucial steps to manage their corporate culture actively. Their focus should be on building a culture that is attractive to the millennial workforce.

Estimates suggest that millennials are willing to compromise on salary and bear an average pay cut of $7,600 in the pursuit of career development opportunities, meaningful work, work-life balance or better company culture (18) Such findings underscore the importance of good corporate culture in attracting as well as retaining millennials. It is, therefore, imperative that during recruitment, organizations direct their efforts towards building and marketing their company culture in order to attract as well as retain millennial candidates (18).

4. **Parents' involvement with millennial children:** Helicopter parents, who have coddled and overprotected their millennial children all through their childhood, have now started hovering over their work organizations. Generation Y, as a cohort, is particularly close to its parents. This closeness assumes the form of increased involvement in the job search as well as post-job activities. In a study conducted by CERI, 32 per cent of the employers (with an employee base of more than 3,688) and 26 per cent of the employers (with an employee strength of 351–3,687) indicated that they had witnessed parental involvement in the recruitment process as well as in the early career stages of college recruits. Employers reported that this involvement was exhibited in the form of activities such as obtaining information about the company, submitting resume on behalf of the

student, promoting their children for a position, attending career fairs, complaining if their children were not hired, making interview arrangements, negotiating salary and benefits, and attending the interviews. Given these trends, several organizations are embracing parental involvement instead of frowning at it. Doing so is beneficial as parents have the ability to influence their children's decisions. Hence, fostering emotional bonds with them would go a long way not only in attracting and retaining talent but also in boosting employee morale. In the California-based headquarters of Google, an event known as 'Take your parents to work day' was recently hosted and it attracted as many as 2,000 parents. Likewise, another organization, Northwestern Mutual, regularly invites parents of college-aged interns for open houses. Such efforts have actually paid off for the company, and the number of interns meeting the productivity benchmarks has risen by a whopping 40 per cent. It is, therefore, recommended that organizations in Asia also take up similar parent-focused initiatives for attracting millennial talent, as millennials in Asia are closer to their parents as compared to their American counterparts (19–21).

The above discussion sheds light on the unique preferences of the millennial generation in terms of recruitment and selection processes. These differences pave the way for new challenges for recruiting organizations. It is the need of the hour that business organizations realize the importance of these millennial trends and make dedicated efforts to address these needs of the millennial workforce. Doing so would go a long way in attracting, engaging, as well as retaining millennial talent, which in turn will help the organization in achieving a competitive advantage over rivals.

STRATEGIES FOR RECRUITING AND SELECTING GENERATION Y INTO THE WORKFORCE

Having deliberated upon the needs and expectations of millennials during recruitment and selection, we now elaborate upon what organizations can do to address these millennial needs and expectations. Some of the strategies that organizations can adopt to improve their recruitment and selection efforts and make them attractive to millennials have been presented as follows.

1. **The role of the organization's official website:** Within the HRM literature, past academic research studies have been conducted to spot the factors that play a vital role in predicting the attraction of millennials towards organizations. A research study conducted in the context of web-based recruitment of millennial employees noted that perceptions of work-life balance as conveyed on the organization's official website and perceptions of website usability were significant predictors of millennials' attraction towards the organization. The findings of this study emphasize the importance of website content in shaping millennials' perceptions of the job as well as the organization. Therefore, it would be advantageous for organizations to develop user-friendly websites. It is equally important for organizations to maintain their websites and update them regularly by posting content that is likely to appeal to the millennial cohort (22).

2. **The role of corporate recruiting videos and photos:** Another empirical research study has demonstrated the importance of novel techniques such as corporate recruiting videos in attracting millennial applicants. Being one of the initial points of contact with prospective

hires, corporate recruiting videos offer a glimpse into the kind of work environment and lifestyle an applicant will experience once he (she) steps into the organization.

Videos featuring meditation rooms, sleep pods, on-site massages and laundry, in-house gyms and so on are especially attractive to young talent. Industry giants today are offering a wide range of unusual perks to their employees. For instance, Google allows its employees to enjoy a host of facilities such as getting a haircut at work, taking showers or taking naps in one of the sleep pods. Likewise, Airbnb provides its employees the opportunity to explore their passion of travel by providing coupons worth as much as $2,000 per year. While these benefits fall under the purview of compensation planning which is discussed at length in the next chapter, it is the proper marketing of these benefits that falls within the scope of the present chapter. In order to attract the best of millennial talent, organizations need to broadcast the perks that they are offering to entice Generation Y applicants. This could be achieved by posting such corporate recruiting videos and images on a wide variety of platforms to ensure maximum coverage (23–26).

3. **The role of recruitment advertisements:** Another research has pointed out the role of recruitment advertisements in attracting millennial applicants. The study employed an experimental research design to assess the impact of different types of recruitment advertisements on applicant attraction. It found that advertisements featuring information pertaining to training and development, financial rewards and career advancement were reported as more attractive by these participants. Similarly, participants in another study were found to be the most

attracted towards organizations whose job posting contained information about a flexible career path and least attracted towards those where job posting allowed only a traditional career path. These findings highlight the importance of the design of job postings in influencing millennials' attraction towards them. Hence, it may be inferred that organizations should carefully design their job postings keeping in view the expectations of millennials. Job postings containing information that resonates with the needs and expectations of millennials would help the organizations to attract more applications from this cohort (27, 28).

4. **The role of job review sites:** While consumer review websites such as TripAdvisor and Yelp are well known for providing customers the opportunity of posting online reviews of the brands that they have shopped from, the concept of employee review websites is relatively less common but is multiplying. Over the past few years, websites such as Indeed and Glassdoor have come up, which allow employees to post anonymous reviews about the organizations that they have worked for. Such reviews play a crucial role in shaping the brand image of the organization amongst the prospective hires. Being technologically active, millennials often go through such review websites while looking for jobs. This is evident from the findings of a recent survey conducted by Software Advice in which 52 per cent of the 4,633 respondents agreed to having used Glassdoor at some point in their job search. Hence, it is necessary for organizations to realize the importance of having a strong and positive presence on such job search platforms. Doing so would not only help improve the visibility of the organization amongst potential applicants

but would also contribute towards the development of a favourable brand image especially amongst millennials. Unlike the official websites managed by the organizations, information posted on these platforms is based upon the experiences of former as well as current employees of the organization, thus enhancing the perceptions of its reliability, authenticity and credibility. In other words, the third-party reviews posted by employees may have an even greater influence on millennials looking for job opportunities. Organizations, therefore, should try to ensure that most of their employees speak well of them on such platforms. This would go a long way in attracting potential millennial talent for the organization (29–31).

5. **The role of embracing diversity and inclusion:** Lately, the meaning of diversity has ceased to remain limited to mere surface-level differences based on age, race, gender and skin colour. For millennials, a participative environment fosters new ideas and perspectives leading to collaboration. Hence, it is often argued that millennials see diversity very differently from Generation Xers and Baby Boomers. The findings of a recent study conducted by the Institute for Public Relations further elucidate this point.

In this research, 47 per cent of the millennial respondents revealed that they considered issues related to diversity and inclusion while searching for jobs, quite in contrast to just 37 per cent of Generation Xers and 33 per cent of baby boomers. These results indicate that millennials value diversity much more than their earlier generations do (32, 33). The benefits of embracing diversity have continued to receive attention from academics as well as practitioners. Past academic literature has observed that employee perceptions of diversity climate are positively related to a host of desirable outcomes such as organizational commitment, psychological empowerment, and group performance and negatively related to undesirable outcomes such as turnover intentions (34, 35). In line with the academic research, practitioner reports by firms such as McKinsey also reveal that companies which feature in the top quartile with respect to embracing diversity related to gender, race and ethnicity are more likely to enjoy higher financial returns vis-à-vis their industry peers. Given the value that millennials place in diversity and inclusion along with the range of benefits that inclusion can generate for the organizations and its members, it is critical for organizations to foster an inclusionary environment. In addition to creating an environment that embraces diversity, it is equally essential for organizations to communicate these efforts to prospective hires during the recruitment phase itself. More attempts need to be made to express that the organization is serious with regard to the introduction as well as the implementation of its diversity and inclusion initiatives. Doing so would be especially appealing to the millennial talent and will help the organization recruit more of it (36–38).

6. **The role of embracing the gig economy:** The past few years have witnessed the magnificent rise of the gig economy, which is characterized by a marked departure from traditional 9-to-5 jobs towards more flexible forms of employment such as temporary employment, on-call work, multiparty employment relationships and part-time work. Given the host of benefits that the gig economy offers to its workers ranging from

flexibility and freedom to a better work-life balance, more and more millennials are getting drawn towards it. This is evident from the results of a recent survey which estimates that millennials are likely to constitute as much as 42 per cent of the self-employed American population by 2020 (39).

The increased inclination of millennials towards alternate forms of work can be explained by the fact that there is a significant amount of overlap between the benefits offered by the gig jobs and the core needs and values of millennials. Given the advantages offered by the gig economy and the millennials' attraction towards these, it is crucial for organizations to build provisions for alternate forms of work. In other words, to attract talented millennials who are avoiding full-time employment for whatever reasons, organizations should make provisions of temporary contracts for which the services of gig workers may be used. Doing so would prove beneficial for not only the workers but also the organizations. While millennials can enjoy the advantages of a gig job by undertaking contractual assignments, organizations can make use of their specialized expertise even without employing them permanently. These advantages of the gig economy for organizations are clear from the recent estimates which suggest that approximately 57 per cent of the organizations that use services of gig workers are saving at least 20 per cent of their labour costs. It has also been reported that nearly 42 per cent of mid- to large-size companies meet seasonal demands with the help of contingent workers. Hence, it would be beneficial for organizations to make provisions for contractual job opportunities that are likely to attract millennials interested in alternate forms of work (39–41).

Having deliberated upon the strategies that organizations can use to attract and recruit the millennial talent effectively, we now present the example of a real-world organization that has actually excelled at recruiting millennials into its workforce.

....

Recruiting Talent 'The Millennial Way': The Use of Gamification by Marriott International

Marriott International, Inc., is the world's largest hotel company headquartered at Bethesda, Maryland, USA. Currently, the company boasts of an exemplary port-folio of more than 6,100 properties spanning across 124 countries in the form of 30 leading hotel brands (42). It operates and franchises hotels along with licens-ing of vacation ownership resorts around the world (43). Recently, Marriott International has been ranked—the second time in a row—as one of the 'best places to work for millennials'. The research was jointly conducted by the consulting firm known as 'Great Place to Work' and the *Fortune* magazine (43). The rankings were based on the anonymous feedback of over 398,000 employees working at 'Great places to work for' certi-fied organizations. The survey covered several aspects of work-life such as millennial employees' experience with their supervisors' competence, fairness and respect in the workplace, along with meaningful work and other elements. These results reflect the overall success of the HR strategy at Marriott International that was aimed at attracting millennials and subsequently engaging, incentivizing and retaining them.

In 2016, around 69 per cent of all hires at Marriott International were millennials (1). The company's philosophy revolves around employee well-being, personal happiness and company pride. According to its executive vice president and global chief human resources officer, David Rodriguez, millennials are particularly attracted to job opportunities where they can feel good about themselves, engage in teamwork and have a passion for not only the job but also the organization. The success of Marriott can be attributed to a range of factors, one of them being the novel recruitment strategy adopted by it in 2011 to recruit the millennial talent. This strategy focused on the use of 'gamification' in the recruitment process.

The company partnered with Evviva (a consultant firm for developing corporate games) and launched a social media game on Facebook called 'My Marriott Hotel' on 6 June 2011, with the aim of recruiting the best talent in hospitality (43). Similar to FarmVille, 'My Marriott Hotel' allows the players to virtually operate their hotel, hire and fire employees, deliver food and clean guestrooms. The players can also create their own restaurants by purchasing the equipment and ingredients within a budget (43). Points were obtained for happy customers, and penalties were imposed for poor customer service. There was a dedicated 'do it for real' button which directed the players to the actual company career page. The company posted this game on its Facebook page and career webpage. The gamification experiment became a key part of Marriott's strategic plan to drive global talent acquisition. It also helped the company to introduce the Marriott brand to emerging markets through global social media platforms (44). Being the first mover in using social media platforms, Marriott created an interest amongst the millennials towards working in their company and the hospitality sector at large (45). A natural question arises at this point: What is the rationale behind this strategy? To understand this, let us look at gamification as a means to recruit talent.

Gamification has increasingly been used by organizations such as Marriott, Deloitte, PwC, and US Department of Defence to recruit, develop and motivate employees (45). Gartner group defines gamification as 'the concept of employing game mechanics to non-game activities such as recruitment, training, and health and wellness'. The growing interest in gamification stems from the fact that organizations all over the world desire to increase the level of engagement amongst their employees. According to Gallup, 71 per cent of the American employees are 'disengaged' at workplace and millennials form the largest portion of it. The report also suggests that millennials feel that they do not have the opportunity to show their best work or have a medium to contribute their ideas and suggestions (46). By using gamification, organizations can not only improve upon the engagement levels but also attract the best talent. Moreover, it is also important to note that millennials will make up 75 per cent of the global workforce by 2025, which gives organizations enough of a reason for adopting this new strategy (47).

A research was conducted by Pew Internet and Elon University by taking inputs from 1,021 internet experts (48). The findings of this research showed that the principles of gamification could improve creativity, participation, learning and motivation. As the millennial workforce is driven by rewards and competitiveness, gamification engages them well. When players engage well, they feel a sense of accomplishment and are willing to do more. Applied in the context of Marriott, 'My Marriott Hotel' effectively engages the millennial talent pool by allowing them the opportunity to manage their own hotels and restaurants virtually. For Marriott, the rationale behind the game is that the company is expanding in growth markets outside the United States. As a result, the company seeks to attract more millennials, and to do so it needs to find new ways to interest them towards careers in hospitality (49). Especially in emerging markets, the hospitality sector might be less established, and by using gamification, the organization can create awareness and interest in adopting it as a career.

Another benefit that gamification offers is that it ensures the right fit between a person applying for the job and the nature of the job. In addition, companies are also using gamification to solve their day-to-day operational challenges such as safety and efficiency. For instance, Walmart uses gamification as a safety training tool to help them retain the safety information they are provided. Deloitte and Cisco use gamification to improve team performance and to impart leadership training to their employees. The famous search engine Google uses gamification to incentivize its employees to submit their expense reports on time (50).

To summarize, gamification has been one of the latest and most influential strategies that organizations are using to attract, engage, retain and motivate the millennial workforce. The full potential of this technique is yet to be discovered. Marriott International, Inc, and My Marriott Hotel game portray an excellent example of how gamification can be used to attract millennial talent and create a long-term strategic advantage for the company.

Discussion Questions

1. Enlist factors behind the success of the gamification strategy for the recruitment of millennial workforce?

2. What other strategies apart from gamification be used to recruit, motivate and engage the millennials working in an organization?

REFERENCES

1. Armstrong, M., & Taylor, S. (2014). Armstrong's handbook of human resource management practice. London: Kogan Page Publishers.
2. Dessler, G., & Varrkey, B. (2011). Human resource management. 15 edition. India: Pearson Education India.
3. Rynes, S.L., & Boudreau, J.W. (1986). College recruiting in large organizations: practice, evaluation, and research implications. Pers Psychol. 39(4):729–57.
4. Bartram, D. (2000). Internet recruitment and selection: kissing frogs to find princes. Int J Select Assess. 8(4):261–74.
5. Sundheim, K. (2013, Apr 2). The internet's profound impact on the recruiting industry. Forbes. Retrieved from https://www.forbes.com/sites/kensundheim/2013/04/02/the-internets-profound-impact-on-the-recruiting-industry/#1e00582e2707. Accessed on 15 Oct 2018.
6. KPMG. (2017, Jun). Meet the millennials. Retrieved from https://home.kpmg.com/content/dam/kpmg/uk/pdf/2017/04/Meet-the-Millennials-Secured.pdf. Accessed on 15 Oct 2018.
7. Morgan, J. (n.d.). The war for talent: It's real and here's why it's happening. Inc. Retrieved from https://www.inc.com/jacob-morgan/the-war-for-talent-its-real-heres-why-its-happening.html. Accessed on 15 Oct 2018.
8. Barney, J. (1991). Firm resources and sustained competitive advantage. J Manag. 17(1):99–120.
9. Lewis, R.E., & Heckman, R.J. (2006). Talent management: a critical review. Hum Resource Manag Rev. 16(2):139–54.
10. Motzie. (2017, Mar 26). 5 ways millennials are changing the recruitment landscape. Mobile Talent. Retrieved from https://info.mobile-talent.com/blog/5-ways-millennials-changing-recruitment-landscape. Accessed on 15 Oct 2018.
11. Daab, J., & Forbes Agency Council. (2018, Apr 3). Are millennials really failing the marshmallow test? Forbes. Retrieved from https://www.forbes.com/sites/forbesagencycouncil/2018/04/03/are-millennials-really-failing-the-marshmallow-test/#3ad1f8b9a276. Accessed on 15 Oct 2018.
12. Stanney, L. (2017). Because we can: a study of millennial impatience and the rise of next day delivery. Doctoral dissertation, School of Media and Communication, University of Leeds, UK.
13. Smith, M.N. (2016, Aug 1). KPMG is shortening its recruitment process because millennials are getting frustrated. Business Insider. Retrieved from https://www.businessinsider.in/KPMG-is-shortening-its-recruitment-process-because-millennials-are-getting-frustrated/articleshow/53489347.cms. Accessed on 15 Oct 2018.
14. Landrum, S. (2017, Jul 7). How millennials are shaping the hiring process. Forbes. Retrieved from https://www.forbes.com/sites/sarahlandrum/2017/07/07/how-millennials-are-shaping-the-hiring-process/#3eaa40562377. Accessed on 16 Oct 2018.
15. How the millennial generation has changed the recruitment process. USA Today. Retrieved from http://classifieds.usatoday.com/blog/careers/millennial-generation-changed-recruitment-process/. Accessed on 16 Oct 2018.

16. Rietsema, D. (n.d.). ATS software: features and benefits. Applicant Tracking Systems. Retrieved from https://www.applicanttrackingsystems.net/ats/features-and-benefits/. Accessed on 16 Oct 2018.

17. Thompson, M. (2016, Jun 23). Goldman Sachs is making a change to the way it hires. CNBC. Retrieved from https://www.cnbc.com/2016/06/23/goldman-sachs-is-making-a-change-to-the-way-it-hires.html. Accessed on 16 Oct 2018.

18. Chew, J. (2016, Apr 8). Why millennials would take a $7,600 pay cut for a new job. Fortune. Retrieved from http://fortune.com/2016/04/08/fidelity-millennial-study-career/. Accessed on 16 Oct 2018.

19. Collegiate Employment Research Institute. Retrieved from http://ceri.msu.edu/publications/pdf/ceri2-07.pdf. Accessed on 16 Oct 2018.

20. Willyerd, K. (2013, Dec 23). Parents may be your secret weapon for recruiting and retaining millennials. Harvard Business Review. Retrieved from https://hbr.org/2013/12/parents-may-be-your-secret-weapon-for-recruiting-and-retaining-millennials. Accessed on 16 Oct 2018.

21. Hofschneider, A. (2013, Sep 10). Should you bring mom and dad to the office? The Wall Street Journal. Retrieved from https://www.wsj.com/articles/hiring-millennials-meet-the-parents-1378856472. Accessed on 16 Oct 2018.

22. Ehrhart, K.H., Mayer, D.M., & Ziegert, J.C. (2012). Web-based recruitment in the millennial generation: work-life balance, website usability, and organizational attraction. Eur J Work Org Psychol. 21(6):850–74.

23. Vaccaro, H. (2017). What millennials want to see: effective corporate recruiting videos for attracting millennials. Fort Worth, TX: Texas Christian University Library.

24. Henry, Z. (n.d.). 6 companies (including Uber) where it's OK to nap. Inc. Retrieved from https://www.inc.com/zoe-henry/google-uber-and-other-companies-where-you-can-nap-at-the-office.html. Accessed on 16 Oct 2018.

25. The Economic Times. You might want to work for Google after seeing these photos. (2017, Feb 16). The Economic Times. Retrieved from https://economictimes.indiatimes.com/slideshows/work-career/you-might-want-to-work-for-google-after-seeing-these-photos/sleep-sleep-sleep/slideshow/57187270.cms. Accessed on 16 Oct 2018.

26. Microsoft's Tree House, Google's Nap Pods: perks offered by new-age cos to break the monotony (2017, Nov 20). The Economic Times. Retrieved from https://economictimes.indiatimes.com/magazines/panache/microsofts-tree-house-googles-nap-pods-perks-offered-by-new-age-cos-to-break-the-monotony/head-out-at-airbnb/slideshow/61723376.cms. Accessed on 16 Oct 2018.

27. Eddy, C.P. (2016). Millennial work expectations: can recruitment advertisements attract this generation to organizations? Doctoral Dissertation, San Francisco State University, San Francisco, CA, USA.

28. Carless, S.A., & Wintle, J. (2007). Applicant attraction: the role of recruiter function, work-life balance policies and career salience. Int J Select Assess. 15(4):394–404.

29. Patel, D. (2017, Jun 29). Millennials love job review sites: leaders take notice. Forbes. Retrieved from https://www.forbes.com/sites/deeppatel/2017/06/29/millennials-love-job-review-sites-leaders-take-notice/#58b25269528b. Accessed on 17 Oct 2018.

30. Brian Westfall (n.d.). How job seekers use glassdoor reviews. Software Advice. Retrieved from https://www.softwareadvice.com/resources/job-seekers-use-glassdoor-reviews/. Accessed on 17 Oct 2018.
31. Lighthall, S. (n.d.). One star, two stars, three stars, four. The tricky business of online reviews. Relate. Retrieved from https://relate.zendesk.com/articles/one-star-two-stars-three-stars-four-the-tricky-business-of-online-reviews/. Accessed on 17 Oct 2018.
32. Johansson, A. (2017, Nov 14). Millennials are pushing for diversity in these three industries. Forbes. Retrieved from https://www.forbes.com/sites/annajohansson/2017/11/14/millennials-are-pushing-for-diversity-in-these-3-industries/#1b699f956a5c. Accessed on 17 Oct 2018.
33. Kochhar, S. (2017, Dec 4). Nearly half of American millennials say a diverse and inclusive workplace is an important factor in a job search. Institute for Public Relations. Retrieved from https://instituteforpr.org/nearly-half-american-millennials-say-diverse-inclusive-workplace-important-factor-job-search/. Accessed on 17 Oct 2018.
34. Chrobot-Mason, D., & Aramovich, N.P. (2013). The psychological benefits of creating an affirming climate for workplace diversity. Group Org Manag. 38(6):659–89.
35. Roberge, M.É., & Van Dick, R. (2010). Recognizing the benefits of diversity: when and how does diversity increase group performance? Hum Resource Manag Rev. 20(4):295–308.
36. Prakash, R. (2017, Sep 21). How to sell to millennials? Be radically inclusive. Entrepreneur.India. Retrieved from https://www.entrepreneur.com/article/298747. Accessed on 17 Oct 2018.
37. Burton, S. (2017, Mar 1). Companies Lacking Diversity Fail Their Shareholders—and Employees. Observer. Retrieved from https://observer.com/2017/01/diversity-workplace-economic-returns-hiring/. Accessed on 17 Oct 2018.
38. Llopis, G. (2017, Aug 30). See inclusion and diversity as a growth strategy, not a cost. Entrepreneur.India. Retrieved from https://www.entrepreneur.com/article/298967. Accessed on 17 Oct 2018.
39. International Labor Organization. (n.d.). Non-standard forms of employment. Retrieved from https://www.ilo.org/global/topics/non-standard-employment/lang--en/index.htm. Accessed on 17 Oct 2018.
40. Monahan, K., Schwartz, J., & Schleeter, T. (2018, May 1). Decoding millennials in the gig economy. Deloitte Insights. Retrieved from https://www2.deloitte.com/insights/us/en/focus/technology-and-the-future-of-work/millennials-in-the-gig-economy.html. Accessed on 17 Oct 2018.
41. Muhammed, A. (2018, Jul). Four statistics showing how business can benefit from the gig economy. Forbes. Retrieved from https://www.forbes.com/sites/abdullahimuhammed/2018/07/31/four-statistics-showing-how-business-can-benefit-from-the-gig-economy/#4903b66b752f. Accessed on 17 Oct 2018.
42. Mcmanus, B. (2017, Aug 1). Great Place to Work® and FORTUNE® Name Marriott International a Best Workplace for Millennials. Marriott International. Retrieved from http://news.marriott.com/2017/08/great-place-work-fortune-name-marriott-international-best-workplace-millennials/. Accessed on 18 Oct 2018.

43. IBS Center for Management Research. Beyond resumes: Marriott using gamification to recruit top talent in hospitality. IBS Center for Management Research. Retrieved from http://www.icmrindia.org/casestudies/catalogue/Human%20Resource%20and%20Organization%20Behavior/Beyond%20Resumes%20Marriott%20Using%20Gamification%20to%20Recruit%20Top%20Talent%20in%20Hospitality-Case.htm. Accessed on 18 Oct 2018.
44. Marriott targets millennials through social-media game: potential employees experience the thrills and spills of kitchen work. Hum Resource Manag Int Digest. 19(7):9-11. Retrieved from https://www.emeraldinsight.com/doi/pdfplus/10.1108/09670731111175506. Accessed on 18 Oct 2018.
45. Meister, J. (2012, May 21). The future of work: how to use gamification for talent management. Forbes. Retrieved from https://www.forbes.com/sites/jeannemeister/2012/05/21/the-future-of-work-how-to-use-gamification-for-talent-management/#5826463e98d3. Accessed on 18 Oct 2018.
46. How Millennials Want to Work and Live (2016). The Gallup. Retrieved from https://news.gallup.com/reports/189830/e.aspx#aspnetForm. Accessed on 18 Oct 2018.
47. Economy, P. (2019, Jan 15). The (millennial) workplace of the future is almost here: these 3 things are about to change big time. Inc. Retrieved from https://www.inc.com/peter-economy/the-millennial-workplace-of-future-is-almost-here-these-3-things-are-about-to-change-big-time.html. Accessed on 18 Oct 2018.
48. Elon University School of Communications 2012 survey. What is the potential future influence of Big Data by 2020? Retrieved from http://www.elon.edu/e-web/predictions/expertsurveys/2012survey/future_Big_Data_2020.xhtml. Accessed on 18 Oct 2018.
49. Meister, J. (2015, May 30). The future of work: using gamification for human resources. Forbes. Retrieved from https://www.forbes.com/sites/jeannemeister/2015/03/30/future-of-work-using-gamification-for-human-resources/#6645efc324b7. Accessed on 18 Oct 2018.
50. Ewen, C. (2017, Jan 11). 6 gamification examples: a real game-changer for recruitment and career services. GradLeaders. Retrieved from https://www.gradleaders.com/blog/post/gamification-examples. Accessed on 18 Oct 2018.

STRATEGIES FOR INCENTIVIZING MILLENNIALS

The topic of employee motivation has continued to intrigue organizational scholars as well as practitioners for decades. It can be safely argued that motivation has been one of the most heavily researched topics in the organizational behaviour literature. This is evident from the fact that a simple search for the keyword 'employee motivation' displays nearly 1.8 million hits on Google Scholar (1). Moreover, the practitioner literature is also flooded with thousands of articles containing tips and techniques that managers may use to motivate their employees. Given the ubiquity of motivation in management literature as well as practice, we delve a little deeper into this concept before initiating a detailed discussion pertaining to motivation in the case of the millennial generation.

The word 'motivation' has been derived from a Latin word *movere*, which means 'to move' (1). The academic literature defines work motivation as 'a set of energetic forces that originates both within as well as beyond an individual's being, to initiate work-related behavior, and to determine its form, direction, intensity, and duration' (2, p. 992; 3). Seminal works in the field have classified work motivation into two broad categories, namely, extrinsic as well as intrinsic forms of motivation. While intrinsic motivation refers to an individual's performance of an activity for no apparent reward except the activity itself, extrinsic motivation drives one to perform an activity because of the presence of several external rewards contingent upon the performance of that activity (4). A recent meta-analytic review of literature spanning over 40 years of past motivation research demonstrated the joint effect of intrinsic motivation and external incentives in predicting employee performance (5). Such findings underscore the salience of both these forms of motivation in governing important organizationally relevant outcomes.

While the consequences of extrinsic and intrinsic motivation have been thoroughly documented in the extant motivation literature, the concept of motivation has received relatively lesser attention from a generational standpoint.

An extensive review of literature allows us to conclude that there is limited academic research that has explicitly studied how different generations need to be motivated differently. A dearth of such knowledge may seriously handicap the functioning of the HR executives in organizations who are directly responsible not just for motivating a multigenerational workforce but also for designing appropriate compensation plans for the same. Without a clear awareness of what exactly motivates the employees belonging to different generational cohorts, it would be a daunting task for practitioners to provide the right set of incentives and perks to different generations of employees. The challenge gets further aggravated by the fact that more and more millennials are stepping into the workforce and they possess an entirely different set of needs as compared to their predecessors. A different set of needs calls for a different set of incentives that would be able to address those needs adequately. Given the fact that millennials constitute a large proportion of the workforce in India (46% of the labour force) as well as the United States (35% of the labour force), they possess substantial bargaining power over organizations who must take care of the needs of the millennial employees in order to survive the cut-throat competition currently prevalent in the business landscape (6, 7). Such an endeavour may be facilitated by the design of the right bundle of incentives that are capable of sufficiently satisfying the unique needs of Generation Y employees.

In light of the above discussion, we set the agenda for the present chapter. This chapter aims to achieve the following objectives. First, it reviews the available academic as well as practitioner literature on millennials to compile a set of findings that shed light on the unique expectations that millennials have from their jobs as well as organizations. Second, it makes use of these compiled findings to present a range of strategies that may cater to the needs of the millennial workforce and may help organizations to incentivize their Generation Y employees effectively. Finally, we conclude with a case study that illustrates the efforts of a real-world organization that actually excelled in incentivizing its millennial workforce.

EXPECTATIONS MILLENNIALS HAVE

Several research studies within the academic literature have attempted to recognize the set of factors that truly reflect the needs and expectations of the millennial employees. Likewise, several practitioner reports have also revealed the elements that millennials truly crave for in their jobs. The key findings of each of these works have been compiled below:

- Capital Group conducted an online quantitative survey in 2017 of 1,200 American adults, of which 400 were millennials (aged 21–37), 400 were Generation Xers (aged 38–52) and 400 were baby boomers (aged 53–71). The findings of the survey revealed that while there is some amount of overlap between the expectations of different generations, millennials additionally have some unique set of expectations from their employers. Eighty per cent of the surveyed millennials believed that employers should provide a retirement savings option. Likewise, 60 per cent of the millennial participants wanted paid time off to volunteer, free lunches and snacks, a mentoring programme and pet-friendly offices. Thirty-four per cent of the Generation Y respondents also considered college savings plan as an important benefit that employers could offer (8, 9).

- Udemy recently published the 2018 Millennials at Work report which was based on a survey of 1,000 adults in the United States falling within the age bracket of 21 and 37 years. The most significant findings of the survey were that 42 per cent of the participants reported that learning and development was the most important benefit they considered after salary while deciding where to work. Additionally, 44 per cent of the respondents said that a flexible schedule was the ideal work arrangement for them and 30 per cent wanted to work remotely full-time (10, 11).

- As a part of a global quantitative study conducted in 2016, Manpower Group recently surveyed a total of 19,000 working millennials as well as 1,500 hiring managers spread across 25 countries around the world. Amongst other questions of the survey, participants also indicated their priorities while deciding when and where to work. It was observed that the top five priorities of millennials while looking for jobs were money (92%), security (87%), holidays or time off (86%), opportunity to work with great people (80%) and flexible working (79%). Moreover, millennials have redefined the meaning of job security. When they refer to job security, what they actually mean is career security. They consider job-hopping as stepping stones to self-improvement and lifelong learning (12, 13).

- Blackhawk Engagement Solutions recently conducted a survey titled 'Happy Millennials: An Employee Rewards & Recognition Study' that sought the views of 1,800 hourly employed or salaried individuals in the United States, of which 350 were millennials. According to the results of the study, 40 per cent of the millennial participants were not happy with the rewards and recognition programmes being offered by their organization. Additionally, 64 per cent of the respondents preferred to be recognized for personal accomplishment instead of team accomplishment. In response to the question about what they wanted to be recognized for the most, 85 per cent of the millennials liked being rewarded for exceeding personal performance levels, 79 per cent for exceeding team performance levels and 80 per cent for receiving a promotion. Moreover, millennials said that even when they received awards, they felt that the element of recognition was missing from the reward (14, 15).

- PwC published a report based on an online survey of 4,364 millennial graduates spread across 75 countries around the world. Participants were asked to rank the benefits that they would value the most from an employer. Training and development topped the list by being the preferred benefit for 22 per cent of the participants, followed by flexible working hours and cash bonuses, which were preferred by 22 per cent and 19 per cent of the participants, respectively. Other benefits that also featured in the list of preferences of participants included the following: free private healthcare (8%), pension schemes or other retirement funding (6%), greater vacation allowance (6%), financial assistance with housing (5%), company car (4%), assistance in clearing debts occurred while studying (3%), maternity/paternity benefits (3%), subsidized travel costs (2%), free child care (2%), access to low interest loans (2%), time off to do community work (1%) and higher wages instead of benefits (4%) (16, 17).

- In 2016, the Banfield Pet-Friendly Workplace PAWrometer conducted an online survey of 1,006 employees and 200 HR decision makers. The findings revealed that 53 per cent of the employees working for pet-friendly organizations and 63 per cent of the HR decision makers in non-pet-friendly organizations reported that they were more likely to stay with the company if it allowed them to bring a pet in the office (18, 19).

  Additionally, a large proportion of employees in pet-friendly, as well as non-pet-friendly organizations, reported that they believed that allowing pets in the workplace improves employee morale, well-being, stress, the guilt of leaving pets at home, work-life balance, loyalty to the company, improved work relationships and an ability to work longer hours (18, 19).

- Wong et al. (20) undertook an academic research investigation to examine the motivational drivers of three generations of employees, namely, millennials, Generation Xers and baby boomers. As a part of the study, data were collected from a sample of 3,535 professionals and managers who were working for moderate-to-large Australian organizations. While Generation Xers and baby boomers were found to be heavily motivated by power and the ability to exercise influence over others, such a need was a very low priority for millennials. Additionally, millennials were observed to be motivated by career advancement and progression, and this need was much higher amongst millennials than in other generations (20).

- Ng et al. (21) conducted a research study to examine the career priorities and expectations of millennials. Data were collected from 23,413 undergraduate students in a Canadian university who were going to step into the workforce. The key findings of the study were that

65.8 per cent of the respondents expected a promotion within 18 months of joining their first job. Also, survey participants were asked to rate the most desirable work-related attributes. Opportunities for advancement topped the list, followed by good people to work with and report to, good training opportunities, work-life balance, good health and benefits plan, job security, good initial salary level and challenging work. The study also noted the role of individual difference variables within the millennial cohort, such as gender, GPA (grade point average) and minority status but added that these individual differences accounted for only a small proportion of the variance (21).

In all, the above discussion is drawn from an extensive review of past academic and practitioner literature on millennials. Specifically, it revolves around the factors that millennial employees desire from their jobs.

STRATEGIES FOR INCENTIVIZING THE MILLENNIAL WORKFORCE

Having discussed at length about what millennials actually want from their jobs and employing organizations, we now divert our attention towards what organizations can actually do to address these millennial needs. While there are several strategies that may be used to attract and retain millennials in the workforce, this chapter focuses on the strategies related to incentives, perks and benefits. The reader may be referred to other chapters for a detailed discussion of the strategies pertaining to other functions of the HR department, such as recruitment and selection and employee retention (Chapters 7 and 9, respectively). The provision of appropriate incentives and perks plays a major role in influencing the engagement levels of the employee, which in turn affect the performance of the employee. What follows is a list of recommendations that may be useful for HR executives who are currently involved in the design of various forms of incentives in their respective organizations, especially those targeted towards addressing the innate needs of the millennial employees.

MONETARY PERFORMANCE REWARDS

Millennials want to feel valued at work, and one of the best ways that organizations can use to express this value is through investment in that employee. Millennial employees are not willing to commit to employers who do not commit to them. It is necessary for organizations to showcase their commitment towards their employees, especially millennials, in order to retain them. This commitment may include, but is not limited to, competitive compensation. Organizations need to take a holistic approach towards the provision of monetary rewards and should also invest resources in providing employees with training and resources for personal development. Hence, organizations should try to create high-performance work systems that synergize the efforts of all the functions of HRM and demonstrate the organization's commitment towards the millennial workforce from multiple angles (22).

Given the fact that millennials thrive on recognition, organizations must also provide opportunities for career advancement as an indicator of their commitment and investment towards employees. This may also mean that they offer clear career ladders to their millennial employees and offer regular pay hikes (annually or biennially) to their workforce.

Doing so helps the millennials feel that their efforts are being recognized and they are progressing in their careers. However, such an endeavour may be facilitated only after the creation of intermediate positions between established ranks. Hence, organizations need to create a taller organizational structure consisting of a sufficient number of ranks to provide regular promotions. Regular promotions imply progress not only in terms of pay but also in terms of status. Hence, the creation of these intermediate ranks and regular promotions may help to cater to the millennials' needs for recognition and achievement. Thus, such efforts may fall under the category of both monetary and non-monetary rewards.

NON-MONETARY PERFORMANCE REWARDS

Anecdotal evidence suggests that millennials value experiences over money. These anecdotes are now being corroborated by actual data and research. A recent survey conducted by Sodexo Benefits and Rewards Services found that as many as 84 per cent of the surveyed millennials were keen on receiving vouchers and experiences of cinema tickets or discounts as their employee rewards. Moreover, 17 per cent of the subjects reported that they wanted to share their experiences with their team, and 25 per cent of them wanted to share their rewards with friends or family (23). Likewise, another survey conducted by the TLF Panel sought the recognition preferences of 1,000 working adults in the UK and concluded that experiential rewarding was crucial in driving productivity across the business (23). Such a conclusion was reached based on the fact that 63 per cent of the high-performing organizations were clearly inclined towards non-cash awards. Organizations wishing to motivate their millennial workforce could opt for the provision of such attractive experiential rewards to their younger employees (23).

Other studies have also noted the value that millennials place in experiences. A recent survey conducted by Harris reveal that a whopping 78 per cent of millennials prefer to spend money on desirable experiences instead of purchasing something desirable (24). These findings carry noteworthy implications for employers who can provide their millennial workforces with experiential rewards. Some such examples may include festival or sporting tickets, VIP access passes for events, couple cruise tickets, passes for body spa at beauty parlours, adventure trekking trips, paid vacation time and so on. These types of rewards are very powerful in motivating the millennial employees and satisfying their innate needs and urges for the things they crave the most.

Other ways of rewarding good performance may be a dinner with the boss, free lunches and pizza parties, or the opportunity to work from the manager's office for a day. These rewards play a major role in making the employee feel respected and recognized, values which lie at the heart of the millennial mindset. Moreover, many of these rewards do not cost much or hardly anything to the organization, but create a very personal and memorable experience for the rewarded employee (24, 25).

....

The Joy of Being a 'Googler'! Incentivizing Employees the Google Way

With the addition of more and more millennials into the workforce, a pertinent question arises: How can organizations motivate their millennial employees so as to achieve mutual goals? In the discipline of HRM, the most common way of motivating employees is the use of monetary and non-monetary incentives. In a way, incentives refer to the rewards given to the employees based on their performance. As discussed above, the regular norms of incentivizing change when it comes to motivating the millennials. Companies are deviating from their usual incentive plans to offer a range of unusual incentives that may cater to needs of their millennial workforce. One company which stands out from the rest in motivating its Generation Y employees is 'Google'.

Founded by Larry Page and Sergey Brin in 1998, Google is an American multinational company which deals with internet-based products and services. It has over 85,000 employees as of 2018 (26). Currently, Google is one of the world's most valuable brands. Another jewel was added to the crown of Google in 2014 when it was named as the 'Best company to work for' by the Great Place to Work institute and *Fortune* magazine for the fifth time in a row (26). Clearly, the exemplary growth of Google in such a short span of time may be attributed to the performance of its creative and engaged workforce. Considering the variety of offices that the company has around the globe, it would be interesting to find out how Google is able to extract such outstanding ideas from thousands of its employees.

Google's model for motivation and incentive management of its workforce is primarily dependent upon two major components: the happiness of its employees as well as productivity. The organization tries to ensure the happiness of its employees by offering a bundle of incentives. Similarly, the productivity component of the model is taken care of by making sure that the work is done with all flexibility, freedom, fun and with employee's creativity. The majority of the employees at Google are young professionals, that is, millennials. A recent survey elucidates three reasons why millennials want to work at Google and other tech giants: career growth, flexibility and a sense of purpose (27). Compared to their older predecessors who were more concerned with the compensational aspects of a job, employees belonging to the millennial cohort are more interested in 'accelerated growth', 'freebies' and 'flexible work timings' (28). According to a recent report published by the Bank of America and Merrill Lynch, nearly 20 per cent of the interviewed millennials reported Google to be their 'ideal employer', followed by Apple at 13 per cent (28). Such facts and statistics demonstrate the success of Google in attracting and motivating the millennial workforce effectively.

Another fundamental dimension of innovative and creative work culture at Google is the fact that it employs a pool of strategies such as giving employees the freedom to explore, relaxing workstations and the right amount of independent time. Google is reaping the fruit of its efforts in the form of a highly entrepreneurial culture and innovative product offerings. Like other tech giants, Google offers incentives to employees in the form of flex spending accounts, health and dental benefits, insurance, tuition reimbursements and vacations. However, some unique perks and benefits offered by it are noteworthy, showing its commitment to keep its employees happy. Some of these benefits are maternity leaves at 100 per cent pay, take-out benefits for new parents, financial support for adopting a child, on-site car wash, oil change, free lunch and dinner and so on. These benefits have been further explained in detail (29).

Twenty per cent flexible work allowance: Flexible work allowance is one of the pioneering techniques of incentivizing the employees. At Google, employees have a higher discretion in terms of their work hours and the company allows them to devote 20 per cent of work time to projects that they believe in (2).

The 150 feet from food rule: Google offices are designed in a manner that an employee does not have to travel greater than 150 feet for food. In addition to free food, the variety of food to choose from is also huge: from healthy foods to gourmet dishes. In addition to the provision for free food, the company also provides free cooking lessons along with team-building exercises (29).

Maternity and parenthood benefits: Maternity pays are available for all Google employees at 100 per cent pay for a maximum of 18 months. In addition, the father and mother of the newborn baby are also given an allowance of $500 for take-out meals in the initial three months that they spend with the baby.

Personal care benefits: A range of facilities are available to the employees at Mountain View, California headquarters of the company. These include the provision of a gym, massage therapy, hair stylist, laundry, fitness training and so on.

Sleeping pods: The millennial workforce has a more flexible attitude with regard to the execution of its responsibilities. In addition, unlike their predecessors, millennials are more open to 'sleeping on the job' which they think is instrumental in boosting performance. Due to this changed attitude, Google allows its employees to take regular naps at the workplace and has installed sleeping pods, where they can relax at work (30).

Pet-friendly policy: Employees at Google are allowed to bring their pet dogs along with them to work. It allows the employees to keep their energies up, without worrying about their pet, and can improve their concentration at work. Since many millennials are delaying marriages and tend to stay alone, pets can help them reduce the loneliness in their lives. The perk of bringing the pet to work alongside highly encourages Generation Y employees.

Death benefits: Google also provides benefits to the spouse and children of its employees. If any employee passes away while working at Google, in addition to the life insurance, the surviving spouse receives half of the employee's salary for the next 10 years. In addition, there is a provision for $1,000 per month for each of the deceased employee's children (31).

Thus, the incentives and benefits offered by Google to its millennial workforce are commendable. Not only are they targeted towards the needs of Generation Y employees, but they also show their employees that the company truly cares for them and their families. Such an approach has a profound impact on employee motivation and productivity, which fulfils the real motive of incentives in the domain of HRM.

Discussion Questions

1. Discuss the ROI for the activities Google uses to motivate its millennial workforce?

2. Design a preliminary metrics to measure the outcomes of such innovative initiatives.

REFERENCES

1. Dörnyei, Z., & Ushioda, E. (2013). Teaching and Researching: motivation. London, UK: Routledge.
2. Meyer, J.P., Becker, T.E., & Vandenberghe, C. (2004). Employee commitment and motivation: a conceptual analysis and integrative model. J Appl Psychol. 89(6):991.
3. Pinder, C.C. (1998). Work motivation in organizational behavior. Upper Saddle River, NJ: Prentice Hall.
4. Deci, E.L. (1972). Intrinsic motivation, extrinsic reinforcement, and inequity. J Pers Soc Psychol. 22(1):113.
5. Cerasoli, C.P., Nicklin, J.M., & Ford, M.T. (2014). Intrinsic motivation and extrinsic incentives jointly predict performance: a 40-year meta-analysis. Psychol Bull. 140(4):980.

6. Fry, R. (2018, Apr 11). Millennials are the largest generation in the US labor force. Pew Research Center. Retrieved from http://www.pewresearch.org/fact-tank/2018/04/11/millennials-largest-generation-us-labor-force/. Accessed on 20 Oct 2018.

7. Research. (2017, May 26). India's millennials to drive growth in four key sectors. Morgan Stanley. Retrieved from https://www.morganstanley.com/ideas/India-millennials-growth-sectors. Accessed on 20 Oct 2018.

8. Millennials demand more from employers and investments. (2017, Aug 29). Capital Group. Retrieved from https://www.capitalgroup.com/our-company/news-room/milliennials-demand-more-from-employers-investments.html. Accessed on 20 Oct 2018.

9. Zimmerman, K. (2017, Oct 1). 5 things we know millennials want from a job. Forbes. Retrieved from https://www.forbes.com/sites/kaytiezimmerman/2017/10/01/5-things-we-know-millennials-want-from-a-job/#31cfa2d78099. Accessed on 20 Oct 2018.

10. Udemy in Depth: 2018 millennials at work report. Retrieved from https://research.udemy.com/research_report/udemy-in-depth-2018-millennials-at-work-report/. Accessed on 20 Oct 2018.

11. Darmody, J. (2018, Jun 27). What do millennials want at work? It's not what you think. Siliconrepublic. Retrieved from https://www.siliconrepublic.com/careers/millennials-future-of-work-udemy. Accessed on 20 Oct 2018.

12. Millennial Careers: 2020 Vision Report. Manpower Group. Retrieved from https://www.manpowergroup.com/wps/wcm/connect/660ebf65-144c-489e-975c-9f838294c237/MillennialsPaper1_2020Vision_lo.pdf?MOD=AJPERES. Accessed on 20 Oct 2018.

13. Marginalia. (2018, Feb 23). What millennials expect from the workplace in 2018. Marginalia. Retrieved from http://www.marginalia.online/what-millennials-expect-from-the-workplace-in-2018/. Accessed on 20 Oct 2018.

14. PR Newswire. (2015, Aug 5). Blackhawk engagement solutions' employee research demonstrates which rewards keep millennials happiest and most productive compared with other employees. Blackhawk Engagement Solutions. Retrieved from http://www.multivu.com/players/English/7590351-blackhawk-engagement-solutions-happy-millennials/. Accessed on 20 Oct 2018.

15. BlackHawk Networks. Retrieved from https://go.hawkincentives.com/The-Happiness-Study.html. Accessed on 20 Oct 2018.

16. A PwC report. Millennials at work. Retrieved from https://www.pwc.de/de/prozessoptimierung/assets/millennials-at-work-2011.pdf. Accessed on 21 Oct 2018.

17. Mccarthy, N. (2015, Nov 12). Which work benefits do millennials value most? Forbes. Retrieved from https://www.forbes.com/sites/niallmccarthy/2015/11/12/which-work-benefits-do-millennials-value-most-infographic/#7b6ca2dc34ff. Accessed on 21 Oct 2018.

18. Pet-friendly workplace PawRometer. (2016, Mar). Banfield Pet Hospital. Retrieved from https://www.banfield.com/Banfield/media/PDF/Banfield-PAWrometer-Summary_032916_FINAL-TM.pdf. Accessed on 21 Oct 2018.

19. Banfield shares data on the positive impact of pets in the workplace. (2016, Mar 28). Retrieved from https://www.banfield.com/about-us/news-room/press-releases-announcements/banfield-shares-data-on-the-positive-impact-of-pet. Accessed on 21 Oct 2018.

20. Wong, M., Gardiner, E., Lang, W., & Coulon, L. (2008). Generational differences in personality and motivation: do they exist and what are the implications for the workplace? J Manag Psychol. 23(8):878–90.

21. Ng, E.S., Schweitzer, L., & Lyons, S.T. (2010). New generation, great expectations: a field study of the millennial generation. J Bus Psychol. 25(2):281–92.

22. Kassab, M. (n.d.). Forget work perks. Millennial employees value engagement. Harvard University. Retrieved from https://www.extension.harvard.edu/professional-development/blog/forget-work-perks-millennial-employees-value-engagement. Accessed on 22 Oct 2018.

23. Small business.uk (2017, Feb 21). Millennial employees value experiences over financial rewards. Retrieved from https://smallbusiness.co.uk/millennial-experiential-rewards-2536972/. Accessed on 22 Oct 2018.

24. Fueling the experience Economy. Millennials. Retrieved from http://eventbrite-s3.s3.amazonaws.com/marketing/Millennials_Research/Gen_PR_Final.pdf. Accessed on 22 Oct 2018.

25. Haden, J. (2017, Dec 21). 25 rewards that great employees actually love to receive. Inc. Retrieved from https://www.inc.com/jeff-haden/25-creative-rewards-that-great-employees-actually-love-to-receive.html. Accessed on 22 Oct 2018.

26. Martin. (2014, Sep 25). The Google way of motivating employees. Cleverism. Retrieved from https://www.cleverism.com/google-way-motivating-employees/. Accessed on 22 Oct 2018.

27. Umoh, R. (2017, Jul 31). 3 reasons why millennials want to work for Google and Amazon so badly. CNBC. Retrieved from https://www.cnbc.com/2017/07/28/3-reasons-why-millennials-want-to-work-for-google-and-amazon-so-badly.html. Accessed on 22 Oct 2018.

28. Kosoff, M. (2015, May 23). Millennials have a clear favorite when asked which tech company is their 'ideal employer'. Business Insider. Retrieved from https://www.businessinsider.in/Millennials-have-a-clear-favorite-when-asked-which-tech-company-is-their-ideal-employer/articleshow/47400879.cms. Accessed on 23 Oct 2018.

29. Yang, L. (2017, Jul 11). 13 incredible perks of working at Google, according to employees. Insider. Retrieved from https://www.thisisinsider.com/coolest-perks-of-working-at-google-in-2017-2017-7#googlers-can-attend-or-help-organize-talks-at-google-a-program-that-lets-employees-bring-in-speakers-who-interest-them-3. Accessed on 2 Feb 2019.

30. 19 of the best job perks and benefits millennials have that their parents didn't. Business Insider. Retrieved from https://www.businessinsider.in/19-of-the-best-job-perks-and-benefits-millennials-have-that-their-parents-didnt/Game-breaks/slideshow/65610068.cms. Accessed on 22 Oct 2018. Accessed on 2 Feb 2019.

31. D'Onfro, J., & England, L. (n.d.). An inside look at Google's best employee perks. Inc. Retrieved from https://www.inc.com/business-insider/best-google-benefits.html. Accessed on 2 Feb 2019.

8

STRATEGIES FOR RETAINING MILLENNIALS

As millennials form the majority of the workforce today, it is time to address the problem next in line, the problem of retention. Millennials are job-hoppers and are not found to stick to a job for more than a few years. For the average American millennial, the median tenure that he/she stays at one job is 1.7 years (1). The high turnover rates are extremely problematic for the management as the functioning of the organization is hindered if a portion of the workforce keeps changing very often. The task of retaining the millennials, therefore, becomes vital in light of the growing millennial workforce.

Retention is important since loss of valuable knowledge workers stalls the growth and productivity of an organization. The question is why do employees change jobs? There are multiple reasons why an employee may leave his/her job. Salary issues, want of better career opportunities, unmet work expectations, desire to change industries, individual emotional conditions and so on are some of the grounds on which individuals wish to exit their job. Millennials regard their own contributions to the organization as a more fulfilling accomplishment than their tenure of work. Hence, the defining characteristics and traits of the millennials must be leveraged to offer fruitful incentives to make them stay.

The strategies and policies used to retain the older generations might prove to be ineffective for Gen Y. This is evidently because of the different work expectations that these generational cohorts have. Their larger than life aspirations from their organization are not fully realized which leads to dissatisfaction and the quest for better opportunities. The fall of expectations is met with desire to move to a place which meets their aspirations, subsequently paving the way for job switching (2). They desire a handsome paying job with learning opportunities and a good working environment, a healthy work-life balance along with time to pursue social obligations and recognition of their work. The bounty of expectations makes them move from job to job on the quest for the job which gives them it all.

Though we know that we cannot bind the millennial employee to one organization, we cannot say that they are not loyal. We can nurture them so as to make them serve a longer tenure for the particular company. To manage millennials, it is important that employers adopt strategies that appeal to the millennial ideology and way of life. Once a millennial has been hired successfully, the focus shifts on retaining them. As long as one plays by the millennial rule book, it is not difficult to retain them for a year or two.

Employers must look to appeal to the characteristics that millennials seek most: horizontal and vertical career advancement opportunities, a desirable location and a strong social network within the company (3). By playing off these factors, firms have the ability to design a unified and robust brand image that encompass millennials' most desired traits. Once this brand image is well established, the company can look to strengthen their communication processes to reach and attract millennials in innovative ways.

In this chapter, we present some of the strategies and practices that have been adopted by organizations across industries to retain millennials. The average tenure of work has been increasing over the years. To decrease the instances of turnover, all levels of managers must work hand in hand, identify the need of the employee and then devise the best possible strategy to retain them. The managers need to build a model that attracts the millennials and keeps them glued to their work.

1. **Internal branding:** The organization must strive to form and maintain a brand image. Internal branding initiatives will ensure that employees are motivated in nurturing of the organizational brand. The employer needs to show themselves in a light superior to all the other organizations, showcasing that they are furnishing their employees with the best they can get. It will help to develop a deeper appreciation for a brand that internalizes their work attitudes and behaviours (4). However, it requires intrinsically motivating HRM policies and practices to develop emotional attachment to the organization and brand. To achieve this, employees must be communicated through value propositions of their organizational brand.

The first step to building an internal brand lies in recruiting employees whose values fit with the organization. This creates an assurance that these individual employees feel closely connected to the organization. Since they identify with the organization as a brand, they will be more attached to the organization and have a deep sense of loyalty towards it. Internal branding aims to develop and link the attitudes and thoughts of the employees towards the organizational brand and make them messengers to the external world (5).

The basis of internal branding lies in delivering the values of the organizational brand by making the employees aware of its significance. This involves communicating the relevance of the brand image to the employees at the right time and at the right length. Trying to build a close cognitive and emotional contact binds the employees to their employers, which they must strive for at all instances. Hence, a major step involves educating the workforce along these lines through proper guidance and training and creating awareness and a desire to act for the organization, when required.

The concept of internal branding also strengthens one's psychological contract with the organization. The individual expectation that employees have with the organization enhances and solidifies into a deeper relationship. The recognition of employee's every need and fine tuning it to the likes of every generation establishes firm ground for the employees to trust the management. The fulfilment of their psychological contract creates a reciprocal relationship where employees find themselves eager to work with an ignited enthusiasm.

It is also suggested that effective financial incentive reward packages must be linked to the acquisition of potential employees. They need to customize the HR strategies taking into account the characteristics, working styles and employment expectations of baby boomers, Generation X and millennials. As already explained, millennials have distinct workplace needs, such as flexible work hours, a fun work environment as well as opportunities for project diversity, career advancement and further learning and other motivating factors like family and personal lives relatively degree of privacy and work-life balance, when compared to Generation X and baby boomers. Therefore, corporate management and HR departments should strive to comprehend their motivations and preferences so as to be able to develop appropriate recruitment processes, selection tools, training and development techniques, rewarding systems and implement them effectively.

Internal branding reflects the organizational brand in their employees at all points, right from selecting the right candidate. The employees need to be treated as internal customers, with a directed individual focus on each member. Just as the organization dedicatedly works for the customer, the employees' needs must also be identified and nurtured. The key lies in synergizing the brand image with the employees and making them carriers of the organization label. The business leaders need to convey the importance of staying with the organization, by focusing on the essence of the brand. This brand image of the company must be reiterated to them time and again to build their recognition of the brand and exude the values at all times.

All in all, effective implementation of internal branding strategies through the contributions of HR policies that address intergenerational distinctions will help employees to become emotionally attached to their organization with greater enthusiasm for the success of both themselves and their employer.

2. **Increasing the digital workspace:** There is no other thing a millennial loves more than a digital workspace. Since technology acts as a driving force for the millennials, they consider it impossible to survive in a workplace that has outdated technical infrastructure. It is the onus of the employer to keep updating the technology and provide the best available technological set-up for the millennial employee. Technology is not only considered a tool but also a valued skill set. They differentiate themselves on the basis of the tools,

software, algorithm and so on that they bring to the table and have a quest to learn new technologies. Sometimes, when costs are attached to acquiring these technologies, employers will strengthen the employer–employee relationship if they procure it for their employees. Having updated technology is not only an investment towards the employees' morale but also a direct advantage to the company's business.

Employers can manoeuvre successful mastery of technical skills, thereby carving a pathway for them to move up the career ladder. The idea of working for an employer who provides them a step to hone themselves is appealing to the millennials. They are willing to work for such professionals where they are at liberty to utilize the most updated form of technological systems. Although the idea of organizations implementing and updating technology for their workforce may be over the top, it is not untrue to say that employees do wish for their employers to adopt state-of-the-art systems. A good 42 per cent of millennials, as per a survey by Robert Walters, feel that it is worthwhile for their employers to invest in the development of new technologies (6). Hence, though a large investment for the company, it can help a bit in easing the problem of turnover due to poor technological infrastructure.

The tech thrust of the millennial is not limited to the provisions made by the organization. They also want to be able to have the permit to bring their own tech tools and systems to work. Not just that, they also want the flexibility to work from their devices from any location. The millennials are proud of their legacy of digital systems and want to be able to make work convenient for them. They always have some smart technological trick up their sleeve to do their work in the quickest of ways. There are abundant software and services available to them for work. The trend of Bring Your Own Device is becoming popular day by day where organizations are encouraging their employees to bring their own systems (7). It offers the privilege to have a common system, incorporating both the individuals' work tools and the company's which increases his productivity, alongside the ease of working from wherever they want, however they want. Millennials have a passion for their work and do not want to be constrained by the parameters of location. They want to be able to work from their own places, which is made possible by technology.

The millennials also want their employers to allow them to use social media for their work. In the above-mentioned survey, 38 per cent millennials want their employers to give them the freedom to use social media (6). Millennials have high social connectedness, and they do not find it any wrong to seek benefit from their social connections. A huge part of their lives is online, where they spend a lot of time on these platforms. It does not seem far-fetched that they might seek to incorporate it in their work aspects as well. Although this threatens the sanctity of work and may endanger valuable productive time in slandering the internet, it is a choice the employer has to make. Undoubtedly, social media, which makes life faster and easy for the employees, can be used for work purposes considering its huge reach and innovative ways.

3. **Work flexibility; work-life integration more than work-life balance:** Both social life and work life are important to them, and they do not want to neglect one for the other. They yearn for the freedom to work at their own

workspace, not just from their office desk. Almost all organizations are offering the provision of flexi-time and work from home. Managers should understand that millennials are all about getting the work done, no matter where it is done from. It is definitely an assumption that millennials are not working if they are not at the workplace, which must be done away with. Hence, millennials should be permitted to work from a remote area, other than the office.

The modern workplace encapsulates a millennials den. Keeping in line with the fun and comfort work demands of the millennial, more and more employers are transitioning from the traditional offices. The system of office cubicles or rooms is being replaced by informal seating spaces. In many offices, especially the start-ups, the offices do not even install work desks, and the employees prefer to sit on the floor or on couches and beanbags. The offices are characterized with open spaces, where people can sit together and work in teams or can have a light chat while working and are accessible to others. Google has the provision of customizable work desks, where one can design their own workstations in the coolest way (8). Millennials are team workers and this work set-up supports collaboration and boosts team spirit.

Workplaces have been redesigned to make them lively. Where traditional Indian offices had a tea vendor distributing tea or a small canteen, or depended entirely upon the shops in the vicinity, modern offices have coffee lounges, cafes, classy restaurants serving multi-cuisine food, micro-kitchens and so on. They also boast of a gaming room, gym, pool, library, prayer room, massage parlour and so on.

4. **Positive and supportive company culture:** Millennials are social beings and want their workspaces to be social centres as well. According to a survey by Robert Walters, 30 per cent millennials considered meeting colleagues to be an important aspect of induction, in contrast to 1 per cent of baby boomers and 15 per cent Generation Xers (6). They want to work in a healthy environment, where their colleagues can be their friends and their bosses their mentors. Opportunities must be given to them to collaborate in work teams where the unique attribute of every member is contrived together in a platter, for organizational productivity. The underlying facet for the employer to remember is to provide the millennials with a place they want to work at.

A supportive work culture, where managers and leaders encourage them and appreciate them, is all they desire. They want their leaders to be more accessible and available to them. They do not acknowledge hierarchy or titles and are not scared to ask questions. They want their leaders to be willing to listen to them and pay individualized attention to them. They want collaborative working environment where only the boundaries of respect exist. They want to work together, in consultation with their colleagues, supervisors, other advisers and so on. They need regular feedback for their work and a sense of direction from their leaders to discharge their duties earnestly.

The millennials require an inclusive culture, where they find acceptance. Managers should do away with stereotypes and categorization on the basis of age groups. One must be seen as an individual, with his/her own values, attitudes, thoughts and skills. Lee Noble, an employee at Lendesk, says, 'Once one does away with all the stereotypes surrounding millennials and our purportedly unique expectations and needs from our employment, we can build a strategy to attract and retain good talent' (9). When the millennial stereotypes and biases are removed from the table, they will look like just another employee, with certain expectations from the employers. The millennials value diversity and concepts of equality, and policies must be made keeping that in mind.

For example, Google uses the term 'Greyglers' (10) for their employees over 40 years of age. A kind of categorization, it attracted a lot of negative publicity and duped Google as 'ageist'. However, it has helped to formulate specialized strategies for the age group, which is a minority, amongst its fresh breed of young employees.

5. **Volunteering and CSR:** For millennials, just work is not a priority. The millennial generation values principles of equality, inclusion and philanthropy. They want to work for the community and work for the upliftment of the underprivileged.

6. **Valuing engagement:** It has been identified that apart from the inevitable career growth need, the other reason why most millennials quit their jobs is a lack of engagement at work. Millennials want extra benefits and perks through social activities, hands-on sessions, recreational time and so on to have a feel good factor while working in organizations. The Robert Walters Survey points out that 75 per cent millennials want an engaging workplace (6). On the contrary, a survey by Gallup shows that 87 per cent of the workforce globally are not engaged at their workplace (11). If disengagement at work is a major cause of burnout

and turnover, then managers should make room for work engagement in their strategies.

7. **Career development and learning opportunities:** Managers must extend support to the career planning and development of the millennials. They want information about their path of progression in the organization at the time of induction itself. In fact, not getting enough developmental opportunities and not being able to fulfil their career goal are fears millennials hold at the workplace. They declare their career aspirations in a straightforward manner, and in return expect the same transparency from their employers. They even want their managers to convey the promotions and bonus structure clearly to them. Professional development of the individual employee is what the business leaders must target and set in motion (12).

First, millennials must be provided with goal-setting opportunities by the right mentorship. Most of them are ambitious, but may lack a proper direction for the fulfilment of their goals. Helping the employees set realistic and achievable goals goes a long way in nurturing their aspirations. Leaders should also promote forming team goals for increasing communicating and shared understanding between their employees. Structured goals will facilitate comradeship and team spirit and will also help to understand each other's skills and orientations. Post goal setting, the millennials should be provided with valuable feedback from time to time. It is time bosses become mentors and guide the millennials effectively to build them as leaders of tomorrow. Mentors should help the mentees in learning the tricks of the business, develop leadership, help to achieve personal goals and along the way fulfil the organizational objectives.

Millennials consider themselves global citizens and are free to work outside India for international projects. Internet penetration has made the world a smaller place and has made networking possible with different communities across the globe. Millennials are no novice to this work trend of virtual businesses and have an aspiration of working abroad. Companies must offer them opportunities to showcase their talents and skills globally and must assign them projects likewise. This acts as a source of motivation for them alongside sharpening their careers. International work transfers are also a good investment for the organization as they cultivate a workforce having global experience and who are well versed with the nuances of international business.

In other cases, to retain the employees, instead of giving them shorter projects, managers should give them a long-term project, which is challenging and rewarding for them (13). A string of small projects tends to make them feel that they have worked long enough with the firm, hence instigating the need to shift. Working on a project for a year and getting handsomely rewarded for it might seem more reasonable. Also, they can be assigned projects that they themselves bring to the company or can be allowed to pick their assignments. This way, they will stay connected to the task and the ownership that they feel will make them contribute with rekindled zest.

Millennials can also be provided with lateral shift options. They can be transferred to other functions or departments within the organization. A version of job rotation, this can prove to be a good strategy since they crave for challenging tasks. Working in a different vertical with the opportunity to learn new things might find fervour with them. Instead of moving to a different organization, they might continue working in the same one (6).

Millennials do consider salary as reward for work, but they are not satisfied with just money. They value learning and development, and unless the organization indulges them with such opportunities, they are not going to stay. The company needs to evolve their work culture to provide sufficient scope for building new skills at the workplace. Activity-based learning and on-the-job training are alluring ways that ensure employees grow up in a learning culture. Other than in-house facilities, employees must also be sent on external trainings, conferences, workshops, seminars, summits and so on to dispense opportunities of career growth and skill development.

8. **Accepting mobility**: Organizations must overcome the fear of Goodbye. Even though it is tough to forgo valuable talent, managements must learn to let their employees go. It is time for them to change the concept of retention. Having too many stringent policies regarding exits might only drive the employees away. On the contrary, being more easy-going and supporting their decisions to move will only further bind them to the organization. Being more accepting towards the subordinate's decision to quit will leave a positive mark on the employee, which will ripple to a positive organizational reputation in the market. It will help to create goodwill in favour of the company which will help to captivate more potential employees. It also leaves the door open for employees to join back (14).

We now summarize the list of findings catering to the managers, mentors and recruiter groups.

RECOMMENDATION FOR MANAGERS (15, 16)

For an organization to effectively manage and retain a talented workforce, the role of managers becomes extremely crucial, especially in the case of millennial employees. The following tips are likely to aid managers in their efforts of managing and retaining the millennial workforce.

- Adopting management style that helps in attracting, motivating and retaining of millennials.

- Investing time and effort to cultivate genuine relationship with employee to coach effectively.

- Building trust amongst the employees towards the management. Trust is a motivational factor for building strong relationships with employees and it also has significant effect on how employees will perceive feedback.

- Adopting a coaching approach, while working with employees, will help to develop employees. Giving them the right to take decision and bestowing personal responsibility to employees will bring independence in providing feedback. This helps millennials to gain new skills on critical evaluation and finding path to answers by themselves.

- Managers should work to tailor their relationships and interactions to the unique needs of their individual employees. Managers should cultivate leading with individual consideration for more effective relationships. Further, employee will also be more open to seek feedback on their performance.

- Put an effort into knowing them professionally and personally. When a manager shows care for his team, it builds a positive atmosphere to achieve professional success in an organization. Millennials feel more comfortable in informal settings compared to formal settings.

- Establish a mentor/coaching relationship and treat them as colleagues, so that you can help them to grow and improve. Position yourself as source of learning; provide tools and learning goals to progress in time. If they realize that knowledge and skills are required to succeed then they will learn their best.

- They do not like managers who are arrogant and unapproachable. Help them in customizing their schedules, work assignments, projects and career paths. Provide consistent and immediate feedback to get them back on track immediately and do not wait for performance evaluations about work. Along with feedback, provide recognition and incentives and rewards for great performance.

RECOMMENDATIONS FOR RECRUITERS (17)

Recruiters are the backbone of a company who have the arduous task of retaining millennials from joining their competitors. Below is a list of strategies that must be adopted in retaining their multi-talented millennials from getting poached by their rivals.

- HR managers are recommended to put special emphasis on perks and benefits while designing pay strategy for the younger generation which is about to enter the workforce.

- It is advisable to tailor-make perks and benefits in terms of retirement and health.

- Men favour profit sharing more than women do.

- There is a strong relationship between experience and practice in the business world and the perception of importance of individual and team contribution to organizational performance.

- HR managers can create a sense of awareness between potential and new employees that performance pay is of crucial importance for organizational success.

- Amongst experienced individuals and respondents with self-initiated need for learning, off-the-job training is one of the most important indirect transactional rewards.

- For organizations that build their competitive advantage on knowledge technologies, it is recommended to design different modalities of education and training outside the organization.

RELATIONAL ASPECTS OF MOTIVATION AND REWARD MANAGEMENT

- Generation Y is dominantly interested in promotion opportunities.

- Although promotion is a prerequisite for motivation and consequently job satisfaction, work-life balance is a factor that has become central and very specific to Generation Y individuals.

- Delicately plan and execute work activities in order to allow employees to maintain the balance between work obligations and private life, especially in case of women who have assigned more importance to their relational element than men.

- Women have generally indicated more inclination towards recognition, feedback information and high-quality leadership. These factors should be taken into account while designing specific HR policies and activities. Since educated women are increasingly entering the workforce, they value recognition as a motivating factor to enhance job performance.

- Highly favour on-the-job training, teamwork and participation in decision-making.
- Implement more teamwork design to their work tasks.
- Leadership quality is crucial in all above-mentioned activities; this generation expects their leaders to be able to apply a more 'coaching' style of leadership as well as to be able themselves to demonstrate the knowledge and skills they ask from Generation Y individuals.

RECOMMENDATION FOR MENTORS

Following are some tips to engage millennial as followers to retain workforce in long term and grow them into assets in the organization (18, 19):

- Leaders will need to adapt and accommodate millennial leadership style. It is required to engage them as followers and eventually develop them as leaders.
- Provide flexible work schedule and give importance to their work-life balance.
- Giving freedom to choose when and where they work is very powerful, so that they do not want to give up the office environment. Organizations provide an option of working from home one day a week.
- Older generation should not misunderstand if they do not find their millennial colleagues in office from 9 until 5 every day. It does not mean that they are not performing.
- Leaders should take advantage of their 'presence' with 'activity'. Since they put extra effort from remote locations.
- Leaders need to allow millennials the flexibility to set their own schedules to work efficiently, considering the fact that quality of performance is not compromised.
- Flexible work programmes complement millennials already blended lifestyle.

- Though there is the misconception of poor work ethics and poor manners, they are extremely talented and well educated.

- Leaders must engage with millennial followers by providing growing experiences, respecting their contribution, utilize mentoring, give feedback and staying flexible. Thereby, leaders can retain millennial as followers who will develop into future leaders.

....

Facebook's Famed Retention Strategies That Make It a Global Brand

In 2013, Glassdoor ranked Facebook as the No. 1 employer brand for having the most number of satisfied employees. It was No.1 because its employees were presented with an exciting work environment to provide creative solutions. Facebook received an amazing rating of 4.7 out of 5 with its tech competitor Google receiving a 4.3. The high ratings along with dedicated HR team have played a pivotal role in making Facebook the crème de la crème of the tech world employers. It has always stressed on unique retention policies taking into account both economic rewards and employee benefits for its employees. Due to these very reasons, Facebook has been successful in protecting its staff from being poached by other companies, resulting in a single-digit turnover rate for many years (20).

Facebook offers unlimited sick days to its employees. This demonstrates the level of trust Facebook imposes in its employees. However, like most tech firms, Facebook has also struggled in hiring and retaining women engineers.

Hence, it has come up with out-of-the-box strategies like close-in reserved parking spaces for pregnant women to make them feel at home away from home. It also offers paid parental leave for both spouses and $4,000 'baby cash' for a new arrival (20).

A study conducted by Lori Goler, head of HR Business Partners working in tandem with Facebook's People Analytics team found out that the company knew the secret to increasing retention amongst its employees. Many millennial employees at Facebook were very happy working with their managers but still left the organization due to personal problems with their position or role. The study also revealed that it is imperative for employees to do work that energize them, even at the cost of a demotion or a lateral move (21). In other words, not everyone wanted expansion of job role or promotion. The study demonstrated that a company should provide opportunity to its employees to be in roles that they relish and find best suited for themselves. Therefore, Facebook offered its employees to choose job roles. A unique example was cited where an employee did the hiring for her own replacement and then moved into a lower level role where she is now thriving (21).

These unique retention strategies have made Facebook stand out amongst its legions of competitors in the Silicon Valley. Such has been its retention policy impact that other companies are following suit with similar programmes of their own to motivate millennial employees to stay longer and create a visible impact for their organization.

Discussion Questions

1. Do you think such strategies of Facebook would be appropriate in manufacturing companies which are, to a greater extent, policy driven?

2. Can the use of 'unlimited sick days' be a curse in disguise for companies? Why or why not?

REFERENCES

1. Fries, L. (2017, May 30). Beyond recruiting: how to retain millennials. The Business Journals. Retrieved from https://www.bizjournals.com/bizjournals/how-to/human-resources/2017/05/beyond-recruiting-how-to-retain-millennials.html. Accessed on 2 Feb 2019.
2. Luscombe, J., Lewis, I., & Biggs, H.C. (2013). Essential elements for recruitment and retention: generation Y. Educ+ Train. 55(3):272–90.
3. Sharer, E., Jones, C.J., Morris, A., Harpel, A., Miesle, A., & Dixon, J. (2016). Recruiting and maintaining millennial talent for The J.M. Smucker Company. Honors Research Projects. 372.
4. Ozcelik, G. (2015). Engagement and retention of the millennial generation in the workplace through internal branding. Int J Bus Manag. 10(3):99.
5. Dechawatanapaisal, D. (2017). The mediating role of organizational embeddedness on the relationship between quality of work life and turnover: perspectives from healthcare professionals. Int J Manpower. 38(5):696–711.
6. Robert Walters. (n.d.). Attracting and retaining millennial professionals. Retrieved from https://www.robertwalters.com/content/dam/robert-walters/corporate/news-and-pr/files/whitepapers/attracting-and-retaining-millennials-UK.pdf. Accessed on 2 Feb 2019.
7. Gianniris, D. (2018, Jan 25). The millennial arrival and the evolution of the modern workplace. Forbes. Retrieved from https://www.forbes.com/sites/forbestechcouncil/2018/01/25/the-millennial-arrival-and-the-evolution-of-the-modern-workplace/#2047d9dd5a73. Accessed on 14 Oct 2018.
8. Inside Google Office. (2014, Sep 28). 15 coolest things you get as a Google employee. Letsintern.com. Retrieved from http://www.letsintern.com/blog/inside-google-office/. Accessed on 2 Feb 2019.
9. Expert Panel, Forbes Business Development Council (2018, May 18). Seven ways to recruit and retain millennials in today's job market. Forbes. Retrieved from https://www.forbes.com/sites/forbesbusinessdevelopmentcouncil/2018/05/18/seven-ways-to-recruit-and-retain-millennials-in-todays-job-market/#3fa3b55869c2
10. Google Diversity annual report 2018. Retrieved from https://static.google usercontent.com/media/diversity.google/en//static/pdf/Google_Diversity_annual_report_2018.pdf. Accessed on 2 Feb 2019.
11. Crabtree, S. (2013, Oct 8). Worldwide, 13% of employees are engaged at work. Gallup. Retrieved from https://news.gallup.com/poll/165269/worldwide-employees-engaged-work.aspx. Accessed on 2 Feb 2019.
12. Elsbury, K. (2018, Mar 1). Five proven tactics for hiring and retaining millennial Employees. Forbes. Retrieved from https://www.forbes.com/sites/yec/2018/03/01/five-proven-tactics-for-hiring-and-retaining-millennial-employees/#48f3b51d2deb. Accessed on 2 Feb 2019.
13. Rossheim, J. (n.d.). How to retain those restless millennials. Monster. Retrieved from https://hiring.monster.com/hr/hr-best-practices/workforce-management/employee-retention-strategies/how-to-retain-millennials.aspx. Accessed on 2 Feb 2019.

14. Kassab, M. (n.d.). Forget work perks. Millennial employees value engagement. Harvard University. Retrieved from https://www.extension.harvard.edu/professional-development/blog/forget-work-perks-millennial-employees-value-engagement. Accessed on 2 Feb 2019.
15. Thompson, C., & Gregory, J.B. (2012). Managing millennials: a framework for improving attraction, motivation, and retention. Psychologist-Manager J. 15(4):237.
16. Martin, C.A. (2005). From high maintenance to high productivity: what managers need to know about Generation Y. Ind Commerc Train. 37(1):39–44.
17. Galetić, L., Braje, I.N., & Klindžić, M. (2015, Dec). Adapting reward strategies to millennials' pay preferences. Fifth European Reward Management Conference.
18. Luscombe, J., Lewis, I., & Biggs, H.C. (2013). Essential elements for recruitment and retention: Generation Y. Educ+ Train. 55(3):272–90.
19. Burkus, D. (2010). Developing the next generation of leaders: how to engage millennial in the workplace. Leadership Advance Online. XIX. Retrieved from https://www.regent.edu/acad/global/publications/lao/issue_19/Burkus_leading_next_generation.pdf. Accessed on 2 Feb 2019.
20. Sullivan, J. (2013, Sep 9). A case study of Facebook's simply amazing talent management practices, Part 1 of 2. ERE Media. Retrieved from https://www.ere.net/a-case-study-of-facebooks-simply-amazing-talent-management-practices-part-1-of-2/. Accessed on 7 May 2019.
21. Huppert, M. (2018, Oct 25). Facebook Knows the Secret to Increasing Retention—And It Starts With Managers. Linkedin. Retrieved from https://business.linkedin.com/talent-solutions/blog/employee-retention/2018/facebook-secret-to-increasing-retention. Accessed on 7 May 2019.

9

LEVERAGING ON THE STRENGTHS OF THE MILLENNIALS: INDUSTRY'S BEST PRACTICES

Millennials are different from the rest of the workforce and operate in different ways. They comprise the largest generation in today's workforce and are forerunners of change. They are leading the baton when it comes to advocating new policies and lifestyles. Their vision of bringing in a positive and influential thought process forces organizations to evolve with time. Millennials are entering jobs and transforming it accordingly to make their organizations work effectively. It is no news that with their dynamicity, they only wish to stay with employers who make them feel valued at the organization.

Companies adopt a plethora of initiatives to attract and retain millennials. Considering their large set of employees to be millennials, it is essential that organizations make room for what these generational cohorts demand. In this chapter, we highlight some of the best practices that have been undertaken by firms, large and small alike, to accommodate millennials. We mention an array of incentives that companies are offering to indulge its tech-frenzy workforce.

New generation leadership: What kind of leaders do the millennials need? They need mentors, leaders who are honest and moral in their dealings. Millennials need strong role models and their leaders must be able to inspire them. They need coaching on a one-to-one basis with individualized attention. To meet the concerns of the millennials, the Gen Xers and baby boomers are evolving the way they manage people.

UNIQUE MARKETING STRATEGIES

Marketing strategies need to change since the generation of buyer changes from Gen X to Gen Y. As more and more millennials and Gen Zs flock the consumer market, the traditional methods of marketing and advertising pave the way for neo-trends. The millennial shoppers are not the same as their previous generations, but are still alike in certain ways. Their tech-savviness and fast lifestyle make them a different breed of consumers to cater to (1). They want a connection with the retailer and the brand and resort to technology to forge a connection.

The millennial shoppers love to shop online, but do not deny themselves the pleasures of the physical shopping experience. They want the best brands at the lowest of prices. They often shop during discounts and sales, and like to use their discount coupons and tickets. They shop in the brick-and-mortar stores and their personal devices alike. Irrespective, they want a smooth shopping experience and prefer to revisit those who make them feel valued.

The millennials rely on their friends and family and trust their user judgement when it comes to using a product. They count immensely on word-of-mouth experience of their counterparts and peers (2). Moreover, they review everything online before buying and are not scared to take action or give negative feedback about a product. They also keep checking social media for discounts, value coupons and best deals. They first enquire about the product offline, then research the stores for best prices, followed by seeking validation from their networks and online reviews, post which they either place the order online or make an in-store purchase, depending upon whichever offer is more attractive.

In order to attract the millennials, marketers and business-men must create a buzz with their products. Their offering must invade the public and personal space of their millennial customer. Millennials consider their interactions with their social network as precious. The marketers need to enter the channels and media where these conversations between millennials occur and information gets generated. These comprise of the social media platforms such as Facebook, Twitter, Quora, LinkedIn, Instagram and so on. There have been times when products have been launched on Facebook, generating quite a customer upheaval. The extent to which their product is 'viral' is also one of the key aspects a person evaluates before making a purchase. It is vital to find out what they need by asking them and involving them directly. They seek experiences, and technology should be integrated with the strategies to provide them that. Mobile apps, games, videos, gift coupons, flash sales and so on all must be incorporated into the marketing strategy. Moreover, gender-based strategies have to be adopted since female millennials shop more than males (3). Needless to say, marketers and retailers must integrate technology in their activities of sale to the millennial consumer.

Companies need not use just social media marketing techniques but also attractive advertising. Advertisements should be such that these capture the attention of the millennial viewer. It requires telling a good story about something they can identify with, such as stories of people. Attempts at inspiring them by narrating the life story of someone like them captures their attention and builds a connection with the product or service. Advertisements need to be creative in such a way as to capture the essence of the product and at the same time generate a hype. Not only that, they are aware and are concerned about the environment and the society. The usage of bio and green products is on the rise because of the millennials' preference to buy them. Associating with a cause or having a social agenda has an impact on the millennials purchase intention (4).

XIAOMI FLASH SALES

Flash sales imply sale of limited quantity of a particular good at a particular time on a given day. The Chinese cell phone manufacturer Xiaomi has catapulted to the second-largest smartphone selling company, by only following its online flash sale selling strategy (5). Within a period of four years, Xiaomi has taken over the long-time market leader, Samsung. Xiaomi launches its smartphones exclusively on e-commerce platforms. It broke the internet with the sale of Redmi Note 5 and Note 5 Pro, smartphones under ₹15,000 segments, launched on the online giant, Flipkart.

The newly launched cell phones garnered good reviews, but were not available in stores in India and were being sold only on the designated site. The sale was extensively advertised on print and online media, providing a lot of publicity to the product. On the first sale, the entire product sold out within three minutes of its commencement. Post the sale, Xiaomi announced having sold 300,000 handsets (6). Thousands of customers begin flocking to the site at the time of the sale, crashing the Flipkart site. So high was the demand for this product that the inability to purchase left many customers unhappy. The uproar over products getting sold out within seconds was to such an extent that some even termed it as a hoax sale, part of a marketing strategy (7).

The soaring sales of Xiaomi's products can be attributed to its flash sale selling and its tech-frenzy buyers who go to lengths to purchase the product they want. Although only a few are able to purchase the smartphones, it builds a notion of scarcity which throws it more into the spotlight. The hype generated is enough to keep the cell phone trending on everyone's social media stories and news feeds for a long time (8). The flash sales also help keep the production in check, with the management knowing how many units to manufacture the next time. The e-commerce websites which tie up with Xiaomi also benefit, where they can increase their consumer reach (9). The undulated attention the product gathers furthers helps to increase its sales, thereby making it a successful product.

UNIQUE RECRUITMENT STRATEGIES

The upcoming workforce's lifestyle preferences are changing the recruitment scenario. They no longer respond to the traditional hiring techniques and are evading the employer's eyes. With the workforce comprising more and more of the younger generation, companies are adopting recruitment techniques that will capture their attention. They are revising their pay structures and are tweaking their incentives to suit the millennial lifestyle. The wallet share for talent-driven activities for companies has increased. They are seeking technology for recruiting and have become open to options like remote interviewing through Skype or other video call apps, video resumes, using social media.

Social media recruitment comprises of building an online presence to enter the list of companies the millennials wish to work for. Potential employees have a strong social media presence, and such recruitment strategies are aimed at tapping them in their natural space. Hence, recruiters take to social media to seek the candidates by themselves building an online presence. And the best part is it can ensnare both active and passive candidates. Passive candidates are employees who are employed and are not searching for a job but would be willing to negotiate if a good opportunity came their way. Social media acts as an effective tool to pursue those candidates.

The newest addition to the recruitment techniques is artificial intelligence (AI). AI is now being roped in to change the face of recruitment strategies implemented by HRs. Sampling candidates' resumes, performing psychometric analysis, finding best fit, smart applicant searching databases, quicker search and selection processes and so on are just some of the ways that AI can help in sharpening the recruitment processes (10). AI-enabled solutions help to swift up the recruitment process and make it free of biases that creep in during the selection interviews. There are now plenty of software and chatbot services available in the market that cater to the hiring needs of HR by helping them to source, screen, shortlist and eventually select the best candidate for the job (11). AI is extremely beneficial to the recruiters by saving on a lot of time spent on searching for the correct candidate, effectively manages the manifold of data and standardizes the functions of the HR.

To attract more and more candidates from the Generation Y, a paradigmatic shift in the company's ideals is needed. Today's candidates want to be able to interact with the organization at any time. Being able to satiate that desire is made possible only through social media. Social media recruiting also presents the opportunity to be able to hire passive talent, one who is not very up front in searching for jobs. Given the amount of time millennials stay hooked onto the internet, social media particularly, it becomes necessary for the employers to reach out to them at these platforms, where they are found the most.

To look appealing to the potential talent for the company, organizations have to showcase themselves as a good brand, one they would want to associate themselves with. Although a shortage of jobs still exists, it is now the onus of the employers to make themselves alluring rather than the candidates marketing themselves. To do this, organizations are capitalizing on their brand. Unless they differentiate themselves from their competitors in their branding strategy, it is likely that they will lose potential talent to other firms. Companies are now increasing their budget ascribed for branding and advertising to hire good employees. They are taking the help of ads in the print, television and online media, video messages, website optimizations, partnering with ranking agencies and so on to come across as more promising organizations.

E&Y

Ernst & Young (E&Y), one of the Big Four, recognizes the platform social media can provide it to consolidate its employer brand. In its quest to become a brand of choice for the upcoming workforce, it designed a new website exceptionaley.com (12). This website was created with the idea of providing the job seekers with information about the company so that they are able to see for themselves if the company provides them what they are looking for. This website provides an entry to the potential candidates into the inside world of E&Y. It has offerings like how being a part of E&Y will help them change the world and what they can expect to receive from the company.

The site also provides them details about the company culture through a section which talks about E&Y policies on diversity, career development, learning opportunities, benefits and so on. These are charted out with videos. The current employees also share their experiences about their life at the organization in the form of attractive videos. Finally, the website also offers details as to how the seekers, both fresh graduates and experienced, can apply and what they can expect to get in return. Overall, the website is a good tool to provide newbies the experience of working at E&Y and showing them what the company is all about, before they even think of joining the company.

McDonald's

McDonalds's has successfully grabbed the attention of the millennials by catching them right at the place they inhabit the most—Snapchat (13). Snapchat is a multimedia platform to which youngsters are glued to, uploading images in the form of 'Stories' or 'Snaps', about themselves and their daily happenings. The fast food giant McDonald's has carefully found its way through it to source candidates for jobs, in a first-of-its-kind recruitment strategy, with the term 'Snaplications'.

Snapchat has a feature which allows users to upload a ten-second video on their accounts as a 'Story'. McDonald's has videos of their employees sharing their experience of working there put up as mini ads on Snapchat, which the viewer sees between stories. Any person interested in applying for a job at McDonald's can simply swipe up on the ad, which redirects to the company website. Snapchat also offers a McDonald's filter option, which users can apply, to see themselves in a McD uniform.

On being redirected to the company Career page, applicants can fill in their details for the job openings, thereby commencing the recruitment process. Alongside, they can also upload ten-second videos in the form of stories to be posted on Snapchat. This out-of-the-box strategy is just one of the new way employers have devised to channelize the younger generation workforce. Youngsters seem to find it simple and easy to apply, and this in no way disrupts the traditional hiring process of the company (14).

Nestlé Purina

Nestlé Purina (15), formed in 2001 as a result of Nestlé's acquisition of Ralston Purina, is the pet care food business of Nestlé. They work to meet the nutritional and dietary requirements of pets and are one of the world leaders in the industry. They boast of a wide range of brands to choose from for the proper care of one's pet, such as Purina Frosty Paws, Purina Cat Chow, DeliCat, Purina Tidy Cats and so on.

Nestlé Purina has reinvented its recruitment process and has become completely tech-driven, which has helped them to improve the quality of talent drawn into the organization. Starting off, the company has a step-by-step detail of the interview process on its website to make the candidates aware of the process. The elaborate description guides the potential candidates to what they should do before, during and after the interview process. They even encourage the candidates to look them up for company reviews on portals like Glassdoor and provide their social media handles for the above purpose.

The online recruitment process allows the candidates to submit their resumes online. Candidates can also track their applications through an efficient applicant tracking system. When most job seekers complain of not being able to ascertain what happens to the resumes once they sent it, the tracking system simplifies the process by showing them exactly where their application is. It is also advantageous to the company as it helps to maintain an active talent pool.

This talent pipeline strategy has enabled it to meet the job requirements before going external with a job posting, reducing the time to fill a position. A behavioural interview method is followed once the candidates are shortlisted. This method usually consists of the panellists asking the interviewee to narrate incidences from their employment in which their ability to handle critical situations are displayed. Keeping in line with the millennials' undaunted inquisitiveness, they encourage them to ask questions post the interview.

Nestlé Purina prides itself in being amongst the first few to adopt the virtual recruiting model (16). This unique model befits the traditional campus recruiting method and opens the way for attracting and maintaining a larger-than-ever candidate pool. They opened themselves to the opportunity technology presented them and harnessed every technology they could lay hands on. As part of their campus recruitment, they focus on connecting with the individuals and mingling with the students they wish to draw into their employee pool. The relationships they nurture with their employees help them go a long way and solve a part of the turnover problem. Virtual Job Fairs, creating social media presence through communication groups on LinkedIn, Telephonic Interviews, Video Interviews, availing cloud services and so on are some of the ventures they undertook to implement virtual recruiting. Moreover, their recruitment team consistently makes use of metrics and to track how and when they can improve upon their ongoing strategies.

UNIQUE TRAINING METHODS

The millennial generation has a penchant for growth and advancement through skill development. This makes organizations make training, learning and development a part of their job offerings; they no longer are optional. The significance of learning and development for the millennials is inevitable. They are a generational cohort for whom skills hold more prominence than rewards. Learning and development opportunities act as potential motivators at work and a ground to stay with the organization. Companies have been organizing regular training sessions, conducted by both in-house corporates and external invitees. It is noteworthy that with the change in the learning mindset, the traditional learning methods may not work for this generation. With their short attention span and their need for speed, it is difficult to keep them engaged for long. The corporate trainers and managers therefore are cognizant of the need to reanalyse what works best for this generation and redesign their strategy accordingly. It lies solely upon the trainers and mentors to ensure that millennials remain glued to the programme and take home something to learn.

The millennials have grown up in different household conditions than their earlier generations, and hence their needs, aspirations and working styles are different. What works for them and what does not must be discerned to devise new learning techniques. Strategies must be synchronized with their characteristics and preferences. Their approach to learning is more practical where they want to fundamentally do things themselves, rather than to just listen to a theoretical session. Training sessions can no longer remain confined to PowerPoint presentations and lectures. They must evolve to incorporate technology-aided hands-on sessions, personalized to suit individual preferences and learning speeds. At the same time, learning must be collaborative and inclusive, where each one learns more through the experiences of others. Millennials are socially hyperactive and will not rebut the idea of learning together as a team. Creating learning units and online learning communities go a long way in helping them grasp the nuances of the training being delivered to them (17).

It is advisable to follow the principles of micro learning. It involves admeasuring the training to a smaller group of individuals, covering parts of the final learning objective. Since the human attention span is less, micro learning provides for learning in short bursts of a few minutes, hence also known as bite-sized training. Millennials find the idea of micro learning cool since it does not involve investing long hours and discards training as a burden. It also gives them more time to absorb the learning and apply it in their work. Millennials have the tendency to switch between tasks, and giving them spot-on short learning resources will be more effective in delivering the learning. They want learning to be fun; hence, micro learning resonates with them.

Learning tools or Performance Support Tools to improvise the training material must comprise of fresh, up-to-date and visually appealing resources which are able to grab their interest. The content must be a mix of videos, presentations, PDFs, exercises, games and so on, which are aligned to the course objectives. The materials must be accessible to the millennials' devices and must provide them remote access. Unless millennials are able to execute the training by themselves, learning will never materialize for them. They must be able to apply their classroom learning to real-time situations using technical assistance.

Individuals should be provided with content curation opportunities, where the material on a particular topic or module is continuously updated. Content curation refers to identifying, organizing and sharing content on an online community or platform. It allows the learners to upload relevant material regarding the course/module and share it with others. It makes the learners more involved in the learning process and empowers them, making them participative in the learning process. This is one good process to ensure the millennials are engaged. Additionally, it renders learning to be a unique social interactive experience through a composite learning environment. Organizations must also provide learning and innovation centres for the employees to develop their creative acumen and implement their learnings. Moreover, learning activities such as brainstorming sessions, group discussions, innovation exhibitions, design thinking workshops and so on must be inculcated as a large part of the course.

A big part of the millennial lifestyles is their cell phones, to which they are glued to most of the times. Mobile learning elements build on to the concept of just-in-time learning, where learners do not have to wait for a prescheduled session to learn something new. Online learning mobile apps guarantee on-demand learning resources, which practically translates to learning on the go. Cell phones can also be roped in to fabricate their learning experience through gamification (18). As a strategic method, this involves devising fun and challenging ways to keep millennials' interests intact throughout the course. Online games can help the learners create their own personal avatars and perform tasks to move up the levels. A dashboard can help them track their progress as well as that of others in their course. Simulation games with ardent visuals and background stories engage the employees and trace their mindset and behaviours. Elements of the game should be carefully crafted for everyone to play at any time on any device, where in between moments of work, they can have a few minutes of frolic. Gamification not just enhances the learning, but also builds a positive competitive spirit with an aim to extrinsically motivate the employees.

Apart from mobile learning, newer trends of virtual reality and AI are catching up with training and learning (19). Chatbots and virtual training coaches are playing the role of instructors just like human instructors. Organizations are incorporating analytics and data-driven solutions to fabricate interactive learner platforms. These utilize data to offer personalized courses and resources and also assess them based on their level of knowledge acquired. Formative assessments that use informal evaluation methods are used to provide qualitative feedback to the learners on a daily basis. Enabled by machine, these are helpful in gauging how much the students have understood and where do they need more work, and what kind of material must be further corroborated to polish their strengths and dispel their weaknesses.

For trainers, it is extremely important to make the trainees/learners interact with them (20). They should concoct a dual-learning environment by harmonizing the leaners to share their own thoughts and knowledge and likewise ask questions when in doubt. Through the course of the training, the trainer must be flexible and be ready to shift from the set pattern of teaching he/she had in mind. To engage the audience, he/she must shift the delivery towards the side the learners show more attention to. Apart from that, being too rigid and monotone hampers effective learning. The trainer should be able to tell a well-timed story, with ample means for the audience to grasp it, only then will the learning bind. Being a little informal during sessions helps to get their attention. When giving them exercises or take-home tasks, trainers should be able to provide them feedback and give an assurance to reach out any time. Also, to pique their interest, not everything must be spoon-fed or conveyed through materials. It is important to leave something for them to explore on their own, as there is nothing that engages millennials more than challenges.

KFC

As a part of their induction process, KFC, the chicken fast food company, has employed virtual reality in the final course of their training programme (21, 22). Called The Hard Way: A KFC Virtual Training Escape Room, the virtual exercise has been improvised to demonstrate the art of baking its signature fried chicken. A pair of virtual hands on the screen demonstrates the entire five-step preparation in a kitchen space. The simulation has been designed with the application of Oculus Touch and Oculus Rift virtual headsets to hear the entire voice-over. The entire picture is supported with the voiceover of Colonel Sanders, the founder of KFC, as the overseer. Once the employees complete the game, they can exit the Escape room, or the VR zone.

The basic reason for the adoption of this technology was to reduce the time taken to illustrate the entire process. Usually, it took 25 minutes for the company personnel to demonstrate but with the VR, it can be completed in just 10 minutes (23). Additionally, it also saves on the wastage of chicken and other resources employed for the demonstration during training. Although it saves time, it is being labelled as just an additional aid to the real training process. The whole experience has been designed to teach workers the original recipe of KFC in a dramatized way. The founder bestowing them with instructions and tricks of the trade adds a touch of tradition in it, making them feel a part of the tribe. Overall, it is a good way to implement VR in training the employees, providing them a different and engaging experience.

Walmart

Walmart, the world's largest retail corporation that provides a one-stop shopping solution, has been continuously implementing new technology to make its workplace more engaging for the millennial employees. To keep in line with its 'people come first' policy, Walmart has come up with various unique schemes. Walmart indulges in the mainstream on-site and off-site classroom teaching along with technologically advanced methods such as virtual reality supported training. Traditional learning practices like job rotation and mentorship are used as on-the-job training by the managers. For the first-two years at the job, management trainees are rotated between departments. Besides the above, there are opportunities for online web-based training (23).

A unique feature that Walmart incorporates is its Training Needs Assessment where a SWOT analysis is performed to identify the organizational areas needful of training. It also has its own learning centre, called the Walmart Academy, where the employees are taught skills required for the job, such as sales, customer service, merchandising and so on. The L&D team of Walmart has partnered with various organizations to develop AcademyEDU, an iPad app. The app functions as a user interface for skill development to employees across various levels. The custom-made app integrates state-of-the-art technology to provide its employees both professional and personal life skills (24).

Walmart has adopted the micro learning form of training and development methodology, replete with VR-based learning activities. To keep their employees informed about the safety at the store, it has designed a computer-simulation-based game, which was made available across stores. The motive of such VR exercises is to provide the in-store employees a hang of how real-time situations occur. It wants its employees to stay prepared to deal with compromising situations at the job. They learn how to manage the customers during rush days. Handling accidents, mishaps and leaning safety procedures is also a part of the drill. They also train on the ways to manage different types of customers (25, 26).

EMPLOYEE WELLNESS PROGRAMMES

Millennials have a penchant for a good workplace culture and a fetish to make work fun. They have more culture mindedness that the other generations and want to work in a good environment. Survey shows that millennials want to stay healthy more than being wealthy (27). Whether it is a startup business or a multinational organizational, millennials desire a lot of working facilities from their employers and are also willing to work for it. Today's business leaders have realized the role of a good work environment and are offering innovative packages and incentive schemes to the millennial employees.

Organizations are continuously improvising their employee benefits and wellness programmes to engage millennials at work. Ideas directly targeted at boosting employees' morale and keeping them more engrossed at work are implemented at the workplace. Not just that, they continually aim to reduce the employees' workload and give them time in between work to recharge themselves. Strenuous work hours have given way to flexitime, and orthodox/tight cultures have broken down to socially open workplaces.

The focus is now shifting from employee benefits to wellness programmes. The task is no more limited to motivating employees and boosting their productivity. The attention of the employers has moved towards keeping their employees happy and stress-free. When research recognized that work was starting to become a cause of stress and depression for the employees, it was inevitable to start looking after the well-being of their employees. Employee wellness is directed at providing a healthy and safe daily working environment to the employees. This involves a threefold focus on maintaining mental and emotional balance, eating healthy and staying fit, and increasing social connectedness.

Workplace now provides space for fitness centres, yoga classes, gym, apart from restaurants and eating zones (28). Yoga and meditation help to keep calm and are essential in acutely demanding jobs. Some organizations have provision for rooftop yoga zones, where the employees can practice at their own free time. Google is known to provide massage therapy to its employees during their work hours to help them relax. Apart from dietary assistance and fitness provisions, some companies also conduct smoking cessation sessions for their employees.

Recently, the world has opened up to the idea of mental health. Talking about depression and stress is no longer a taboo. As more and more organizational members become vocal about stigma at workplace and the need for therapy, organizations feel the need to come to the rescue of their employees. To give its long-standing due to employees' mental fitness, organizations are laying stress upon staying happy at work.

The millennials aspire to stay emotionally fit and have a well-balanced life. Their attitude towards everything is very transparent, due to which the society is also evolving to be more accepting. They are unabashedly opening up about their fears and embracing their insecurities. At the workplace too, owing to the millennials' life attitude and work ethics, the social stigma attached with mental illness is decreasing. The millennials want to work with passion and the minute work starts to become a burden for them, they do not hold themselves back and readily quit their jobs.

The main agenda is to alleviate the employees' reluctance to speak about their mental health due to fear. Leaders and managers can play a great role in this by framing employee-friendly organization policies and provisions to those undergoing stress and trauma. Immediate supervisors who interact on a daily basis should seem more sympathetic towards employees who are dealing with such issues. They should learn to recognize the signs and be more approachable if someone wants to speak to them. The colleagues and team-mates must be impartial towards those speaking up and learn to accommodate those individuals, reverberating the principle of inclusivity (29).

Workshops and talk sessions, simply to raise awareness about the subject and make their employees free to talk, are being organized. Sometimes these services are extended to the families as well to help them deal with their family member's conditions (30). Apart from that, there are also provisions of a counsellor or a therapist within the organization for the employees to consult with.

Draper Inc.

Draper Inc., a company manufacturing athletic systems and shades, places huge emphasis on the fitness of its employees.

It organizes annual health fairs and a host of competitions such as the weight loss challenge and walking competition, amongst others. Winners are awarded with a cash prize, along with gift cards. These competitions and sessions such as Weight Watchers merge enjoyment and competitive spirit, which makes working out a social activity (31).

The company also has a dedicated wellness park, complete with a gym, workout space, Zumba centre, volleyball and tennis courts and a running track. Trainers present on the site monitor the session of each employee and help him or her stay healthy. Its advantage is that employees have their own schedules to work out, overthrowing the one-size-fits-all approach, and their individual fitness needs are catered to by specialists (31).

REFERENCES

1. Donnelly, C., & Scaff, R. (2013). Who are the millennial shoppers? And what do they really want? Outlook: The Journal of High-Performance Business, (2). Accessed on 2 Feb 2019.
2. Synchrony Financial Report, 2014. Retrieved from https://investors.synchronyfinancial.com/financial-results/annual-reports/2014/an-2014/2014-annual-report.aspx. Accessed on 2 Feb 2019.
3. Forbes Coaches Council. (2017, Aug 28). Eight marketing strategies to attract modern millennials. Forbes. Retrieved from https://www.forbes.com/sites/forbescoachescouncil/2017/08/28/eight-marketing-strategies-to-attract-modern-millennials/#62d362d250f3. Accessed on 2 Feb 2019.
4. Kulkarni, C. (2018, Jul 21). 4 strategies to use when marketing to millennials. Entrepreneur India. Retrieved from https://www.entrepreneur.com/article/312408. Accessed on 2 Feb 2019.
5. Yang, Y. (2018, Mar 23). Flash sales, social media savvy helped Xiaomi topple Samsung as India's No. 1 smartphone supplier. South China Morning Post. Retrieved from https://www.scmp.com/tech/enterprises/article/2138503/flash-sales-social-media-savvy-helped-xiaomi-topple-samsung-indias. Accessed on 2 Feb 2019.
6. Lucic, K. (2018, Feb 23). First Redmi Note 5 Pro flash sale angers Indian consumers. AH. Retrieved from https://www.androidheadlines.com/2018/02/first-redmi-note-5-pro-flash-sale-angers-indian-consumers.html. Accessed on 2 Feb 2019.
7. Shahid, M. (2018, Mar 9). Xiaomi allegedly scammed the Redmi Note 5 and Redmi Note 5 Pro flash sale. TechGenYZ. Retrieved from https://www.

techgenyz.com/2018/03/09/xiaomi-scammed-redmi-note-5-redmi-note-5-pro-flash-sale/. Accessed on 5 Feb 2019.

8. Gangwar, A. (2018, Jun 29). Is Xiaomi losing customers because of flash sales? Beebom. Retrieved from https://beebom.com/xiaomi-losing-customers-flash-sales/. Accessed on 5 Feb 2019.

9. Mathur, V. (2014, Sep 6). Why does a phone go out of stock within seconds of going on sale? Livemint. Retrieved from https://www.livemint.com/Industry/N9u9LgpBPphua8nejlNqCK/Why-does-a-phone-go-out-of-stock-within-seconds-of-going-on.html. Accessed on 5 Feb 2019.

10. Forbes Coaches Council. (2018, Aug 10). 10 ways artificial intelligence will change recruitment practices. Forbes. Retrieved from https://www.forbes.com/sites/forbescoachescouncil/2018/08/10/10-ways-artificial-intelligence-will-change-recruitment-practices/#55192fbc3a2c. Accessed on 5 Feb 2019.

11. Seseri, R. (2018, Jan 29). How AI is changing the game for recruiting. Forbes. Retrieved from https://www.forbes.com/sites/valleyvoices/2018/01/29/how-ai-is-changing-the-game-for-recruiting/#63692f611aa2. Accessed on 5 Feb 2019.

12. Ernst & Young. Retrieved from https://www.exceptionaley.com/#home-be-exceptional. Accessed on 6 Feb 2019.

13. Huppert, M. (2017, Jun 15). 'Snaplications' are a thing: how companies like McDonald's and Grubhub are using Snapchat to recruit. LinkedIn. Retrieved from https://business.linkedin.com/talent-solutions/blog/recruiting-strategy/2017/snaplications-are-a-thing-how-companies-like-mcdonalds-and-grubhub-are-using-snapchat-to-recruit. Accessed on 6 Feb 2019.

14. Calfas, J. (2017, Jun 13). McDonald's is using a new method to recruit young employees—Snapchat. Fortune. Retrieved from http://fortune.com/2017/06/13/mcdonalds-snapchat-jobs-2/. Accessed on 6 Feb 2019.

15. Vevey (2001, Jan 16). Nestle and Ralston Purina announce the creation of a major international pet-care business. Nestle. Retrieved from https://www.nestle.com/media/pressreleases/allpressreleases/purina-16jan01. Accessed on 6 Feb 2019.

16. Nestle. Why a virtual recruiting model? Retrieved from https://www.nestle purinacareers.com/blog/why-a-virtual-recruiting-model/. Accessed on 6 Feb 2019.

17. Jenkins, R. (n.d.). How to effectively train millennials in the workplace. Inc. Retrieved from https://www.inc.com/ryan-jenkins/how-to-deliver-training-that-transforms-millennials.html. Accessed on 7 Feb 2019.

18. Simek, E. (n.d.). 5 innovative employee training techniques you must consider. Userlane. Retrieved from https://blog.userlane.com/5-innovative-employee-training-techniques-to-consider/. Accessed on 7 Feb 2019.

19. Weiss, D. (2018, Mar 7). The top 7 corporate training innovations making the biggest impact in 2018. eLearningIndustry. Retrieved from https://elearningindustry.com/corporate-training-innovations-top7-impact-2018. Accessed on 7 Feb 2019.

20. Fouts, M., & Forbes Coaches Council. (2017, Nov 3). The secret to successfully train millennials. Forbes. Retrieved from https://www.forbes.com/sites/forbescoachescouncil/2017/11/03/the-secret-to-successfully-train-millennials/#503685726741. Accessed on 7 Feb 2019.

21. Filloon, W. (2017, Aug 23). KFC's new employee training game is a virtual reality nightmare. Eater. Retrieved from https://www.eater.com/2017/8/23/16192508/kfc-virtual-reality-training-oculus-rift. Accessed on 8 Feb 2019.

22. Eva, K. (2017, Aug 24). KFC have created a VR escape room for employees and we're now absolutely terrified. VR focus. Retrieved from https://www.vrfocus.com/2017/08/kfc-have-created-a-vr-escape-room-for-employees-and-were-now-absolutely-terrified/. Accessed on 8 Feb 2019.

23. Training and development in Wal-Mart assignment help. Retrieved from https://www.assignmenthelpexperts.com/training-and-development-in-wal-mart-assignment-help. Accessed on 8 Feb 2019.

24. Box Europe (2018, Feb 14). Employee training rendered personal for the Walmart family. Box. Retrieved from https://medium.com/boxeurope/employee-training-rendered-personal-for-the-walmart-family-d8beddddefbe. Accessed on 8 Feb 2019.

25. Stevenson, M. (2018, Jul 5). How Walmart and other companies improved learning to continuously invest in people. HR Exchange Network. Retrieved from https://www.hrexchangenetwork.com/employee-engagement/articles/how-walmart-and-other-companies-improved-learning. Accessed on 8 Feb 2019.

26. Henry, A. (2018, Jan 22). These companies are utilizing virtual reality training, why aren't you? Industrial Training International. Retrieved from https://www.iti.com/blog/these-companies-are-utilizing-virtual-reality-training-why-arent-you. Accessed on 8 Feb 2019.

27. Verlinden, N. (n.d.). How to engage millennials in employee wellness programs. Digital HR tech. Retrieved from https://www.digitalhrtech.com/engage-millennials-infographic/. Accessed on 8 Feb 2019.

28. Rise Staff (2017, Apr 16). 10 great examples of workplace wellness programs. Rise. Retrieved from https://risepeople.com/blog/workplace-wellness-programs/. Accessed on 8 Feb 2019.

29. Meyer, K. (2016, Jul 11). How we rewrote our company's mental health policy. Harvard Business Review. Retrieved from https://hbr.org/2016/07/how-we-rewrote-our-companys-mental-health-policy. Accessed on 9 Feb 2019.

30. Kohll, A. (2016, Apr 21). 8 things you need to know about employee wellness programs. Forbes. Retrieved from https://www.forbes.com/sites/alankohll/2016/04/21/8-things-you-need-to-know-about-employee-wellness-programs/#6b6833e740a3. Accessed on 9 Feb 2019.

31. Draper. Retrieved from https://www.draperinc.com/. Accessed on 9 Feb 2019.

UNDERSTANDING AND STRATEGIZING MILLENNIAL JOB SEARCH PROCESS

Job search is an investment of time to find employment after graduation from universities or find new employment due to discontent in the current position. Today's millennials are ambitious, energetic and assertive enough in seeking greener pastures for new opportunities that enable them to move up the ladder in the organizational hierarchy of companies. They bring with them values and new ideas to the organization and are not prepared to wait until they hear a response from companies. When they apply for newer roles, they seek details of the position right away in the first communication that they have with the employer. They prefer to be contacted directly as 'Business Speak' turns them off instantly (1).

Often times, searching for an appropriate job can be a demanding experience for millennials. A recent LinkedIn survey found out surprising facts about job search attitudes and habits. It found that 90 per cent of the professionals surveyed said that they were open to new positions in the market with 63 per cent stating that they feel flattered when they are being reached out for opportunities (1). When candidates apply for a job, they mostly look at three primary things: information, speed and compensation (but not just money) (1).

Millennial candidates also do not want a long and arduous process and hope for quick recruitment that does not take more than two to three months from the submission of application (1). They ideally prefer about three interviews (84% of respondents said they are happy with three interviews) with 65 per cent saying that a bad interview experience makes them lose interest in the job (1). The interviews must be turned into experiences—not transactions for millennial job seekers. One way companies can do this is by engaging them through social media. This can paint a positive picture of the future colleagues that they would get to connect with when joining the company.

Compensation today is no more relevant to millennial job seekers. Just as companies want a good fit, millennials seek the same. A research study found out that though compensation was the most preferred choice amongst candidates who were in the process of a job change (47% of the respondents cited it), better skills fit (37%), growth opportunities (36%) and challenging work (36%) were next in the list as the reasons for seeking a change in job positions (1). Millennials increasingly prefer working in a place where they can connect with the culture and, most importantly, do great work.

DIFFERENT STEPS OF JOB SEARCH

Having a proper strategy in place during a job search is of utmost importance for millennials today. Once the strategy is in place, the most important part is of defining the target. Choosing the target companies depend on the background and educational qualifications that a millennial possesses. In an article in *Forbes* (2), strategies were identified on how to create a job search target.

1. **Identify your audience:** At first, the candidate must know which industries he/she intends to work in. Whose problems does one intend to solve (decision makers, clients and so on)? Can sub-industries be identified? Can customer demographics be defined? Can the audience's biggest pain points be highlighted?

Example: I want to work in the wearable device industry so that I can use my expertise in creating technology to improve health issues. A major challenge is to create devices that are affordable for the general population. However, there are security concerns related to wearable technology in certain environments which must also be addressed.

2. **Market:** Are the required skills needed for the market changing? Does the industry prefer more specialists to generalists? Is demand for growth from a technological, cultural, political or an economic point of view shrinking? These are the questions that would answer the overall job market prospects of the candidate.

Example: The wearable technology market is projected to be valued at $34 billion by 2020. Schools are looking for cost-effective ways to bring this technology to classrooms, with greater privacy and security when engaging with these devices.

3. **Geography:** What would be the ideal job location for the role? Is the job location far away from hometown? Is it located in a city or a suburban area?

Example: My ideal job location would be Silicon Valley with its healthcare tech start-ups. It also has a thriving AI industry necessary for the inter-collaboration between the healthcare and the tech industries.

4. **Companies:** Which companies offer roles where I can create an impact? Is it a large company which has a lot of structure or a small one where I can create greater impact? Is the company willing to experiment with their product portfolios or are more focused on getting a greater market share?

Example: Check the job board for the roles in the Silicon Valley area and then cross check the company profile. Do the mission, vision and objectives of the company match your preference? Based on that, make a prompt selection.

5. **Culture:** What type of office culture generally suits you? Do you prefer the friendly atmosphere of a large organization or the intense and energetic atmosphere of a start-up?

   Example: Because of family pressure, I would prefer to work in an atmosphere which is less intense, but still allows me to innovate with my new ideas for the healthcare industry. I prefer working in a collaborative environment which would bring more new ideas in the workplace and help meet deadlines.

6. **Expertise:** What skills do you bring to the market? What differentiates you from other job market candidates? Are there any special skills that can be utilized by the company of your choice?

   Example: With 12 years of marketing experience and deep knowledge of distribution channels, I can help drive the strategies required for successful product positioning, pricing and competitive analysis. I also have cross-functional (sales, marketing, legal) domain knowledge due to my previous role as a legal adviser of a company giving me a unique advantage in negotiating deals.

7. **Function:** How will you use your expertise in solving the problems of the customers associated with the company?

Example: I am seeking marketing strategy roles in the wearable device industry where I can significantly contribute to the Silicon Valley companies such as (A, B or C) looking to grow their market in the education sector. Additionally, I can also provide legal and strategic support to break the entry barriers in the wearable device market.

INFLUENCE OF EMPLOYER BRANDING ON JOB SEARCH

With advancement in technologies in knowledge-based economies around the world, companies are innovating to attract the best of talent and retain them in the workforce. The millennial workforce today is no longer loyal to their employers, and hence there is a high turnover rate in companies (3). Finding the right talent today is the hardest part of successfully executing the vision of a company. Millennial job seekers are no more swayed by starting bonuses and impressive perks; instead, they are more concerned about the employer brand in the market.

Today, employment sites such as Indeed, Glassdoor and Monster offer a new level of transparency through its star ratings, reviews and conversations about companies. This has brought the millennial job seekers into a level-playing field with job givers. In recent research conducted in Glassdoor from where 4,600 people were surveyed, job seekers highlighted that good rating of a company and compensation benefits factored heavily when searching for a job. The research also showed that just like in the case of e-commerce, where consumers preferred recent reviews about products and services, job seekers, too, look for fresh reviews—not older than six months (4).

In Glassdoor, for example, 'Company Reviews' and 'Salaries' are top navigation menu items. It also helps the millennial job seekers to prepare for interviews through the questions asked in the 'Interviews' section.

In order to lure the best talent away from a competitor's workforce, certain steps must be followed.

1. **Treat your employer brand like you treat your corporate brand and manage its online reputation:** Employers must give the same level of importance to job sites such as Glassdoor, Indeed and so on, as they do to their LinkedIn profile. Reviews to these popular sites must be responded to with courtesy and with a positive attitude. It would enable prospective employees to know that the company seriously cares about what is troubling the employees and that they are doing their level best to fix the issues (4).

2. **Have a low rating? Find out why and fix it:** Try and gain insights from reviews about the problems that persist and discuss them in monthly department meetings. Try and resolve them because if there is a valid issue, chances are that there must be resentment amongst the current staff as well. Companies must make sure to pay attention to their employee's views because they have the power to influence the employer brand with their opinions, either online or via word of mouth (4).

3. **Ask current employees to submit reviews:** Companies must try to gauge the pulse of their current workforce by engaging with them. They should try to create a representative picture of employee experience and get fresh

reviews from them so as to make insightful changes in the company (4).

4. **Align your brand management efforts with HR:** There may be a case when a customer has a bad experience while talking to a company representative (say, Ramesh) of an organization which forces the customer to write negative reviews about the employee. There should be a mechanism which triggers the HR to send a training module to Ramesh to update himself on how to handle difficult customers without the interaction going southwards. This kind of employee redressal mechanism builds confidence amongst the employees as they feel supported, and are armed with tools they need to succeed in their workplace (4).

INFLUENCE OF SOCIAL MEDIA ON JOB SEARCH

A growing number of organizations today use social media for knowledge transfer from public networking sites to internal communication in organizations. Use of LinkedIn to recruit millennials has become the norm in many organizations looking for an all-around performer. It allows the user who is in search of a job to be more 'presentable', for example, through participation in professional groups, connection with alumni, human resource professionals, mentors and so on. The use of social networking websites has also been adopted in management education (5). Job search today is a time-consuming, arduous and demanding process which involves gathering information from various websites about potential jobs in the market (6). The job search period involves perseverance and unending energy. In a study conducted by the Bureau of Labor Statistics in 2005, a person in the United States changes his/her job on an average 10.2 times over a period of 20 years (7).

Social media also enable recruiters to search for 'passive millennial candidates' for middle- and higher-level roles. Passive candidates are the ones who are currently not looking for a job but may be interested in one at a later stage. This strategy is often referred to as 'poaching' or 'talent raiding' necessary to hire talent for senior management roles. Passive millennials generally spend more time on personal-based social media apps such as Facebook than LinkedIn, whereas the opposite is true in case of active millennials. Also, job boards are perceived more favourably by 'active' candidates who invest more time in them and hence are more inclined to use them. Millennial job candidates must always be vigilant about posting background details or videos that may hamper one's candidature. Brad Schepp, co-author of *How to Find a Job on LinkedIn, Facebook, Twitter and Google+*, adds:

> Make sure any profiles you write are free of typos, the information is coherent and applicable to your industry [or job you're trying to land], and your photos present you in a favorable light. You can verify the applicability of the information by checking profiles of others in the same field. (8)

Another article in the *Business Insider* (9) lists six recruiter confessions on social media habits that can cost a millennial one's job.

- **Recruiter confession #1—badmouthing employers or co-workers:** Badmouthing about colleagues in a public sphere reflects badly on the job-seeker as employers doubt whether he/she is a team player who is going to support the organization. One must be especially careful in venting their frustration in social media as it can have serious repercussions.

- **Recruiter confession #2—getting too personal:** Sharing of personal information should not be done in professional websites like LinkedIn, especially religion. A 2014 Carnegie Mellon study showed significant discrimination against Muslim applicants relative to Christians, which highlighted a particular behaviour pattern in recruitment, hampering millennials belonging to a certain religion.

- **Recruiter confession #3—contradictory posts:** A car accident forced an employee to quit her job and was unable to return for three months. This story can be heart-wrenching. 'But shortly thereafter, the hiring manager found pictures of her waterskiing on vacation, which told a slightly different version of the story', says Liz D'Aloia, founder of the Dallas-based mobile recruiting company HR Virtuoso. Therefore, one must be frank and honest about one's personal lives and refrain from sharing personal videos/pictures on social media platforms which can give a different story altogether.

- **Recruiter confession #4—spelling and grammar mistakes:** Millennial job seekers must be especially prompt in making sure their resumes are error free, because a survey by Jobvite found that 66 per cent of recruiters rejected candidates due to their poor grasp of English. One must use a spellchecker before shooting them off to prospective employers.

- **Recruiter confession #5—questionable content:** Job seekers must be very careful about what they post in social media. Pictures related to illegal drugs or sexual posts can be a misfit for companies that pride themselves in being an organization of social change. According to a headhunter named Nick Corcodilos, 'Your reputation is based on how you present yourself—it's your stock-in-trade.'

- **Recruiter confession #6—being a bully:** Companies always solicit a candidate that is smart, obedient and forever remains loyal to the core values that the organization espouses. Companies never tolerate snarky individuals who can create unnecessary problems for them. Hence, Corcodilos says, 'Raise the standards of your behavior, and write things that will be helpful and make others feel good.'

CAMPUS VERSUS NON-CAMPUS JOB SEARCH

Job search is generally of two types: campus and non-campus. In the United States, companies visit on-campus to hire candidates mostly for internships. Most job seekers do not get a permanent position in the on-campus hire. Only in exceptional situations are they offered a role when companies visit campus. Most job searches follow the normal pattern where millennials apply in the 'Careers' or 'Jobs' section on the company website. After that, the applications are scrutinized. If there are a large number of applications for a single position, 'Keywords' specific to the job role are typed in to distinguish the resumes which match the job profile with the ones that are not a precise match. Once suitable candidates are selected, phone screening and subsequent interviewing take place, with the best candidate hired at the end of the process.

In South-Asian countries and more specifically in India, however, most of the millennials after graduation from top-notch universities get full-time placement through on-campus recruitment. Companies visit the campus and are given specific time slots during which they pre-select the candidates based on their Cumulative Grade Point Average (CGPA) and other activities (co-curricular or extra-curricular) and invite them for interviews and group discussions (if applicable). After the process is over, the deserving millennial job seekers are given full-time placements and join their respective companies after they graduate.

....

Naukri.com: Helping Millennials Search Their Dream Jobs

Frequent job changes and even changes in the streams are a common trait amongst the millennial workforce. Consequently, the new generation of millennial workers explore the labour market differently than the older generation. According to the World of Work study by Monsterboard, online search was the preferred medium of job search for millennials. This research, conducted in July 2016, with over 4,000 millennial respondents, reported that 65 per cent of the millennials look for online job boards (10). Thus, job boards have become a popular source of recruitment for companies.

Naukri.com is one of the most well-known job boards in India founded by Sanjeev Bikhchandani in March 1997 (11). As of 2016, the company had a database of over 49.5 million registered job seekers with an average growth of 11 thousand resumes being added daily (12). It provides a floorless or virtual employment exchange and provides services such as database access, advertisement to hirers amongst others.

In order to use Naukri.com, candidates need to build their profile in the portal by uploading their resumes and professional pictures. Recruitment agencies can then view the profiles and, depending on their requirement, source the data through the portal. When the recruitment cycle starts and there is a need to hire for a particular position, a 'keyword' search is done based on which several profiles are shortlisted. The best profiles are then filtered where the candidate/candidates are called and discussed the opportunity in detail. If he/she is interested, the cost to company details along with the notice period are taken down and then the profile is shared with the company for further shortlisting. After that, the candidate is invited for interviews (telephonic or on-site or both). If the candidate successfully completes the interview process, an offer letter is issued, based on which the candidate submits his/her resignation in the parent company and then serves the notice period after which they join the new company.

The millennial workforce tends to experiment with the type of work they like to do. Their expectations with their work organizations is also fairly higher. As they are more adaptive to change and are more innovative, the way in which they look at work is dramatically different. They tend to like shorter recruitment processes, focus highly on the company's culture of working, and with the wider availability of niche online job boards, they tend to seek specific domain jobs. Also, with the advent of mobile technology and apps, online job boards have been more accessible at their fingertips (13). Seeing the changes occurring at the demographic front, Naukri.com has also changed its strategies and has taken steps in a direction to attract more millennial traffic. The company launched its mobile app early in 2012 and soon it received more than 23 per cent of its traffic on mobile apps.

Thus, Naukri.com plays the role of a mediator between the millennial job seekers and the hiring company by facilitating the recruitment process of deserving candidates in the job market. From a viewpoint of strategy, firms willing to ease the hiring process for the millennials may focus more on the generation-specific factors. Additionally, companies like Naukri.com provide an example of the successful implementation of the same.

Discussion Questions

1. Discuss other generation specific factors which can help companies to target the millennial workforce.

2. Outline social media strategies Naukri.com can use to further its reach to the millennial customers.

....

Recruitment at IIMs

The IIMs are a group of 20 government, autonomous management institutes in India. As per the IIM Act, 2017, they have been declared as institutes of national importance. After India's independence in 1947, the Planning Commission, which was formulated to oversee the development of the nation, recommended establishment of fine institutions for providing management skills. Consequently, the first IIMs were opened in Calcutta (now Kolkata) and Ahmedabad in 1961 (14).

With the success of older IIMs, many newer IIMs were established in different parts of the country.

IIMs are characterized as providing a platform for recruiters to directly visit the campus and recruit the talent. Such placement activities in IIMs have garnered significant attention due to offers of high salaries to the graduates. Placements in IIMs are of two types: summer and final placement. Summer internships play an integral role in the holistic development of postgraduate programme (PGP; equivalent to MBA degree) students where they get to spend 8 to 10 weeks in their chosen organization. This enables them to innovate and challenge new ideas and learn about the particular industry that they are interested to work in, which equips them to be more receptive to market needs and decide on their specialization by the second year (15).

After the students complete their summer internship, they prepare a report and share their learning of the organization before they register for the second year. IIMs generally enjoy extensive corporate support for the summer internship programme, as a result of which students get immersed in a diverse and intense learning experience. The benefit of this summer placement program is that it gives the company the chance to evaluate interns over a long period in real business-like situations, based on which they can make pre-placement offers and hire them full time.

Final placements generally happen during the last term of a graduating year where distinguished companies from India and around the world visit the IIM campuses across the country to hire the best talent. IIMs renowned alumni who have held key positions in top corporates worldwide help in building a sustainable competitive environment to recruit candidates from their campuses. Placements in IIMs have always been a student-driven affair. IIM Ahmedabad, for example, follows a unique cohort-based system with an objective to provide a better student–recruiter fit. This process has twin bene-fits: to enable recruiters to evaluate students over a longer duration and to give the students a variety to choose from different career options (15).

Since a majority of the students are from the millennial gen-eration, the placement process is tailored according to their needs. Students can choose the subjects they intend to study in the second year. This allows them to make their own unique profile according to their interests, industry require-ments and deciding their own career paths. The process also helps to create skill diversity amongst the students, which is appreciated by the recruiters. The recruiters are then invited to make their corporate presentations and provide a holistic picture of the job to the students. Such initiatives ensure that the students are informed about the company's work culture, policies, job descriptions, salary offered and so on. In a way, the recruiters also cater to the generational characteristics of the millennial workforce.

Thus, unique in its own sense, placement activities at all the IIMs provide a platform for their students to ease the job search process and allow companies to directly strategize their recruitment and attain a competitive edge. Aimed at the modern millennial workforce, the placement process is also a tailored example of how business schools can also provide a platform to ease the job search process, especially for their millennial students.

FIGURE 10.2 FINAL PLACEMENT GANTT CHART IN IIM AHMEDABAD (15)

Final placements	January	February	March
Corporate presentations			
Submission of résumés			
Short-listing			
Pre-processes and interviews			

Source: IIM Ahmedabad PGP placement process.

Discussion Questions

1. What other initiatives IIMs can take to further improve the job search process of their students?

2. Discuss the negative implications of campus placement activities. Devise strategies to overcome them.

REFERENCES

1. Arruda, W. (2017, Jul 24). The three things today's job seekers want, according to LinkedIn. Forbes. Retrieved from https://www.forbes.com/sites/williamarruda/2017/07/24/the-three-things-todays-job-seekers-want-according-to-linkedin/#6dddaa596e05. Accessed on 18 Mar 2019.

2. Graham, D. (2018, Jan 24). Ready, set, switch! how to define your job search target so you land the role. Forbes. Retrieved from https://www.forbes.com/sites/dawngraham/2018/01/24/ready-set-switch-how-to-define-your-job-search-target-so-you-land-the-role/#42d05371d717. Accessed on 16 Mar 2019.

3. Verhoeven, H., Mashood, N., & Chansarkar, B. (2009). Recruitment and Generation Y: Web 2.0 the way to go? Proceedings of the Tenth International Business Research Conference, Dubai, United Arab Emirates, pp. 1–14. Retrieved from https://www.researchgate.net/publication/228427686_Recruitment_and_Generation_Y_Web_20_the_way_to_go. Accessed on 20 Mar 2019.

4. Fertik, M. (2018, Aug 6). Attract talent with a strong employer brand. Forbes. Retrieved from https://www.forbes.com/sites/michaelfertik/2018/08/06/attract-talent-with-a-strong-employer-brand/#9bc092492474. Accessed on 18 Mar 2019.

5. Thomas, M., & Thomas, H. (2012). Using new social media and Web 2.0 technologies in business school teaching and learning. J Manag Dev. 31(4): 358–67.

6. Swider, B.W., Boswell, W.R., & Zimmerman, R.D. (2011). Examining the job search-turnover relationship: the role of embeddedness, job satisfaction, and available alternatives. J Appl Psychol. 96:432–41.

7. Bureau of Labor Statistics. (2005). Retrieved from http://www.bls.gov/nls/nlsfaqs.htm#anch. Accessed on 23 Jan 2019.

8. Smith, J. (2013, Apr 16). How social media can help (or hurt) you in your job search. Forbes. Retrieved from https://www.forbes.com/sites/jacquelynsmith/2013/04/16/how-social-media-can-help-or-hurt-your-job-search/#36f121e87ae2. Accessed on 16 Mar 2019.

9. Triffin, M. (2016, Jan 30). Recruiters explain 6 social media habits that could cost you the job. Business Insider. Retrieved from https://www.businessinsider.com/6-social-media-habits-that-could-cost-you-the-job-2016-1?IR=T. Accessed on 16 Mar 2019.

10. Lichtendahl, R. (2016, Dec 14). How millennials look for jobs. VONQ. Retrieved from https://www.vonq.com/recruitment-insights/blog-millennials-jobs-search/. Accessed on 20 Mar 2019.

11. Anand, V. (2012, Sep 8). Don't live someone else's dream: Naukri.com chairman Sanjeev Bikchandani at Mind Rocks Summit. India Today. Retrieved from https://www.indiatoday.in/india-today-mind-rocks-youth-summit-2012/story/dont-live-someone-elses-dream-naukri.com-chairman-sanjeev-bikchandani-at-mind-rocks-summit-copy-115467-2012-09-07. Accessed on 20 Mar 2019.

12. Pal, S.B. (2018, Apr 5). 7 best job sites in India (comparison and inference). Sheroes. Retrieved from https://sheroes.com/articles/best-job-sites-india/NzA2MA==. Accessed on 13 May 2019.

13. Landrum, S. (2017, Jul 7). How millennials are shaping the hiring process. Forbes. Retrieved from https://www.forbes.com/sites/sarahlandrum/2017/07/07/how-millennials-are-shaping-the-hiring-process/#4e2de90b2377. Accessed on 20 Mar 2019.

14. From Ahmedabad to Shillong: MBAUniverse.com relives the IIM journey (2016, Jul 25). MBA Universe. Retrieved from https://www.mbauniverse.com/article/id/1256. Accessed on 13 Mar 2019.

15. IIM Ahmedabad PGP Placement. Retrieved from https://www.iima.ac.in/web/pgp/placements/placement-process. Accessed on 20 Mar 2019.

11

SUCCESSION PLANNING OF MILLENNIALS IN FAMILY BUSINESS

By 2020, millennials will make up almost 50 per cent of a nation's workforce, thus uprooting the baby boomers from a position they have held since decades (1). In everyone's life, there comes a time to retire and undergo a smooth transition. Research has shown that only a little more than 30 per cent of family-owned businesses survive the transition from the founder to second-generation leadership (2). However, in many cases, businesses tend to fail due to a lack of preparation to hand over the reins of the company to the incoming younger CEO.

Every country is filled with stories of succession planning failures. In India, for example, the family feud of the Ambani brothers for control of India's largest private enterprise ultimately led to the division of the conglomerate, the ripples of which are still visible in the Ambani family business today (3). Research has shown that in order to avoid such disputes, succession planning programmes must be prepared to help reduce failure rates during intergenerational transitions (4). Next-generation leaders generally face a set of challenges unique to family-owned businesses. They not only have the added burden of sustaining a successful business but also have the challenge of negotiating complexities of family and ownership systems that have traditionally been an integral part of family enterprises (5).

A critical aspect of succession planning is one's ability to let go and pass it to the next-generation millennials. Senior members must focus much of their time in implementing strong mentorship programmes, creating research and educational opportunities for their colleagues and motivated millennials (6).

It should add more diversity across operations and management departments by building a platform from where working professionals get inspired to carry out new ideas and innovations. This helps in building a progressive culture in organizations, which bodes well for a successful transitioning in a family-owned business in the future.

STEPS OF SUCCESSION PLANNING

Complex histories and intimate cultures in family businesses can sometimes be difficult to understand for outsiders. Today, they are less traditional and more modern in their adoption of technologies in their day-to-day business affairs. By following certain steps, they can create a viable succession plan for their financial independence and continued growth (7).

Step 1: Establish Goals and Objectives

One must establish personal retirement goals by developing an objective vision for their business. A team of professional advisers must be groomed by identifying goals, both personal and business, in order to drive the next wave of leaders.

Step 2: Establish a Decision-Making Process

One must improvise in resolving disputes by involving family members in decision- making processes. This helps in improving governance mechanisms in organizations and can lead to a successful succession plan involving family members.

Step 3: Establish the Succession Plan

One must identify active and non-active roles for each family member, which would help in stratifying the workload of the family business. This is possible only through emotional support provided to family members at the time of need. This leads to the build-up of next-generation leaders who have established credentials to take the company in the right direction in the future.

Step 4: Create a Business and Owner Estate Plan

Leaders must also have a review plan whereby taxes are minimized and delays are avoided in the transfer of stock to the remaining owners or spouses. It must develop a proper buy/sell agreement that is fair and reflective of the actual value of the business. Matters related to taxation, sale or transfer of ownership, death or divorce must be handled with care and objectivity.

Step 5: Create a Transition Plan

If the business is to be purchased in the short run, financial options must be considered, including financing from an external party or self-financed from the retiring owners on a deferred payout basis. One must also develop a timeline for implementation of the succession plan. This allows a rapid transitioning of millennial leaders who are ready to take over the business and bring laurels to the organization in the future.

CHALLENGES TO SUCCESSION PLANNING

Succession planning is one of the challenges that every company faces. It is not something that is done overnight. A classic case is that of Apple, which was hit with a succession dilemma when its company CEO Steve Jobs fell ill in 2011. It left the boardroom in a flurry, with employees worried about who will sit at the helm of the tech giant, should Jobs be unavailable. Hence, the shareholders of the company put forward a proposal which required the firm to have a 'written and detailed succession planning policy' in the future in the event the CEO falls ill again (8). Succession planning of companies is a complex matter which involves meticulous preparation for successfully passing on the baton to the next generation. Hubler (9) in an article in the *Family Business Review* described 10 obstacles to succession planning. The obstacles are described in the increasing order of difficulty in overcoming them (9).

10. Poor expression of feelings and wants: Very often in family-owned businesses, feelings and wants of the members are not expressed freely, which leads to poor and ineffective communication. For communication to be effective amongst family members, people need to be vulnerable, only then can they have the capability, experience and confidence to take risks. Although family members always have expectations of each other in an emotional sense, when these very expectations are not met, they think that it is because they are not worthy of it.

9. When differences are seen as a liability rather than an asset: This is a common problem in family-owned businesses around the world. In most cases, differences between members are personalized, which should not be the case because differences create exciting opportunities as new thoughts emerge. The 'Hubler's Speck of Dust Theory' goes like this:

'Family members often think about small business differences as issues they do not want to bring up with family members. Because they want to maintain family harmony in the context of family-owned businesses, family members often inadvertently create the very problem they are trying to avoid by not discussing their business differences'.

8. **Indirect communication:** Indirect communication is one of the most prevalent problems in family businesses. When differences occur in a family business, it is mostly due to the indirect communication between members which can be solved if members are willing to communicate directly. This has serious ramifications on the nature of family relationships.

7. **Entitlement:** This is an issue often seen amongst the younger generation. The millennials might use their name as an entitlement to achieve advantages which can break the morale of deserving candidates. This can also take place with senior members in family-owned businesses, who believe that they have the right to continue for eternity without giving the younger generation their fair share of leading the company.

6. **Scarcity:** One of the most difficult issues in family-related businesses is scarcity of financial resources, which can lead to inefficient succession planning. Further, lack of appreciation, recognition and love are the underlying problems that lead to emotional scarcity. The way such issues can be solved is to have family members talk directly about what they expect from each other.

5. **History:** History is a big factor in family-owned businesses around the world as it captures the struggles and achievements of a business from start to where it is now. But oftentimes, families overlook their business history, especially those who are having a hard time creating their future. Therefore, one must both learn from the business mistakes and celebrate the positive aspects of their family-owned business history to move forward with their goals.

4. **Other-oriented regarding change:** One of the major challenges in succession planning is to help clients take full responsibility for their businesses. In a family-owned business, it is

common to find people who expect others to change in order to bring about a positive transformation in the organization. This is always a recipe for disaster because individuals must take self-responsibility in successfully contributing to the family business. They should not expect others to do the needful as their priorities might often be different from those of the higher management.

3. **Control:** Having a sense of control in the family business is of paramount importance for a budding entrepreneur who has spent a major part of his life in the business. As mentioned earlier, change is difficult even when it is positive. Many a time entrepreneurs think that bringing in a change in the company can actually change them and in the process take away their companies, which can be a tricky situation to be in. Therefore, it is much more prudent to assist entrepreneurs in developing new dreams by supporting them in their business, their leisure time, and their philanthropy to effectively deal with the issue of control.

2. **Lack of forgiveness:** In a family business involving multiple stakeholders, it is almost impossible not to have identity clashes with one another when the stakes are high. It is very tough being in business together when one does not have the capacity to forgive. Therefore, being part of religious activities, for example, can be an icebreaker, since most religions around the world have 'forgiveness' as a core philosophy that is often helpful in such cases.

1. **Lack of appreciation, recognition and love:** Lack of appreciation, recognition and love is the number one obstacle in family-owned businesses. The baby boomers often seek recognition from their millennial adult children, never admitting it in front of them. Similarly, the millennial generation has the

same issue. They look for recognition from their well-wishers for their accomplishments. Family members must strive to express love in a genuine way with their compatriots, rather than assuming that they are being loved. This enables a healthy 'relationship build-up' amongst members in family-owned companies.

STRATEGIES FOR SUCCESSION PLANNING

Current leadership needs to identify potential millennial leaders. Preparing for a transition leadership now can enable a smooth transfer of power later. Research by Professor Stephen Miller has identified factors that promote next-generation leader development, a key finding of which showed that the degree to which next-generation leaders assume personal responsibility for their actions and decisions is strongly related to their emotional and social intelligence competencies, which, in turn, is a major driver of their leadership effectiveness (5). The Forbes Coaches Council (10) has identified different methods (strategies) to develop the next-generation millennial leaders:

1. **Do not wait to start:** Companies must look to the millennial generation for the transfer of soft skills and new ideas to keep the organization profitable. For this, they need to start early and develop leadership think tanks and new idea sessions that fastens a progressive transitioning of the new blood in the company hierarchy.

2. **Develop a buy-and-build strategy:** Companies must evaluate their core team and decide where they want to buy talent in areas where there is less skill set, and build a long-term team of new talent in order to build a future pipeline of established leaders to take the organization forward.

3. Train senior leaders how to effectively coach and mentor: Senior leaders when developing a succession plan very often do not know how to proceed with it. Therefore, they need to update soft skills such as coaching, mentoring and taking ownership of responsibilities that help them to train younger talent in the future.

4. Encourage collaboration: Collaboration between cross-generational leadership should be encouraged through formal mentoring and skills-based volunteer programmes. This builds a strong connection and demonstrates the value of diversity through a cross-cultural and intercultural exchange.

5. Leverage the success of mentoring: Mentoring is an essential tool through which baby boomers can leave a legacy of their own in an organization. Pairing boomers with millennials can help in bridging the knowledge gap and lead to a strong leadership pipeline in the future.

6. Cultivate multigenerational training programmes: Organizations that have a glance at the future should put emphasis on multigenerational development programmes to transfer wisdom and skill set between the younger generation and boomers.

7. Use sustainable leadership programmes at all tiers: The use of self-assessment and 360-degree feedback tools provides a baseline from which employees can continually improve. These programmes help in the upward mobility of a new hire to a C-suite.

8. Identify and develop needed skills and competencies: Top skills needed for the job must be developed in the cadre through an action learning component to develop the next set of leaders.

9. **Handle your succession plan execution with respect:** Active boomers should not get discouraged and made to feel as if they have an expiration date attached to their forehead. Their expertise, experiences and wisdom must be shared with high potential millennials for better succession planning.

10. **Create opportunities for emerging leaders to take the lead:** Leaders in middle or lower levels must be given an opportunity to make a difference and lead on initiatives that matter for organizations. They must be given room to ask key questions that will help them deliver on key company objectives and grow professionally.

11. **Find new carrots:** Millennials, Gen X and Gen Y are more comfortable in the use of technology and have worked in the corporate world devoid of pensions. These blokes do not follow a one-company career track as they are more entrepreneurial in nature. These carrots must be motivated to develop them into next-generation leaders.

12. **Offer access to stand-alone courses or tuition assistance:** Stand-alone courses that offer leadership training to millennial job seekers would enable companies to attract young talent and retain them in the workforce. Very few companies at present invest in talent, and hence there is a high turnover rate in companies.

13. **Remember to delegate:** Baby boomers who are at the top tier of multinationals must delegate some of the responsibilities to middle-level management. In most cases, millennial future leaders get hampered by the fact that boomers are not letting go of their job until 70 and this demotivates them to continue further.

....

Cadila Healthcare: Sharvil Patel

A majority of the millennial successors of Indian business families are going abroad to gain a wide spectrum of knowledge about their field. Most often after completion of their degrees from prestigious universities, they gain either work experience or research experience to understand the intricate details of their research topics. Once they have mastered the concepts, they come back to join their family business to make an enormous impact. One such example is that of Sharvil Patel, the newly appointed managing director of Cadila Healthcare Ltd. Sharvil is the son of Pankaj Patel, chairman of the company, who handed over the reins to his son in 2017. Sharvil obtained his PhD from the University of Sunderland for his work on breast cancer at John Hopkins, Bayview Medical Center in the United States (11). He has been steadfast in his commitment to research and ensuring compliance so that Cadila can stay in the forefront of ground-breaking experimentation in medical care.

Cadila was founded in 1952 by Ramanbhai Patel along with Indravadan Modi and is headquartered in Ahmedabad, India. In 1995, the partners split; while Modi moved to a new company, Cadila Pharmaceuticals Ltd, Patel became the holder of Cadila Healthcare Ltd. Cadila Healthcare Ltd filed for an IPO in 2000 on the Bombay Stock Exchange. Today, the company is one of the largest pharma companies in India with a revenue of ₹119.05 billion in 2018. It majorly focusses on the manufacturing of generic drugs (12).

Cadila has always been known for its strict inspection schedules and fixing the long-standing quality concerns that have plagued Indian drug makers. Apart from that, the launch of Zydus Wellness under Sharvil's watchful eyes has led to a turnaround in the consumer healthcare business of the company. In the long run, Sharvil is focused on bringing innovative drugs, which includes a range of biosimilars. This would propel Cadila's US business revenue to move up to nearly 50 per cent, due to the long list of approvals that they are slated to get from the US FDA (13).

After Sharvil joined the company, he was given a target of achieving $1 billion of revenue for the company (11). This gave him a great opportunity to know the business in detail and helped him work across teams to understand the strategies required to obtain their revenue goals. In order to achieve the objective, the first thing he did was to unfold the 70 projects under research, market, commercialization, finance, HR and so on which came under the $1 billion target (11). In 2018, Sharvil acquired the Kraft Heinz India business and aims to launch more than 40 generic drugs in the United States (14).

Although the strategic and guiding decisions of the company are taken by the current chairman of the company, Pankaj Patel, Sharvil responsibly holds the position of managing director and takes decisions pertaining to day-to-day operations of the company. He is a third-generation successor of Cadila, he aims to build ambitiously on the empire created by his father and grandfather.

Discussion Questions

1. With the aid of Sharvil's example, enlist steps of succession planning used by the company.

2. What are some challenges the company faces due to succession planning? How can it be resolved?

....

Reliance: Isha Ambani

The value of an idea lies in the using of it.

—Thomas Edison

It was an idea that changed the landscape of the telecommunication sector in India. Back in 2011, Isha Ambani, daughter of India's richest man, Mukesh Ambani, came home for her holidays in Mumbai when she was undergoing her undergraduate studies at Yale University in the United States. She was working on the assignments of her coursework when she complained to her father about the slow internet speed in their home. The millennials in the Ambani household, Isha and Akash, knew that everything would be digital in the new world unlike in the old world where people made money only by connecting calls. Thus, the revolutionary idea was born, and Jio was launched with much fanfare in September 2016 (15). Since then it has already become the biggest telecom game changer in India.

Prior to joining her family business, Isha Ambani entered McKinsey & Company in New York as a Business Analyst after her undergraduate studies (16). This was done as a preparation for a later role in the Reliance Industries group, most probably in the consumer-facing business. Family businesses in India generally encourage their forthcoming generation to get international exposure. P. Thiruvengadam, Senior Director, Deloitte India, said that 'It is proven that children of business families learn more if they work outside family companies in their initial stages' as they tend to pick the nuances of how an organization works far better in external companies (17). Hence, Isha Ambani's international exposure has put her in great stead to lead India's largest family enterprise in the foreseeable future.

Isha's father, Mukesh Ambani, heads the Reliance group. Reliance Industries group is an Indian conglomerate with business in energy, petrochemicals, textiles, retail, telecommunication and natural resources. The holding company Reliance Industries Ltd (RIL) is one of the most profitable companies in India and the first to cross the market capitalization of $100 billion in 2007 (18). Reliance Jio Infocomm Ltd (Jio) is the telecom company of the group. Currently, it offers 4G network services in India and is the third largest mobile network operator.

Millennials like Isha Ambani are far more creative, ambitious and impatient to become the best in the world. She convinced her father that the age of broadband internet has come and is going to be the defining technology where India cannot be left behind. Since then, she has been a hands-on leader who represents the large section of millennial workers in Jio. Such has been her impact that shareholders present at AGM urged the millennial siblings (Isha and her brother, Akash) to take up the mantle and take Reliance Jio to newer heights. An instance where she showed her remarkable leadership qualities is when she launched Reliance's fashion e-commerce subsidiary Ajio's initiation operations (19), which has changed the landscape of fashion clothing for women in India.

Discussion Questions

1. What are the hardships for the succession planning in the case of RIL?

2. Does the strategies for succession planning for a public listed firm change with the change in culture?

252

REFERENCES

1. Kosterlitz, M., & Lewis, J. (2017, Dec). From baby boomer to millennial: succession planning for the future. Nurse Leader. 15(6):396–98. Retrieved from https://www.sciencedirect.com/science/article/abs/pii/S1541461217302616. Accessed on 23 Mar 2019.

2. Grassi, S.V., Jr & Giarmarco, J.H. (2008). Practical succession planning for the family-owned business. J Pract Est Plan. 10(1):27–60.

3. Kansal, P. (2012, Mar). Succession and retirement planning: integrated strategy for family business owners in India. XIMB J Manag. 9:23–40.

4. Cadieux, L. (2007). Succession in small and medium-sized family businesses: toward a typology of predecessor roles during and after instatement of the successor. Family Bus Rev. 20(2):95–109.

5. Gangal, N. (2018, Feb 16). Preparing the next gen is an important aspect of succession planning: Douglas Shackelford. Forbes India. Retrieved from http://www.forbesindia.com/article/indias-family-businesses/preparing-the-next-gen-is-an-important-aspect-of-succession-planning-douglas-shackelford/49457/1. Accessed on 26 Mar 2019.

6. Firestone, K. (2018, Aug 7). How one CEO prepared her organization for her retirement. Harvard Bu Rev. Retrieved from https://hbr.org/2018/08/how-one-ceo-prepared-her-organization-for-her-retirement. Accessed on 26 Mar 2019.

7. Evans, M (2013, Aug 28). 5 steps to create a viable succession plan for your family business. Forbes. Retrieved from https://www.forbes.com/sites/allbusiness/2013/08/28/5-steps-to-create-a-viable-succession-plan-for-your-family-business/#411f7fb176f2. Accessed on 25 Mar 2019.

8. Maharaj, A. (2011, Jan 11). Most companies are clueless when it comes to succession planning. Business Insider. Retrieved from https://www.businessinsider.com/succession-planning-do-it-right-right-now-2011-1?IR=T. Accessed on 22 Mar 2019.

9. Hubler, T. (1999, Jun). Ten most prevalent obstacles to family-business succession planning. Family Bus Rev. 12(2):117–21. Retrieved from https://journals.sagepub.com/doi/pdf/10.1111/j.1741-6248.1999.00117.x. Accessed on 25 Mar 2019.

10. Forbes Coaches Council. (2017, Aug 17). To develop the next generation of leaders, plan ahead. Forbes. Retrieved from https://www.forbes.com/sites/forbescoachescouncil/2017/08/17/to-develop-the-next-generation-of-leaders-plan-ahead/#1d603da57652. Accessed on 20 Mar 2019.

11. Das, S. (2017, Jul 13). Emerging markets to be third pillar of our business: Cadila's Sharvil Patel. Business Standard. Retrieved from https://www.business-standard.com/article/companies/emerging-markets-to-be-third-pillar-of-our-business-cadila-s-sharvil-patel-117071300765_1.html. Accessed on 25 Mar 2019.

12. Bureau. (2018, May 25). **Discussion Questions** FY18 standalone net up 65%. The Hindu Businessline. Retrieved from https://www.thehindubusinessline.com/companies/cadila-healthcare-fy18-standalone-net-up-65/article23989492.ece. Accessed on 13 May 2019.

13. Rajagopal, D. (2017, Jul 19). Cadila's new MD Sharvil Patel aims to double revenues in 5 years. The Economic Times. Retrieved from https://economictimes.

indiatimes.com/industry/healthcare/biotech/pharmaceuticals/cadilas-new-md-sharvil-patel-aims-to-double-revenues-in-5-years/articleshow/59660942.cms. Accessed on 25 Mar 2019.

14. ET Now. (2019, Feb 26). This year, Zydus to launch at least 40 generics in US markets: Sharvil Patel. The Economic Times. Retrieved from https://economictimes.indiatimes.com/markets/expert-view/this-year-we-would-launch-at-least-40-generics-in-us-markets-sharvil-patel-zydus-cadila/articleshow/68166151.cms?from=mdr. Accessed on 27 Mar 2019.

15. PTI. (2018, Mar 16). How Jio was born: tired of poor internet speed, Isha Ambani mooted the idea. Business Standard. Retrieved from https://www.business-standard.com/article/companies/how-jio-was-born-tired-of-poor-internet-speed-isha-ambani-mooted-the-idea-118031600357_1.html. Accessed on 25 Mar 2019.

16. ET Online. (2018, Oct 25). Ivy League, high-society galas, and Jio: Isha Ambani is more than just the Reliance heiress. The Economic Times. Retrieved from https://economictimes.indiatimes.com/magazines/panache/ivy-leagues-high-society-galas-and-jio-isha-ambani-is-more-than-just-the-reliance-heiress/articleshow/66316196.cms. Accessed on 25 Mar 2019.

17. Vijayraghavan, K. (2014, Apr 18). Mukesh Ambani's daughter Isha joins McKinsey; preparation for role in RIL? The Economic Times. Retrieved from https://economictimes.indiatimes.com/news/company/corporate-trends/mukesh-ambanis-daughter-isha-joins-mckinsey-preparation-for-role-in-ril/articleshow/33874328.cms. Accessed on 26 Mar 2019.

18. Dhar, K. (2018, Aug 23). Reliance Industries becomes first Indian company to cross ₹8 lakh crore market cap. Business Today. Retrieved from https://www.businesstoday.in/markets/stocks/reliance-industries-ril-first-indian-company-to-cross-rs-8-lakh-crore-market-cap/story/281569.html. Accessed on 13 Mar 2019.

19. Isha Ambani Biography. (2017, Mar 9). Isha Ambani's important role at Reliance Jio. Retrieved from http://www.ishaambanibiography.com/articles/isha-ambani-important-role-reliance-jio/. Accessed on 25 Mar 2019.

Dheeraj Sharma is Director at the Indian Institute of Management, Rohtak, Haryana. He is also a professor at the Indian Institute of Management Ahmedabad (on leave). He has taught at numerous educational institutions, including in Europe, Asia and North America. Dr Sharma has a doctoral degree with a major in marketing and a double minor in psychology and quantitative analysis from Louisiana Tech University.

Dr Sharma has authored over 100 research papers in leading international journals and conferences. He has published eight books, including one with SAGE. Some of his books are *Principles of Marketing*; *Business to Business Marketing*; *Leadership Lessons From Military* (SAGE Publications); *Consumer Behaviour: A Managerial Perspective*; *Cross-Cultural Perspective in Global Marketplace*; *Proceedings of Academy of Marketing Science*; *Global Business*; and *Swinging the Mandate: Developing and Managing a Winning Campaign*. Dr Sharma continues to serve as a board member in several PSUs and public limited companies.

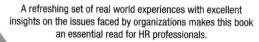